ON MODERN
AUTHORITY

ON MODERN AUTHORITY

THE THEORY AND CONDITION OF WRITING
1500 TO THE PRESENT DAY

THOMAS DOCHERTY

Lecturer, Modern English and American Literature,
University College, Dublin

THE HARVESTER PRESS · SUSSEX
ST. MARTIN'S PRESS · NEW YORK

First published in Great Britain in 1987 by
THE HARVESTER PRESS LIMITED
Publisher: John Spiers
16 Ship Street, Brighton, Sussex
and in the USA by
ST. MARTIN'S PRESS, INC.
175 Fifth Avenue, New York, NY 10010

British Library Cataloguing in Publication Data

Docherty, Thomas
    On modern authority : the condition of
    writing : 1500 to the present day.
    1. Literature, Modern—History and
    criticism   2. Authority in literature
    I. Title
    809'.93355   PN56.A8/

    ISBN 0-7108-1017-2
    ISBN 0-7108-1154-3 Pbk

St. Martin's Press, Inc.
ISBN 0-312-00942-9
Library of Congress Cataloging-in-Publication Data
CIP Applied for

Typeset in 11 point Garamond Roman by
Photo·graphics, Honiton, Devon

Printed in Great Britain by
Biddles Ltd, Guildford and King's Lynn

THE HARVESTER PRESS PUBLISHING GROUP
The Harvester Group comprises Harvester Press Ltd (chiefly publishing
literature, fiction, philosophy, psychology, and science and trade books);
Harvester Press Microform Publications Ltd (publishing in microform
previously unpublished archives, scarce printed sources, and indexes to
these collections) and Wheatsheaf Books Ltd (chiefly publishing in econ-
omics, international politics, sociology, women's studies and related social
sciences).

For Agnes Collum

Le sujet d'un poème lui est aussi étranger et aussi important que l'est à un homme son nom.

(Paul Valéry, *Cahiers*)

There is nothing mysterious or natural about authority. It is formed, irradiated, disseminated; it is instrumental, it is persuasive; it has status, it establishes canons of taste and value; it is virtually indistinguishable from certain ideas it dignifies as true, and from traditions, perceptions, and judgments it forms, transmits, reproduces. Above all, authority can, indeed must, be analyzed.

(Edward W. Said, *Orientalism*)

Contents

Introduction: Poiesis as Rhetorical Criticism

Good style

helluva hard tay read theez init
stull
if yi canny unnirston thim jiss
           clear aff then
gawn
get tay fuck ootma road

ahmaz goodiz thi lota yiz so ah um
ah no whit ahm dayn
tellnyi
jiss try enny a yir fly patir wi me
stick thi bootnyi good style
so ah wull
         (Tom Leonard, from 'Six Glasgow Poems')

contemporary semiotics has rightly destroyed residual ideas concerning the simple location of meaning or even of the author. But though a text is discontinuously woven of many strands or codes, there is magic in the web. The sense of an informing spirit, however limited or conditioned, is what holds us. ... at the end of Ray Bradbury's *Fahrenheit 451* (as filmed by Truffaut) each exile from the book-burning state adopts the name of a text he has learned by heart and which he represents: one person is now called *David Copperfield*, another *Emile*, or even *Paradise Lost*. ... The extinction in this symbolic situation of the personal names of *both* author and reader shows what ideally happens in the act of reading
        (Geoffrey H. Hartman, from 'The Fate of Reading')

Can prose become poetry
through typographical
rearrangement? I
rather think it can.
        (Edwin Morgan, in *Times Literary*
           Supplement, 28 January 1965)

1

The Legitimacy of Reading

This is a book about meaning; more particularly, it is about the production, construction, interpretation and 'enactment' of meanings. Thus it is also, and perhaps despite its title, a book about reading; more specifically, it is about critical readings and their 'authorisations'. Before striding into the historical readings produced here, it is apposite to consider the meaning of *reading*, or rather, the meaning of an activity which I shall call *lecture*. The word 'reading' derives from the Old English *raedan*, and there the etymologist finds suggestions of 'considering', 'discerning' and even 'advising' as basic to the sense of the word. At some fundamental level, then, the meaning of 'reading' is already interwoven with residual ideas concerning the exercise of a critical consciousness: a reader is an agent, involved in activity, and not a mere passive recipient or 'patient' who suffers or 'understands' the text. Further, considering the meaning of the activity of lecture, an intimate relation between the notion of reading and that of legitimacy begins to appear. This link is crucial to a theorisation of authority, especially in the post-Gutenberg age of print.

'Lecture', itself another word for reading, derives most immediately from the Latin *lector*, which denotes primarily a reader who reads aloud. Its most common usage was in a context in which clear social relations of authority were established: the *lector* was a slave or servant who read aloud to a master. Considered in the light of this, the notion of literary authority comes under some speculative pressure. For it should be noted here that the person normally thought of, in contemporary theory, as the 'reader' or audience is actually the one who, as master, is in the historical position of 'authority'; while the person dictating or rehearsing the text (nowadays considered as the position of 'author') is in the place of slave or servant and reader, with no personal authority, and no ability to inaugurate or initiate the text or its lecture. Clearly, there are two spheres of authority here: the master has political and even historical authority (the ability to initiate and control historical situations), while the slave occupies a position which we would normally recognise as being that of 'literary' authority, the position of *scriptor* or writer. A contemporary understanding of reading and authority would see this as an unbearably paradoxical situation: the *scriptor* is in the position of *lector* or reader, and is a slave or patient upon whom history, controlled by other agents, unfolds itself; the reader or audience, as master and agent of this history, occupies the position of 'author'. This is partly explicable in terms of technology: Roman society and culture was predominantly oral, and its literate culture was based on chirographic practice, or on manuscript rather than on print. The literate print culture, the Benjaminian 'age of mechanical reproduction', is, in historical terms, largely an aberration of sorts, located between what Ong calls 'primary' and 'secondary' orality.[1] Print complicates the issue of authority; and the paradoxical arrangement outlined here is of fundamental importance in the theoretical understanding of what might be called 'modern authority', by which I mean literary authority in the post-Gutenberg age (an age which lasts at least until Samuel Morse's first telegraphically communicated message between Baltimore and Washington in 1839).[2] In print culture, relations between 'authors' and 'readers' is complex and, as I shall argue, fundamentally 'critical'.

Lector itself is cognate with *lex*, a Latin word which is frequently translated as 'law'. But, in the first instance, *lex* signifies a rather more preliminary and provisional stage in the establishment or inscription of a law when a proposing magistrate or assembly might put forward a proposition or motion for debate, prior to its written codification in a constitution. In parliamentary systems of government, which derive from the republican democratic model of Roman law, the equivalent of the *lex* is the preliminary stage of a bill, which has to go through a number of critical readings before passing into the *jus scriptum*, the written legal constitution.[3] Interestingly, of course, this immediately offers a second paradox. According to this 'legitimising' procedure in the lecture of a bill, *bulla* or *lex*, reading comes before writing. The reading of the *lex*, the activity of lecture, comes before inscription of a written text or constitutional *jus scriptum*, the law. The proposing *lector* here, although in the position of *scriptor* or author (and even perhaps in the position of

author understood as inaugurator, initiator of the *lex*) does
not yet authoritatively 'dictate' the law as such. Rather, the
lector offers a λεξισ, a phrase, as a first move in a dialogical
situation leading to the establishment of the law as written.
It is as if the *lex* had to be read before being written; it has,
in fact, to undergo the activity of lecture (with its implications of criticism and dialogue) before being enshrined
as written document, constitutive of social and historical
relations, or of laws which regulate such relations.[4]

One further item of etymological information is of importance and will clarify the extent to which criticism is integral
to the activity of reading. *Lex* not only has a foundation in
the Greek λεγω, λόγοσ, but also in an Indo-European root,
leg- or *lig-*, connoting binding or fastening together, and
with legal implications of ob*lig*ation. This mutates into the
two Latinate forms, *ligere* and *legere*, meaning respectively
'to collect, to select' and 'to read'. Reading involves ideas of
sorting or arranging: se-lecting, in fact, in order to confer
an arrangement of sorts on the materials found, invented or
col-lected on the page. The Germanic *Lesen* contains both
these notions of sorting and reading in the one word; and
the sense which is common to both conceptions of the word
Lesen is precisely an idea of 'examining' (as in *raedan*). This
is a primary sense which I want to return to contemporary
notions of reading. While reading, the text is not osmotically
assimilated, nor passively 'received', but requires critical consciousness, critical attention or examination, and selection
with collection. For instance, the repeated themes and motifs,
recognisable signs in the text, will be collected together, and
items will be taxonomically selected for ranging in each such
collection: repeated instances of a proper name, say, will be
collected, while a series of descriptions pertinent to this name
(as opposed to descriptions of a field or landscape, say) will
be selected to constitute the description of a named character.
If reading involves such activities, then it radically involves
the examination and critical *edition* of a text; and, fundamentally, it must be viewed as an *activity*, undertaken by
a historical agent. In this activity, the contemporary reader
recapitulates both positions in the Roman legal model outlined here (*lector/scriptor*), and performs an act which can

only really be described as criticism. This criticism in turn is instrumental in the legitimisation—or better, authorisation—of the legible or the read; that is, this criticism constructs and produces the *auctor*, authority or agency which is engendered through the text and its reading. In this collocation of lector and scriptor, print culture in the age of silent reading interiorises the dialectic of literary and historical authority. What we normally think of as the text can now be seen, not as locus of monumentalised enshrined authority, but as 'pre-text'; and through the reading of this pre-text, there arises the possibility of historical agency on the part of the reader. This is to say, in fact, that 'texts' are not usefully considered as 'containers' of history, but rather as pre-texts for material and historical activity. History is not 'in' the text; rather, the text becomes the condition of history and fully enters into the generation and production of that history.

The historical trajectory of the Roman legal model is instructive, and in one way at least is analogous with what happens to authority at the moment of transference from a predominantly oral or chirographic culture into a print-dominated one. During the period of the republic, the assemblies formed the ground of all legislation. These assemblies, however, although nominally open to all Roman citizens, were actually dominated and controlled entirely by the patricians. In the early years of the republic, especially when the plebeians were struggling to make their voices heard, there was a great deal of civil unrest. The plebeians formed their own assemblies, in which they enacted *plebiscita*, which were, in effect, their own legal system. For it was not until *Lex Hortensia* had been passed, in 287 BC, that *plebiscita* became binding, obligatory or legitimate (i.e. legible, read and heard) for all classes of Roman citizen. By this time, however, questions of social authority and political legislation had already changed their cast. In the early years of the republic, the Senate approved laws only after they had been read, criticised (perhaps amended) and voted on in the popular assemblies. But by the second half of the fourth century BC, the Senate had already arrogated enough power to itself to be able to reverse this procedure. Whereas reading had been prior to writing, the *leges* open to scrutiny before being passed into the *jus scriptum*, now senatorial writing of the law was to come first. Senatorial assent to the reading of the *leges* was succeeded by the senatorial assumed right of initiative in proposing, and writing, laws themselves. Magisterial assent and the popular voice were correspondingly reduced in importance.

This brings us into proximity with our own contemporary conception of literary authority. For the senate now, in writing the law, become themselves 'authors' in our modern sense, no longer answerable directly to the logically anterior political and historical authority of the assemblies. Rather than their 'readers' or audience (the magistrates and people at large) being able to change, with authority, the text of the law to suit their historical condition more closely or desirably, they simply had to follow, as closely as possible, the monumental written law or authority of the Senate: the text was now written without their consultation, consent or authority. Later still, of course, when Augustus established the age of imperial Rome in 31 BC, this senatorial power and authority passed into the even more restricted arena, in the consciousness of one person, the emperor. A subtle but vitally important change had been effected. Instead of authority being de-legated among the people at large (the reader/audience), it now became more and more concentrated into the hands or pen of the one proposer of laws, the authoritative emperor, imperial legislator or writer. The legislator was no longer a reader, a serving *lector* asking for the vocal assent of the people to a given provisional proposition, but rather was now a 'dictator', a writer demanding only the legitimisation of the law as written. Such legitimisation, or 'valid reading', meant complete agreement and active accordance with the consciousness of the imperial authority. Our contemporary notions, perhaps no longer shared with quite the same conviction, of the author's 'rights' over the meaning of her or his text, have their roots in a historical situation analogous to this one. When Gutenberg, along with Johann Fust, printed the 'Forty-two line Bible' in Mainz in 1448, the age of the proprietorial literary author, an author understood in terms similar to the Roman imperial authority, began in Western Europe. As Ong describes this:

> Print created a new sense of the private ownership of words. Persons in a primary oral culture can entertain some sense of proprietory rights to a poem, but such a sense is rare and ordinarily enfeebled by the common share of lore, formulas, and themes on which everyone draws. With writing, [and Ong here means printed writing specifically] resentment at plagiarism begins to develop. ... Typography has made the word into a commodity. The old communal oral world had split up into privately claimed freeholdings.[5]

The idea of authorial 'rights', or 'legitimate authorial privileges', as Fowler calls it, is specifically an effect of print and not at all a theoretical necessity or logical axiom.[6]

One justification for the etymological excursus here into ancient Rome is that the issues which it raises are central to the theorisation of authority in the modern period in Europe. The conflict between writerly authority and political or historical authority (broadly, the authority of writing and that of the voice, typographical literacy versus vocal orality as it were) is central to an age in which, after Gutenberg, writing itself has become more of a social issue, related to questions of power (thus provoking massive state and political censorship and control of written material), and also at a point (the Reformation) when transcendent notions of authority (as vested in the Pope) are being questioned and replaced by more genuinely 'historical' understandings of self-assertion and self-determination.[7] By roughly 1607, when Shakespeare produced *Coriolanus*, the Roman conflict of authorities became entirely comprehensible to an English audience; and not very long after this, a war which was similar to those civil disturbances of Rome, was 'enacted' or fought out in England precisely over such questions of authority.

Shakespeare's Coriolanus, it should be recalled, requires and asks precisely for the 'voices' of the people when he stands for the consulship in Rome. At that moment, he depends upon their authority for the legitimisation of his own name, title and position. He needs their voices (a word which is cognate with 'votes') in order to legitimise his authority as the named Coriolanus. As D.J. Gordon indicates: 'voice like *vox* has a technical sense in grammar: a voice means *word*, what is uttered, and the voice, utterance, that Coriolanus is asking for, is his name'.[8] Names, indeed, are important in the play, as a sign of free self-authorisation. When Coriolanus forgets the name of the poor man who sheltered him, the man remains imprisoned; the man is forgotten with the name.[9] At this moment, then, the state of Rome faces what Habermas calls a 'legitimation crisis',[10] which is what happens in the political system when there is an insufficient 'input' of mass loyalty to maintain the system as an integrated whole. Importantly, the legitimation crisis, following on from what Habermas calls a 'rationality crisis', takes a specific form: 'The legitimation crisis ... is directly an identity crisis'.[11] The character here is in that critical stage, hovering between identities as the historical Caius Marcius and the quasi-mythical 'Coriolanus'. In asking for the voices of the people to give him his name, Caius Marcius is aspiring to remove himself from the mire of mere historical, dialogical or consensual authority, and to assume a position of transcendental individuated authority; for the precise name he is asking for is itself a *myth*. The name 'Caius Marcius' denotes the merest historical accidents of birth and existence; 'Coriolanus', on the other hand, denotes transcendental and mythic essence. In his own assumption of this mythic name, his own resolution of the 'legitimation crisis', he strives to assume a position of authority not only in history (as an element in the Habermasian consensus) but also *over* history.[12]

In some respects, the assumed position of Coriolanus is quite like that in which contemporary culture locates the literary author. Coriolanus is supposed now to be a self-legitimating source, an origin in which the essence of the historically produced 'text' is to be found. More pertinently here, the play dramatises precisely the kind of subversion of democratic authority by the imperial *scriptor* which Rome had witnessed. When banished, he turns on the people who had refused their vocal assent to his identity, and strips them of their voices entirely, in an act of revenge in which he identifies himself not as 'Coriolanus' but as 'Rome' itself:

> Coriolanus: You common cry of curs, whose breath I hate
> As reek o' th' rotten fens, whose loves I prize
> As the dead carcasses of unburied men

That do corrupt my air, I banish you.
And here remain with your uncertainty![13]

In his 'inverse' banishment of them, he becomes Rome himself, leaving the people behind in the vagaries and uncertainties of history unprotected by the civic ritual of the *polis* or city walls. Further, those he leaves behind are reduced from the status of humans, with the possibility of authorial action vested in their voices, to the status of the merest inconsequential producers of noise, interference: they have no voice and become at best mere barking magistrates.

Coriolanus implies two contrary constitutions of authority. In the first, readers (an audience, people at large) have a voice, and in that possibility of vocal assent to a proposition, they have historical authority, the power to enact that 'text' or subscribe to it. Here, as in the republican democratic Roman legal model, reading is in some sense anterior to writing; and the voice is logically prior to print or writing, at least insofar as the writing or transcription depends upon the voice or vocal assent of the reader being given. The orientation here is from provisional script to fundamental voice, or from text to history. When this is subverted into the second mode of authority, as in *Coriolanus*, the imperial author imposes an orientation which is precisely contrary: from one dictatorial voice to the enshrined and monumental codification of that speech in the written constitution of the law. In this case, writing, ascribed to one individuated transcendent consciousness, precedes reading and determines or delimits what can be said, what is legible and legitimate. Correspondingly, there is a movement away from the vagaries of a history constructed through a Habermasian or Weberian 'rational consensus', and towards the imposition of a transcendentally established code, or essentialisation of human social values and relations, be it in the Justinian Law of the Twelve Tables or any other arbitrary code of historical conduct. A theorisation of modern authority must take this fundamental conflict of orientations as its ground.

Clearly, then, some theoretical clarification of the relation between author and reader in the modern era of print culture is required. My argument here intervenes in the area between the respective positions of Macherey and de Man regarding these relations. Near the beginning of *Pour une théorie de la production littéraire*, Macherey puts forward as a basic hypothesis that: 'lire et écrire ne sont pas deux opérations équivalentes ou réversibles: il faut éviter de les prendre l'une pour l'autre'.[14] This is partly in reaction against the Barthesian tendency to confound the two roles, a position which Macherey sees as inherently anti-historical. On the contrary, de Man, who would perhaps have been more at ease with such a Barthesian position, if rigorously applied, manages to conflate the two roles in his brief consideration of a passage in Proust's *À la recherche du temps perdu*. In the reading constructed by de Man, of a scene of reading in the 'dark coolness' of Marcel's room, he demonstrates, among other things, precisely the opposite thesis to that advanced by Macherey, arguing that 'the distinction between author and reader is one of the false distinctions that the reading makes evident'.[15]

The proposition put forward in my own argument mediates between these two courses. While acknowledging that the material reader and author are in some fundamental historical way separate positions or poles, as in Macherey (I am not T. S. Eliot, nor was meant to be, for example), I reverse or confound the positions usually ascribed to these roles (which is part of the impetus of de Man's thesis). The reader, the critical consciousness located in history, is the position which authorises or legitimises the text or its reading. The author is the 'co-respondent' of this reader, and writes or transcribes the text in the face of its own critical reading, a legitimisation of the provisional *lex*, or, following Barthes, *lexie*, which establishes the very possibility and condition of the text itself. The text, then, does now indeed come to us as, in Jameson's phrase, the 'always-already-read';[16] but whereas he means to suggest by this that texts come to us already saturated with cultural interpretations and cluttered by prejudicial or ideological judgements, I want to add the important corollary that the text is actually produced as 'always already read' *before* it has been written or 'legitimised'.

As the etymological excursus at the opening of this introduction makes clear, these ideas are not entirely new, although they may seem shocking to an age which understands print as a norm, and a culture which does not question the intellectual effect of print. Kenneth Burke suggests another possible source for similar theorisations of authority, again with primary reference to cultural artifacts which hover between existence as written composition and sound, in Boethius on music. He writes that:

> Boethius excludes performers from the number of real musicians, since they are merely slaves, obeying orders. The composers are also excluded, since they are merely inspired, and the Muses are responsible for their contribution. Then there are the critics. 'They alone are the real musicians, since their function consists entirely in reason and philosophy, in a knowledge of modes and rhythm, of the varieties of melodies and their combinations'[17]

This maps fairly congruently onto my own position here, but with the important proviso that the critic is also aware of her or his own historical position. This critic should be concerned to produce more philosophical voices, more music in this instance; it would be the function of literary criticism at the present time, by analogy, to produce more potential readers and more voices able to partake as conscious and critical agents in the construction not of more texts, but of more history.[18] If poets are, in Shelley's phrase, 'the unacknowledged legislators of the world',[19] then it is the function of criticism to produce more poets, not necessarily in the sense of more imperialist individuated authors, but in the sense of more voices which can actively take part in this legislation, this procedure of historical authorisation of social activity.

Intentionality: Writing Rites, Speaking Rights

The Boethian musical analogy brings into question the materiality or ontological status of the text. For the musical score is not itself the music that we hear; it must be 'enacted' or played, and can vary from one execution to the next, depending upon conductorial interpretation of the score, or any of a number of other contingent matters. By its nature, performance art is variable, and its grounding 'text' mutable. Thus Bob Dylan, for instance, frequently changes pacing, phrasing and even the words of his songs in each performance; and a line like 'Sometimes even the President of the United States must have to stand naked' takes on new significance after Watergate. According to Philip Hobsbaum, the writings of the poet from whom Dylan took his name, Dylan Thomas, lack sense until they are 'injected with meaning' in Thomas's recitation of them.[20] Some contemporary music has exploited this situation: Messiaen's *Quattuor pour la fin du temps*, for instance, invites the listener, through its complex varietal measure-times, to construct a different text, as it were, on each hearing; and the chance-dominated compositions of Cage, or some of Stockhausen's works are almost guaranteed to be performed differently, to subtend a different text, on each rendition.[21]

Re-applying the analogy to the literary text, it begins to appear that the written artifact is not itself a hermetic, self-sufficient entity; what is written can be considered as some kind of 'pre-text' of its performance. In short, there are no texts, only interpretations or performances; and such 'performatives', to borrow a term from linguistics, are in some sense like Austinian perlocutionary acts.[22] The important thing to comment on here is that such acts take place primarily in the sphere of material history: they are enactments, as it were, of or on a pre-text. Clearly, this kind of problematisation of the status of the literary text has much to do with the confusion of 'voice' and 'writing'. Ong has remarked on the relation of sound to historical experience: 'Sound exists only when it is going out of existence. It is not simply perishable but essentially evanescent'. By contrast, 'The alphabet implies that matters are otherwise, that a word is a thing, not an event, that it is present all at once, and that it can be cut up into little pieces'.[23] Here, sound is to the Saussurean *parole* as alphabetic writing is to *langue*: the typographic font, as it were, holds immanently every possible *parole*, and exists then at the level of the *langue* itself. Sound, or the voice, is in the domain of historical specificity in a way that typographical print is not. When Derrida deconstructs the binary opposition between speech and writing, in *De la grammatologie*, and shows that speech itself is in some sense logically dependent upon the anterior possibilities of the written, the most significant import of the deconstruction is that the written text is itself constitutive of the historical possibilities of speech. As Ong puts it, 'writing restructures consciousness'. Interpretations on or of pre-texts (which are now all we have) are first and foremost manifest in historical action, enactments or performances of meaning. They corroborate, modify or, potentially at least, change radically the social practice of the interpreter, who constructs an interpretation under the pretext of either justifying or questioning the assumptions or ideology within which her or his historical life unfolds. In the first instance, then, literary pre-texts produce the articulation or enactment of a historical ideology; in the second instance, they can be instrumental in delegitimising such an ideology, and affecting historical practice of intentional agents, meaningful speakers. The relation of writing to voice requires further analysis.

The period which saw the development of movable type in Europe coincides with the moment which Huizinga characterises as the 'waning of the middle ages'. He writes of the 'violent tenor of life' in the late fifteenth century as a dominant element affecting human consciousness. To deal with the violence which is material history, people resorted to excessive ritual:

> Every event, every action, was still embodied in expressive and solemn forms, which raised them to the dignity of a ritual. For it was not merely the great facts of birth, marriage, and death which, by the sacredness of the sacrament, were raised to the rank of mysteries; incidents of less importance, like a journey, a task, a visit, were equally attended by a thousand formalities: benedictions, ceremonies, formulas.[24]

Writing itself is one such rite. 'Print encouraged the mind to sense that its possessions were held in some sort of inert mental space', as Ong puts it. The same could also be said, of course, of artificial oral formulas as well; they too remove speech, the voice, from the realm of the merely historical and accidental into the transcendental space represented by

the typographic fount, the space which 'legitimises' or even
inaugurates and authorises all spoken historical discourse.
The voice is, as it were, taken out of history and relocated
in the apparatus of 'literature'.

This is pertinent to contemporary theorisations of the
ontological status of the text. Many Marxists of an Althuss-
erian cast, such as Eagleton and Macherey, anxious to save
history in some sense, suggest or argue for not only the
disappearance of the 'text' as such, but also for the disappearance or redundancy of literature: 'literature does not
exist', at least not in the sense that insects do, writes
Eagleton.[25] From an entirely different point of view, so-
called deconstructionists such as Bloom and Hartman also
worry themselves about the status of the text. These both
write with approval of Gershom Scholem, and Bloom follows
this 'belated Jewish Gnostic' closely enough to reiterate his
point that 'there are *no* texts, only interpretations'.[26] In this
Bloom is actually following a fairly conventional line of
orthodox Talmudic scholarship. There are no fundamentally
monumental 'scriptures', no written texts as essentialised self-
sufficient wholes: 'It is incumbent on every scholar to add
to the Talmud and to contribute to the work, although it
can never be finally completed', as Adin Steinsaltz puts it.[27]
There are, rather, really only a series of oral enactments or
articulations, comprehensible perhaps as historical gestures
of debate, criticism and even modification of the pre-text.
For Bloom, there may well be inscriptions, written artifacts
at some unspecified level of ontic existence, but they are
only 'strong', valid or legitimate (i.e. susceptible to reading)
insofar as they generate the possibility of the historical articulation of a will on the part of their readers, who may themselves then become revisionist writers. 'Revisionism', a bad
term in some orthodox Marxism, is for Bloom high praise.
Such an approach might even locate a principle of revisionism
in the fundamental texts of Marxism; and may want to
suggest that Marx himself, or perhaps more appropriately
Engels, was the first 'revisionist' of Marxism.

Hartman, too, despite his uneasy alignment with what he
has called the 'school of Derrida', a school from which he
frequently plays truant, has fairly consistently emphasised

the importance of the historical realm of voice as well as that
of writing or textuality:

> Writing destabilizes words, in the sense that it makes us aware at one
> and the same time of their alien frame of reference (they are words of
> the other or come to us already interpreted, trailing clouds of meaning,
> each one a representamen) and of the active power of forgetfulness (a
> kind of silencing) which it enables and which, in turn, enables us to
> write. Yet to talk about writing as such or about language as such is
> too abstract, just as to talk about literary language per se is too isolating.
> At some point the affective power of voice, as well as the relation of
> particular words to that resonating field we call the psyche, must be
> considered. Semiotic analysis of the word in the word, even when as
> penetrating as Derrida's, with his method of putting statements *en
> abyme*, cannot reach that field of pathos or power. The interpreter, at
> least, has also to understand the wound in the word.[28]

This 'wound' is itself the violence of history, which Hartman
wants to reactivate, at least to the extent that it resounds,
with pathos, in the consciousness of the interpreter. It is not
a question here of simply privileging speech over writing
once more, as if in wilful ignorance of Derrida. The ghost
of authorial intention may be making its presence felt, but
even such a ghost as this requires the mediating voice of
another speaker for its historical realisation; and this is where
a fuller theorisation of intentionalism in literary interpretation is required.

In almost every defence of the theoretical position which
states that interpretation should be concerned with the reconstruction or discovery of an anterior authorial intention, there
is a confusion between the ritualised text and the historical
consciousness of another individual. Most defenders of intentionalism derive their position from something akin to
Austin's and Searle's linguistic theory of speech-acts. But a
written text, although significant, is no more a speech-act
than is any other kind of non-verbalised historical activity,
like shaking hands, striking an adversary or eating. In a
recent 'refinement' of his hermeneutical position, Hirsch, for
example, simply asserts that there is no difference between
speech and writing,[29] axiomatically refusing to consider this
theoretical difficulty any further. In David Newton-de Molina's
recent selection of papers *On Literary Intention*, those who

follow in this broad line follow Hirsch in the confusion of voice and writing. Cioffi, for instance writes that 'there is an implicit biographical reference in our response to literature'; Sparshott makes a clear analogy of understanding a text with understanding another human consciousness; and Skinner offers perhaps the clearest example of the confusion:

> To know a writer's motives and intentions is to know the relationship in which he stands to what he has written. To know about intentions is to know such facts as whether the writer is joking or serious or ironic or in general what speech-act he was performing. To know about motives is to know what prompted those particular speech-acts, quite apart from their character and truth-status as utterances. [30]

In these formulations it is as if the text, *qua* written text, simply erased itself as we read, being articulated in the voice of the poet. The illusion is that the poet 'speaks' to us, but simply through a medium which veils her or his intention. This medium is taken to be language itself, irrespective of the various technological mediations of that language. The text becomes not even a substitute or parallel for a speech-act, but becomes theoretically accepted as itself constitutive of a speech-act: it is as if books, like humans, really did 'say' things.

Clearly, however, something happens to discourse when it moves from one technological medium to another. It is not very likely that Wordsworth, say, even using a 'selection of language really used by men', would ever have actually *said*, in conversation, 'I wandered lonely as a cloud/That floats on high o'er vales and hills'. [31] The medium may not itself be the message, in McLuhan's celebrated phrase, but it does affect the discourse which it is supposed to serve. In writing, to use Derrida's term, there is a 'dangerous supplement' which threatens to confuse or interfere with a mythic direct transmission from sender to addressee of any 'message'. This supplement is to be found in the 'font' of the typographic *langue*, as the meanings not of a human consciousness but of the language, the written medium, itself. Ricoeur has similarly argued that when discourse makes the rite of passage from speech to writing, 'What the text signifies no longer coincides with what the author meant; henceforth, textual meaning and psychological meaning have different destinies'.[32] It is precisely these different destinies which the interpretative 'intentionalist' confuses, or refuses to distinguish. Following the researches of David R. Olson, Ong agrees that 'orality relegates meaning to context whereas writing concentrates meaning in language itself'.[33]

This is a theoretical crux which most intentionalist theory, as can be seen in the examples cited here, wants to avoid. In this, the history of hermeneutical activity is enlightening. Schleiermacher, for instance, posits two possibilities for interpretation, the 'grammatical' and the 'technical', corresponding closely to Olson's two possibilities. Either meaning is to be found in common cultural areas, such as language itself (the 'grammatical' interpretation), or it is to be found in the singularity or genius of the writer's message (the 'technical', Olsonian 'contextual' interpretation). Schleiermacher argued that the task of hermeneutics was the adoption of the technical recovery of the authorial singular genius. When taken over by Dilthey, this same orientation was maintained, and the hermeneutic enterprise remains firmly psychological, because, as Ricoeur argues, 'it stipulates as the ultimate aim of interpretation, not *what* a text says, but *who* says it'.[34] By and large, this is the same orientation as that ascribable to intentionalist orthodoxy in criticism since Dilthey. What is at stake in this approach is the reconstruction of an identity, an authorial name, which will then be used as legitimisation for the meaning proposed for the text. While this may, theoretically, be admissible, on condition that the critic or interpreter may coexist in the same context as the 'speaking author' of a discourse, it is not so easily maintainable once that discourse has been modified in its transcription into a print culture devoid of specific context. In print, or writing, the location of meaning is not so incontrovertibly located in the consciousness of a speaker; for in fact there is no speaker, and no 'speech-act' in the Austinian or Searlian sense. Rather, the potential of meaning is located in the typographic font of linguistic possibility itself. The interpreter, in reading, is not in an intersubjective context established by the relation of two individuated human consciousnesses; rather, the 'context' is that between the given written document and the

series of other texts, written or possible, which surround it
and differ from it.

When Geoffrey Hartman finds 'outrageous punning' in
the writings of Christopher Smart, for instance, he may
seem to be 'changing' the text which he is supposed to be
interpreting. He discovers the word 'Ruach' (the Hebrew
word for the inspirational breath of God) in, or more precisely 'in front of', Smart's word 'Roach' (a kind of fish).
The orthodox intentionalist might want to argue that this is
simply changing the text to suit an interpretation which is
being imposed on that text, against the explicit will or intention of its writer: Hartman might as well substitute 'anchovy'
for 'Roach'. If so, of course, Hartman might also find that
this word too is mutable, and can become 'an-chov-y' with
an echo of 'Jove' and hence 'Jahweh' in its central section.
At this point, the intentionalist calls 'Enough!' perhaps.[35]
Hartman is no longer discussing 'Smart's text'. But this is
precisely the area of theoretical difficulty; for where is 'the
text', and what 'con-texts' help define it? For the intentionalist, the answer seems to be clear: the context is that
established between the consciousness of interpreter and
another human consciousness, that which is transparently
expressed in the audible or recoverable voice of the speaking
writer. But writing has complicated this: the hypothetical
pure voice, pure consciousness has been vitiated by the possibilities of language as 'encased' in typographic print.

The 'historicist reconstructionist' is concerned with the
establishment of a stable meaning for the text, as guaranteed
by the discovery of the identity or name of the writer, and
as heard in the context of the writer's 'conversation' with the
interpreter. When Hirsch revised his terms 'meaning' and
'significance' in 1972, he still did not change his basic
position. Now Hirsch argues, 'Meaning is what an interpreter
actualizes from a text; significance is that actual speaking as
heard in a chosen and variable context of the interpreter's
experiential world'.[36] Here, however, 'meaning' still resides
within the monument of the hermetic text, sealed off from
the vagaries of language as such. The interpreter 'actualizes'
or activates no longer a fixed, eternal and monumentalised
meaning; instead, she or he activates part of the text's poten-

tial meaning, which now begins to reach out to encompass a number of possible meanings, some of which may even 'disregard' conscious authorial will. The main point, though, which has remained from the Hirsch of 1967, is that the text itself works as the legitimising voice of authorial consciousness; meaning still resides in this text, just as it did (and still effectively does) in the vocalised consciousness of its speaking author. Further, this meaning is supposed to be logically prior to any construction of mere significances. But, again, this position requires examination.

One logical extension of a proto-Hirschian position is to suggest an end to commentary or interpretation as such; the text, being the locus of meaning, should simply be reproduced and allowed to speak for itself; or rather, the author should be allowed this liberty. The preparation of critical editions of reliable texts follows this kind of line. This scholarly approach is concerned, it seems at first blush, with the stabilisation of texts and their construction as unchangeable monuments. But the historicist reconstructionist who aims to reproduce such a pure text, such a pure codification of an authorial vocalised consciousness, is faced with the same *interpretative* difficulties as the Hartmanic critic. For any reconstruction of such an imperial authorial text is dependent upon its 'significance', dependent upon the critic or editor lending her or his own voice to the poet; the critic or editor cannot simply 'hear' the voice of another speaking consciousness. An example will clarify this. In her edition of Donne's *Elegies and Songs and Sonnets*, Helen Gardner tampers with the text of 'The Ecstasy'. In line 67 of this poem, she disregards all previous textual authorities, which give 'Which sense may reach and apprehend', and construes instead 'That sense may reach and apprehend'. The full enormity of such a change is made apparent in her appended commentary:

1.67 *That sense may reach and apprehend.* Against the *consensus* of 1633 and all manuscripts I have emended 'Which' to 'That'. Copyists tend to treat the two forms of the relative as interchangeable, and I am assuming that 'Which' was substituted under the mistaken notion that 'That' was the relative and not the conjunction. The relative here gives poor sense because 'sense' does not 'reach and apprehend' affections and faculties but 'reaches and apprehends' the object of perception by means of affections and faculties. If we read 'That' (in order that) the action of the souls parallels the action of the blood.[37]

This 'emendation', then, is made in concert with a desired interpretation, or 'significance', and yet passes into the substance of the 'meaning' of the text. In principle at least, there is no great difference between this and the manoeuvres of Hartman on Smart, punningly 'emending' the text. A fundamental difference, however, is that Gardner here regards herself as a supposedly naive copyist, the merest transmitter of Donne's voice and conscious intention. When she writes that copyists confused the two forms of the relative, she omits to mention that it is in fact she, as copyist, who is performing this manoeuvre, in pragmatic conformity with the construction of a desired meaning for the text. Here, commentary has entered the text in a manner predicted by the 'typical' deconstructionist. This fundamental difference offers two varied approaches to intentionality. On the one hand, confusing the text with a human vocal consciousness, the scholarly editor such as Gardner pretends to submit herself to the voice of Donne, but actually interpolates her own voice to make Donne 'say' what she wants him to say. The text is then given with the full institutional authorial weight of the name of Donne; it is the consciousness designated by the name 'John Donne' which legitimises the meaning of this text, supposedly. On the other hand, Hartman acknowledges the meaning of the text, using it to construct a meaning or significance which cannot simply be legitimated by the name and identity of Christopher Smart, nor even by those of Hartman himself. Instead, the commentary or interpretation which Hartman constructs here has to be legitimised, if at all, with reference to the system of language itself, and, more importantly, by his own historical readers; that is, by other historical voices and consciousnesses. This, of course, is not meant to devalue the historicist reconstructionist approach to literature as such; simply, it is meant to theorise it and demonstrate that far from offering clear access to a historical truth, 'what Donne *really* said, or really *meant* to say', it is itself intrinsically bound up with pragmatic criticism, and with the voices and articulated desires of the editor/ interpreter. The point of such an argument is to suggest that the 'Gardnerian' approach, sanctioned by proto-Hirschian and 'commonsense' intentionalism, ignorant of the effects of typographic writing, is an attempt to foreclose history and reduce interpretation to the safe ritual of reproducing monuments to past 'truths'. The reader of Gardner's Donne is in one sense denied a voice in the construction of historical meaning around the text: Donne (according to Gardner) has already constructed that unchanging meaning, that essentialised truth which is located within his consciousness and metaphorically reproduced in the scripted text. Like the plebeian in imperial Rome, all we can do is acknowledge such an intention as a preformed entity constructed by another consciousness. We may wish to argue ethically about the propositions within the poem; but here, if we refuse to assent to the text as 'dictated' by Donne's consciousness, what we are doing is not so much textual interpretation but rather indulging in ethical debate, a supposed 'second degree' of criticism. Further, we do not construct an ethics 'with' Donne in this, so much as in defiance of Donne, weighing our own authority, the weight of our own name and authorial reputation, against the institution of Donne's 'canonised' name. The alternative to this, of course, is to acknowledge our own voice working in collaboration with the text, working on or through the 'pre-text' of Donne's poem, and using that to construct a non-ritualised historical meaning; that is, allowing it to impinge upon our consciousness and self-consciousness.

The Ethics of Interpretation: Genealogy and Gender

Hirsch, in his revised position, pins much hope on an ethical argument:

> let me state what I consider to be a fundamental ethical maxim for interpretation, a maxim that claims no privileged sanction from metaphysics or analysis, but only from general ethical tenets, generally shared. *Unless there is a powerful overriding value in disregarding an author's intention (i.e. original meaning), we who interpret as a vocation should not disregard it.*[38]

The ethical grounding of this proposition is to be found, argues Hirsch, in Kant:

> When we simply use an author's words for our own purposes without respecting his intention, we transgress what Charles Stevenson in another context called 'the ethics of language,' just as we transgress ethical norms when we use another person merely for our own ends. ... Kant held it to be a foundation of moral action that men should be conceived as ends in themselves, and not as instruments of other men. This imperative is transferable to the words of men because speech is an extension and expression of men in the social domain, and also because when we fail to conjoin a man's intentions to his words we lose the soul of speech, which is to convey meaning and to understand what is intended to be conveyed.[39]

There are a number of difficulties here. Firstly, in a modern print culture the words in question are not 'the author's words' in a strictly possessive sense: the author, at most, 'borrows' the words which the common lexicon is generous or gracious enough to afford to an author. The typographic font is a public fountain, and cannot be drunk dry of potential fluency or meaning as its words are used up or 'possessed' by 'authors'. Further, the communication model proposed by Hirsch here has little to do with the facts of human communication (especially verbal communication). The model suggests that each human is, as it were, a 'box' or repository of intentions, which are then 'poured out' into an encoded or metaphorical shape (a sentence, say), and subsequently 'poured in' to another 'box', the addressee, who was, as it were, empty of all possible intention prior to this influential 'communication' of ideas. But people simply do not communicate on this model or anything like it. As Ong puts it, in his description of the post-Agricolan mind, which thinks in terms of this kind of 'place logic', 'the whole mental world has gone hollow'; and, in more general terms, he attacks this 'mediumistic' model of Hirsch and others when he writes:

> Human communication, verbal and other, differs from the 'medium' model most basically in that it demands anticipated feedback in order to take place at all. In the medium model, the message is moved from sender-position to receiver-position. In real human communication, the

sender has to be not only in the sender position but also in the receiver position before he or she can send anything.[40]

This is perhaps a more simple way of explaining the Derridean notion of *s'entendre-parler* as fundamental to communication.

Even if we were to concede these points, however, the fundamental ethical position of Kant, in the hands of Hirsch, begins to assume the posture and import of a rather dubious ethics. Kant's notion that people should be regarded as ends in themselves, rather than means towards an end, to be manipulated by other people, is fundamentally 'liberal'. Hirsch argues, following this, that we should not simply use 'an author's words' for our own ends (confusing text and consciousness at this point) but should rather respect that author's intentions. But if the critic *simply* ignores her or his own intentional capabilities, her or his ability to assume a position of historical agency, in order to mediate, rehearse or even discover this authorial intention, as if it existed as a solidly self-sufficient monument, then the critic is becoming the means or medium which allows the author to attain her or his end, which is presumably the influential pouring of a message into the minds of the now passive recipients. Hirsch then becomes simply the unresistant medium or means through whom an authorial end is supposedly obtained. That is to say, his position turns out to be profoundly *anti-Kantian*. This hermeneutical position subtends the very possibility of authoritarianism, which the Kantian precept is supposed to negate. Further, it is not simply the authoritarianism of 'the author' which is thus obtained; rather, since we are dependent upon the mediation of Hirsch for knowledge of this authorial will or intention, we are placed in the position of passive, non-resistant and even unconscious receivers of Hirsch's, or the critic's, authoritarianism.

There is a religiosity to the enterprise, self-contradictory though it is in terms of ethics: Hirsch writes of the 'vocation' of interpretation. Following the mediumistic model of communication upon which the theory rests, the interpretative reader of a text becomes fundamentally 'enthusiastic' (full of the gods). The patient reader, passive recipient of the influential message being poured forth from an 'author' (and where did she or he get their message from; who 'influenced' them?) is posited as an entity devoid of consciousness, or at least devoid of the possibility of intentional agency: we are the merest vessel, or cog in the machine through and across whom the authorial intention enacts itself. We are supposed to await 'possession', then, by a quasi-angelic author; and, like all media, when we rehearse or 'speak' the text (the authorial message), the voice discovered is not ours but a bizarre parody of the author's. To rehearse the intention of another like this, almost unconsciously, is in fact profoundly uncritical; and clearly, as I have argued, it opens the way towards an ethics of authoritarianism over unconscious 'subjects', readers who would now better be described as objects.

This ethical question impinges upon questions of epistemology in interpretation. Many critics of a Hirschian cast might want to argue that the text, and more importantly its author, subtends the possibility of acquiring knowledge; but knowledge is not simply an end in itself: it is a root of authorisations, and of power, in the sense that we have not only 'knowledge about' things, but also the 'knowledge to' perform actions, 'know-how'. The production of knowledge, then, can itself become instrumental in the production of authority, precisely reversing the orientation of the Hirschian position. A theorisation of the role of 'knowledge-production' in interpretation can profit from a consideration of knowledge at the beginnings of modern science.

Blumenberg remarks on a distinguishing trait of modern science and philosophy. He contrasts it with ancient philosophy, where 'The signature of the epoch following Plato and Aristotle is the common possession of the characteristic Hellenistic idea of philosophy, which can be described as its *therapeutic* conception'.[41] Theoretical curiosity, as Blumenberg calls it, is instrumental in providing spiritual fulfilment; the function of science or philosophy is eudemonic. In the Enlightenment in Europe, however, this began to change, as did many other human self-conceptions in the post-Copernican age. Now, Blumenberg argues:

> Truth has become the result of a renunciation for the modern age also, a renunciation that lies in the separation between cognitive achievement and the production of happiness. This separation could be accepted as

a temporary one as long as the integration of theoretical accomplishments still seemed attainable or indeed insofar as one considered one's own present situation to be quite near to the summit of the ascent. But this separation also begins—with increasing doubt about the convergence of knowledge and happiness—to be set up as an ideal: Lack of consideration for happiness becomes the stigma of truth itself, a homage to its absolutism.[42]

Another way of expressing this position might be to frame it in terms of the historical juncture at which 'knowledge of' is displaced by the greater importance of 'knowledge to': knowledge of the truth, a truth which contributes to the happiness of the knowing subject, is displaced in importance by the increasing relevance of a knowledge which is instrumental in actually shaping or constructing a 'truth' and its concomitant happiness for the 'knower'. Such a change in the complexion of science and philosophy occurs in the wake of the Copernican revolutionary displacement of the earth from centrality to eccentricity. With this, according to Blumenberg, the medieval *cosmos* is threatened with disintegration. The stable world-order is now riven with internal conflict and has become once more, to use the terms of Blumenberg, *chaos*. But such a disintegration of stable certainty, of *cosmos*, invites the existential historical construction of order, and makes such an activity a basic human theme, indeed a definition of the human. Blumenberg writes:

> The escape into transcendence, as the possibility that is held out to man and has only to be grasped, has lost its human relevance precisely on account of the absolutism of the decisions of divine grace, that is, on account of the dependence of the individual's salvation on a faith that he can no longer choose to have. This changed set of presuppositions brings into the horizon of possible intentions the alternative of the immanent self-assertion of reason through the mastery and alteration of reality.[43]

The change in the application of knowledge, then, is linked to what might be termed the beginning of the modern, and historical, age. For Blumenberg, the modern age stirs itself into active potential in the confrontation of the cosmological schemes of the pro-Copernican Nicholas of Cusa and the post-Copernican Giordano Bruno of Nola. For Nicholas, time and its corollary, change or displacement, are the merest irrelevancies of human measurement:

> For the Cusan, the Incarnation of the Word was the supplementation and perfection of the Creation, *complementum et quies*, as he says in the sermon *Dies sanctificatus*. Only in this divine self-insertion into the Creation does God's power fully actualize itself (*quiescit potentia in seipsa*). The duality of generation and creation is closed at this juncture and integrated into the unit of God's self-expression. But this pre-supposes that time, by which an interval is laid between the Creation and the Incarnation in the midst of history, is a purely human measure of successiveness, which is imposed on the inner and essential unity of the divine action.[44]

For Bruno, on the other hand, thinking in the wake of the Copernican displacement of the earth and its humanity, there is a relativisation of human existence. If one world deserves to exist (as it manifestly does in the material existence of the earth), then all possible worlds do likewise deserve existence. And this notion of the plurality of worlds 'is based on the metaphysical assurance that the Divinity gave up everything and turned it over to the world, in which therefore anything can become of anything'.[45] Not only have we realised, theo-logically, the notion of the *deus absconditus* in this, the hidden god which will play such a large part in European thought and the Jansenist tradition; we have also, in more literary terms, transferred from the age of medieval allegory to that of modern metaphor ('anything can become of anything'). For Nicholas of Cusa, God or some tran-scendental essence could be discerned behind and in all things. For Bruno, such eternal or atemporal essence has disappeared; or rather, it existed only insofar as it was created or constructed by human and *historical* intervention. In short, through the Copernican revolution, access to the truth of nature is threatened if not entirely lost, while access to history is gained, but such historical existence threatens the human with a real, unritualised, unallegorical and unsch-ematised possibility of an absurd death. Here, then, lies the fundamental modern cleavage between epistemology and eudemonia. The Marxian notion that philosophy in the past had tried to understand the world while the point now was to change it, is axiomatic in Blumenberg's delineation of

modern humanity, whose aim is now 'the mastery and alter- ✓✓
ation of reality'.

Lyotard's distinctions between 'narrative' knowledge and
'scientific' knowledge overlap with these Blumenbergian
notions. Narrative knowledge looks rather like the pre-
Copernican state in which all people, through the rehearsal
of (oral) narratives 'know their place' in the cosmic order
of things. Such narrative knowledge needs no 'scientific'
validation: it is self-legitimising because, like an Austinian
performative, the very act of narration does in fact what it
claims to do in the narration itself. As Lyotard puts it,
narrative knowledge 'certifies itself in the pragmatics of its
own transmission without having recourse to argumentation
and proof'.[46] In the succeeding age of modern science, the
legitimation of 'scientific' knowledge becomes crucial in the
persuasion of people of the validity of the truths advanced
by the scientists and philosophers. Science, post-Copernicus,
produces a metadiscourse, a discourse of legitimation alongside itself, and this is, for Lyotard, 'a discourse called philosophy'.[47]

Opposing Talcott Parsons's optimistic notion of society as
a machine to the Marxian notion of society as radically split
internally, Lyotard constructs a further binary coupling of
knowledges. On the one hand, knowledge can be functional,
and can be instrumental in the efficient maintenance of the
Parsonsian social mechanism. Here individual happiness is
sacrificed to a philosophical 'realism'; and the realism in
question is actually the supposed inevitable reality of the
workings of the machine. Knowledge is instrumental in the
production of efficiency, as in computation. Opposed to this
is what Lyotard calls 'critical knowledge', through which
attempts can be made to 'change' or deregulate the machine
in the pursuit of the creation of happiness among the components of the machine; that is, cognitive and critical agents.
Logically, for Lyotard, the alternative 'seems clear: it is a
choice between the homogeneity and the intrinsic duality of
the social, between functional and critical knowledge. But
the decision seems difficult, or arbitrary', at least in logical
terms.[48] However, with what Lyotard sees as the resurgence
of the narrative mode of knowledge in the post-modern age

of 'secondary orality', a decision of sorts 'legitimates' itself, or urges itself upon the theorist. And this choice is, it seems, openly ethical; although it has modified the less theoretical ethical stance of Hirsch. As Lyotard explains this: 'The mode of legitimation we are discussing, which reintroduces narrative as the validity of knowledge, can thus take two routes, depending on whether it represents the subject of the narrative as cognitive or practical, as a hero of knowledge or a hero of liberty.'[49] Thus 'Knowledge is no longer the subject, but in the service of the subject: its only legitimacy (though it is formidable) is the fact that it allows morality to become reality'.[50] The Kantian ethical question can now reappear, then, in the formulation of the relation between knowledge and power, knowledge and authority (in literary terms), and knowledge and the state (in political terms). Lyotard in fact rehearses precisely the Kantian precept of the relation between means and end, but with a greater degree of theoretical sophistication than it appears in the argument of Hirsch:

> This introduces a relation of knowledge to society and the State which is in principle a relation of the means to the end. But scientists must cooperate only if they judge that the politics of the State, in other words the sum of its prescriptions, is just. If they feel that the civil society of which they are members is badly represented by the State, they may reject its prescriptions. This type of legitimation grants them the authority, as practical human beings, to refuse their scholarly support to a political power they judge to be unjust, in other words, not grounded in a real autonomy. They can even go so far as to use their expertise to demonstrate that such autonomy is not in fact realized in society and the State. This reintroduces the critical function of knowledge. But the fact remains that knowledge has no final legitimacy outside of serving the goals envisioned by the practical subject, the autonomous collectivity.[51]

The seeming ethical choice, then, between being a 'hero of knowledge' or a 'hero of liberty', between the conception of knowledge as based in cognition or fundamentally involved in historical practices, is resolved at this point. For knowledge is in the realm of the practical and is instrumental in the production of authority. It is not the case that we can just have knowledge of a text, say, or of an authorial intention; such knowledge is, as it were, always already engaged in a practical historical situation: it is either functional in upholding some transcendentally conceived system (the mechanical model of society, say), or in critically probing such a system. In opposition to Hirsch, then, it seems incumbent upon the critic to adopt what might be termed an 'oppositional' stance to the literary text. There can be no 'innocent' knowledge of authorial intention: such cognitive knowledge is being practically used to uphold a system which is to a greater or lesser degree authoritarian, as in the conservative notion (as propagated by Parsons in America; or by Scruton and the *Salisbury Review* in England) of the functional society and its norms. Instead of having or discovering knowledge of an anterior and self-sufficient state of affairs (the text, an authorial intention), we can have a mode of knowledge which is not concerned with knowledge about the self-legitimising and thus powerfully authoritative Truth, so to speak (for that truth, in the post-Copernican age, has disappeared), but rather with the production of critical *meanings*. The meanings produced in this case will not be those of an anterior imperialist kind of author, whose intentions and authorial stance are legitimised in an act of 'mediumistic' reading, but will rather be informed by the intentions of the reader, involved in a practical, historical, secular activity of exercising critical consciousness, assaying to construct essayistic meanings. Such an essay, of course, should also be instrumental in generating a historical voice for others, if it is to be genuinely 'libertarian', and should thus oppose the incipient authoritarianism of the Hirschian (and indeed almost every) historicist reconstructionist or intentionalist orthodoxy.

This may appear at first blush to be simple wilful misprision in critical theory; as if I was suggesting that one should always contradict, as directly as possible, an inferred authorial intention. But the point is that even in the interpretative construction of such an intention, there is, if the interpreter is conscious and exercising the critical faculty, an intrinsic 'oppositionalism' at work. It is through our differences from and with an author or a text that we can produce meaning at all in any historical sphere. Said corroborates such a critical stance:

> Were I to use one word consistently along with *criticism* (not as a modification but as an emphatic) it would be *oppositional*. If criticism is reducible neither to a doctrine nor to a political position on a particular question, and if it is to be in the world and self-aware simultaneously, then its identity is its difference from other cultural activities and from systems of thought or of method. In its suspicion of totalizing concepts, in its discontent with reified objects, in its impatience with guilds, special interests, imperialized fiefdoms, and orthodox habits of mind, criticism is most itself and, if the paradox can be tolerated, most unlike itself at the moment it starts turning into organized dogma. 'Ironic' is not a bad word to use along with 'oppositional'. For in the main—and here I shall be explicit—criticism must think of itself as life-enhancing and constitutively opposed to every form of tyranny, domination, and abuse; its social goals are noncoercive knowledge produced in the interests of human freedom.[52]

Here, criticism takes its place not as a functional element in the maintenance of any particular social organisation, but rather as constitutive of a Habermasian production of a 'rational society', on Weberian lines. Considering Weber's notion of rational authority, Habermas opposes the thought of Niklas Luhmann with that of Johannes Winckelmann. The former corresponds roughly to the conservative position of Parsons, arguing that social normatives are legitimised simply through the legality of their constitution (i.e. under the authority of the state, say); for the latter, this is not enough, and a rational consensus which will itself legitimate or validate the authorial stance of that legality is necessary. Meaning, then, is to be produced not simply as a consensus of irrational or ill-informed opinion (classical bourgeois democracy), but depends upon the exercise of a rational will. Norms of action are then validated through communal discourse, the Habermasian consensus. In such discourse we must be assured

> that participants, themes and contributions are not restricted except with reference to the goal of testing the validity claims in question; that no force except that of the better argument is exercised; and that as a result, all motives except that of the cooperative search for truth are excluded. If under these conditions a consensus about the recommendation to accept a norm arises argumentatively, that is, on the basis of hypothetically proposed, alternative justifications, then this consensus expresses a 'rational will'.[53]

Such a libertarian approach may indeed be too much to expect in the realities of capitalist politics, or indeed in political society as such. But, following Gramsci's distinction between 'political society' (what we normally consider to be 'the political', i.e. state institutions which have a direct bearing on polity) and 'civil society' (where less coercive power-dominations are the rule, as in the organisations of human unions and the manifest aspects of a culture), it is right to ask if it is not too much to expect in the 'civil' and cultural realm of textual criticism.[54] The production of knowledge, in the form of productive and therapeutic meanings, is at stake here, and is to be ethically valorised over the incipiently authoritarian expression of individual and uncritical 'opinion'.

This 'oppositional criticism', then, can now be seen to have ethical, if not political, implications. Opposing a dominant authority is conventionally thought to be 'revolutionary'. But if this criticism is indeed revolutionary in any sense, it is so in a quasi-Trotskian sense, for the revolutionary mode of criticism which I am outlining here is implicitly repetitive. Mehlman has remarked on the closeness of revolution and repetition. Adopting a stance, against Habermas it might seem, in which rhetorical persuasion itself is seen as a subtle form of violence, Mehlman writes of the 'violence of interpretative activity', and here comes close to Bloom's argument that 'Gnostic exegesis of Scripture is always a salutary act of textual violence, transgressive through and through'.[55] But transgressive criticism, or oppositional criticism, is seen as wilful violence only from the point of view of a consciousness which understands or accepts dogmatically that texts are monuments (which must not be 'defaced'), monuments to the quasi-sanctity of another consciousness, that of an author (who is to be 'obeyed' simply by dint of being 'authoritative'). But Mehlman argues, correctly, that:

> A text is less a monument than a battlefield. The interpreter's task, then, is to situate his own efforts strategically at the crux of that struggle and to ally himself with that stratum of the text generative of the greatest intensity. But to the extent that one has been able to work within the node or matrix of the various forces, the pursuit of the 'battle' will take the form of a rigorous positing of the lines along

which and the conditions under which the work may be *rewritten*.[56]

Here, then, the revolutionary critic strives to 'rewrite' the text. Another way of expressing this is to suggest that this critic is simply trying to rehearse—that is, to read or articulate, give a historical voice to—the particular text in question. Such a 'repetition', with an implicit degree of revolutionary revisionism, is absolutely fundamental to an understanding of authority in the modern age.

There is a further notch in the ethical substratum of these propositions. As I remarked above, it is the monumental name of the author which is fundamentally being 'healthily' maintained in most orthodox intentionalist critical strategies. In the modern European age, this is itself of ethical importance. The critical question focuses on the notion of critical 'fidelity' to the text under discussion; which, in intentionalism, becomes critical fidelity to an author or authorial progenitor, as it were.

I remarked, following Huizinga, that in the violent age of late medievalism in Europe (a violence which, of course, has not really left us since) writing was a ritual of protection against the vagaries of historical, death-orientated existence. Another such ritual was the domestic family, the so-called 'nuclear family unit'. Therapeutics was more than a philosophical issue in late-Renaissance England; in the sixteenth and seventeenth centuries several health laws were enacted in London to counter both the threat of plague and also that of syphilis (distinguished for the first time from leprosy). Clearly, the presence of such threats to life were conducive to the production of a 'philosophy of domesticity' or privacy. The establishment of a clearly demarcated, walled, private domestic unit works as a mode of protection against material historical disruption: the 'house' (meaning both the building and also the metaphysical organisation of the family) protects the individual against the historically disruptive threat of 'nature'. King Lear, for instance, is expelled from both kinds of house in Shakespeare's play. Having been progressively stripped of all ritual (power, robes, retinue, clothing, voice and protective shelter from the storm), he is left to roam the heath, expelled from the house and exposed to the possibility of death. But this is no isolated instance of such a dialectic of ritual and history. King Lear's condition is a prominent motif in modern writing, where the struggle against a death-orientated history is frequently seen in terms of the establishment, real or fantasised, of the protective ritual of a private, identifiable domestic unit or self, located in the family house.

The presence of syphilis in England leads to the establishment of a more regulated, 'legitimated' sexuality as socially normative. 'Legitimacy' (acting not only in accordance with the health laws but also in accordance with an ideology of 'safe privacy', regulated sexual behaviour) becomes itself 'normative'. In socio-sexual terms, then, the construction of a 'house' in the sense of an identity, an identity gained from an identifiable (repetitive) genealogical and 'legitimate' (even physiognomically 'legible') lineage comes to form a dominant crux in terms of civil and even political authority. For a stable genealogy protects, above all else, the mythic, even talismanic, name of the father from possible dissolution across history. The name, if maintained 'safely' and legitimately across centuries, contrives to make a mockery of the historical progression towards death; this name is a ritual, like writing, which establishes a realm of the transcendental within which the real (historical) bearers of the name find their 'house' or home or identifiable self. The father, at least at the level of his name (coterminious now with his selfhood, however) lives on in the repetition of that name in primogenitive, privatised heredity, in his son. The name, further, legitimises the familial 'issue'. When Eagleton writes that 'The father signifies what Lacan calls the Law',[57] he is misleading, for it is actually (and importantly) the *name* of the father which is important in the Lacanian analysis: 'C'est dans le *nom du père* qu'il nous faut reconnaître le support de la fonction symbolique qui, depuis l'orée des temps historiques, identifie sa personne à la figure de la loi'.[58] An intentionalist criticism, which aims simply to rehearse or repeat the intentions of an author as a mode of self-validation or self-legitimisation, works to preserve the purity of the talismanic name of the father (name of the author) as a guarantee of its veracity. But such a position is difficult to maintain, either logically or ethically.

In the family romance situation, the son of a father must strive to establish his own paternal authority, in fathering a privatised 'house' of his own. But success in such an enter- prise entails its own failure, paradoxically; for what the son inadvertently maintains is precisely the name of his father, as an origin which guarantees the validity of his own authority. No filial authority is possible in these terms; rather, simple conformity to an ideology or 'law' is main- tained, even at the very moment of rebellion against such an orthodoxy. But daughters can fundamentally betray the Lacanian law, for they can produce bastards, 'illegitimate issue' as it were, through their own labour. This is itself incidental to the establishment of a genuinely 'rival' authority to that of the orthodox name of the father, and in the production of the 'illegitimate' the daughter can produce an element whose home is the genuinely historical, unamenable to ritualisation.

The name of the father, then, and criticism which aims to uphold the 'purity' and legitimising powers of the name of an author, both work to maintain or preserve the supposed 'purity' and 'unadulterated' condition of the author's con- sciousness. In other words, this kind of critic does not 'talk back' to literature, does not engage with its discourse. Pushed to the logical limit, such criticism does not even 'hear' the poet. It operates in the realm of what Ihde calls 'Cartesian linguistics':

> When I listen to an other I hear him speaking. It is not a series of phonemes of morphemes which I hear, because to 'hear' these I must break up his speech, I must listen 'away' from what he is saying. My experiential listening stands in the near distance of language which is at one and the same time *the other speaking* in his voice. *I hear what he is saying*, and in this listening we are both presented with the penetrating presence of voiced language which is 'between' and 'in' both of us. ... A 'Cartesian linguistics' however, does not hear. It supposes its listening to hear 'bare sounds', 'acoustic tokens', which in an undiscovered 'translation' are mysteriously or arbitrarily united with the disembodied and elusive 'meanings'.[59]

To 'listen' to the poet, or to offer some recognition to a text, necessitates some interaction in the production of that text, not the mere analysis of its 'acoustic tokens' as from a transcendental position uninvolved with the text. Further, even if it were possible to 'hear' the text in these quasi-Cartesian terms, it is a mistaken assumption to propose that the authorial text itself is made up of an aggregate of such 'tokens', produced from a consciousness which is equally individuated, equally transcendental. For dialogue is fundamental even to the establishment of monologue. Even in an oral culture, a sustained monologue could not be constructed without interlocution, real or imagined ('heard' by the speaker). Ong writes that 'An interlocutor is virtually essential: it is hard to talk to yourself for hours on end. Sustained thought in an oral culture is tied to communication';[60] and it is equally fundamental to communication in a print culture, as attested to by Bakhtin, for instance. Logically, then, the notion of the pristine purity of an authorial consciousness, embodied in the ritual safety of the transcendental name of the father (or author), cannot be maintained. Ethically, its maintenance would also contrive to arrest the historical authority of the present-day reader, or daughter, to establish a meaning or meanings for the world in which she finds herself; that is, it purports to prevent a kind of (oppositional, critical, undogmatic) historical voice or speech. Perhaps even more importantly, the recognition of this kind of (symbolically, at least) female voice as fundamentally constitutive of modern historical authority as such, is much required, both logically and ethically.

There is a further ethical dimension here. When Oliver Taplin reviewed Kermode's *The Classic*, a text which contests intentionalism in its critical practice, Taplin's metaphors betrayed precisely the ethical stance which I am questioning. Having assumed that the author has certain 'rights' over the created text, Taplin argues that communicative authorial intentions are a precondition of our possession of the author's gift. He goes on: 'To deny him the role of purposeful addresser is narcissistic egocentricity and despotic provinciality. In a Professor of Literature it is no less than filial ingratitude';[61] and, according to Taplin's reading of Kermode, 'the unfathered text must be amenable to an infinity of unforeseeable meanings',[62] a state of affairs which

Taplin thinks will paralyse an author. This betrays the acceptance of precisely the kind of genealogical authority, what
might be called a 'tyranny of (falsely self-legitimising)
origins', which I am arguing is logically and ethically untenable. Taplin asks: 'is the critic to take over from the author
as the creator of meaning? That would be the epitome of
provinciality'.[63] The case, clearly, is not so clear-cut as this
makes out: the critic is concerned with the production of
historical (civil and political) meanings, and quite clearly
should be; but this critical approach does not suggest that
the author *did not* strive to create such meanings. Simply, in
the medium of print, such meanings become 'pre-textual',
the raw material, as it were, out of which the reader or critic
strives to fashion a meaning (and a meaning not in the
'possession' of either 'author' or 'critic' as individuals). Taplin
presumably is contrasting provinciality with a decorous
urbanity; and this is germane to the debate here. For the
city, like the family, constitutes a similar kind of ritual
protection against history; and can become equally tyran-
nous, as with all centralisations of power and authority. De-
legation of such authority to 'the provinces' is surely in
principle a good ethical thing; and once more, it depends
upon the preparedness of 'provincials' (whose voices, being
'provincial', have frequently gone unheard) to oppose critically the incipient tyranny of centralised civic and political
authority, vested in 'City Fathers'. The literary equivalent
of such centralisation, of course, is that which centres the
meaning for a text in one point, the consciousness of one
supposedly single author at the time of her or his writing.
It is precisely such repressive 'urbanity' which criticism
should be countering.

Modern Rhapsody: Phenomenological Hermeneutics

When Socrates addresses the rhapsodist at the beginning of
Plato's *Ion*, he suggests that the reciter or reader of Homeric
verse is only successful insofar as she or he occupies the
spirit of the authorial poet. With respect to Homer, Socrates
'envies' Ion 'because you fathom his inmost thoughts. For

he is no rhapsodist who does not understand the whole scope and intention of the poet, and is not capable of interpreting it to his audience'.[64] The irony here becomes apparent as Socrates goes on to attack not only the presumed knowledge of Ion but also that of his precursor the poet Homer, who is deemed to know little, if anything, of the matters of which the poetry treats. The Ionic rhapsodist, then, is supposed to be a kind of Enthusiast ranter, suppressing the very consciousness which the text's recital is supposed to reveal. Plato offers a contrary gloss on the position in the *Phaedrus*. There, Socrates claims that his starting to talk in a dithyrambic strain (i.e. to construct poetry) is entirely due to the presence of his audience/reader, Phaedrus. Reading, then, it is here suggested, determines and defines the poetic act. Among the conclusions towards which this text draws comes a very illuminating idea, relevant to the present thesis:

> he who thinks that in the written word there is necessarily much which is not serious, and that neither poetry nor prose, spoken or written, is of any great value, if, like the compositions of the rhapsodes, they are only recited in order to be believed, and not with any view to criticism or instruction ... this is the right sort of man.[65]

Thus the principle of authorisation for the meaning of a text here is, as in my own propositions, to be located in the activity of critical reading. It is not that a text substantiates or 'authorises' a particular interpretation; rather, it is precisely the contrary, and the activity of reading itself, in the production of meaning, both literary and cultural, authorises, legitimises (even 'canonises') a text.[66] The seeming ironic implications of *Ion* can now be clarified. In an act of writing, the writer, although deeply involved in the dialogical exercise of critical consciousness, delivers or writes more than she or he can hope to know; for what is delivered, what is 'made' from this 'pre-text', depends to a large extent on the historical reception and interpretations which are produced in response to its critical reading. That is to say, as in Ihdian conversation, meaning resides in the *other* of the dialogue, an otherness which is revealed not by writing so much as by voice, historical articulation of purpose and meaning.[67] In de Manic terms, authors and readers alike are blind to the

profundity of their own insights, for such insights depend
upon the alterity of the dialogical interaction of consciousness
which accrues around a text.

Exemplification will clarify this, and should indicate that
'meaning' here is construed in terms of a critical activity, not
as an immanent or blatant substantive. Meaning is not some
inert *thing*, but something we *do*. 'Message clear', by Edwin
Morgan, is a modern poem, dependent for its very shape on
the fact of its production as an element of a print culture;
and it is also a poem in which critical commentary has
entered, or even supplanted, the 'text' (see opposite[68]).

The poem exists as a kind of partial palimpsest, and the
erased spaces in it demand the critical activity of *Lesen*, a
reading which edits, selects and collects the various fragments
into some semblance of sense. There are a number of ways
of discussing this text. Firstly, one 'reconstruction' from the
fragments might suggest that the document simply lists the
phrase 'i am the resurrection and the life' some fifty-six
times: a kind of parodic Iserian closure of the 'gaps' or
erased letters in the text might suggest this kind of reading.
Secondly, it might be suggested that the 'words' which the
fragments, read sequentially, comprise provide a kind of 'ur-
text', critically exposing the 'clear message' which is contained in the phrase, 'i am the resurrection and the life'. Here
the text performs a kind of critical exposure of the 'words
beneath the words' in the Saussurean/Starobinskian sense,[69]
and reveals the 'clear message' encapsulated within the mystic
phrase. Thirdly, it might be argued that the text should be
read as a struggle towards clarity. The poem, according to
this, charts the movement towards the elaboration of the
biblical phrase; reading the text produces a faltering, hesitant,
perhaps *infant*ile speech in its reader, but moves with increasing speed and ease towards the final 'clear' message which is
only fully enunciated, or vocalised, at the end. But at this
point, the phrase itself, of course, becomes obscure or mysterious once more, and the phrase (indeed, the poem) requires
renewed or further critical reading. Fourthly, the poem can
be read as an enactment of revelation; and this reading is
perhaps the most comprehensive, for it includes at least the
other three posited here. According to this, there is a steady

```
        am              i
                             if
i am                      he
      he r      o
      h    ur  t
      the re           and
      he re           and
      he re
    a             n  d
      th  e  r
i am     r               e ife
               i n
           s    ion and
i              d     i e
    am  e res  ect
    am  e res  ection
                 o          f
      the                 life
                 o          f
    m   e         n
         sur e
      the             d    i e
i        s
         s    e t   and
i am the   sur      d
    a   t  res   t
                 o          life
i am he r                 e
i a          ct
i      r   u    n
i   m  e  e   t
i            t            i e
i       s    t  and
i am th        o      th
ı am    r          a
i am the   su    n
i am the   s    on
i am the  e   rect on    e if
i am     re      n   t
i am       s    a      fe
i am       s  e  n    t
i   he  e          d
i   t e  s   t
i      re      a  d
    a  th re       a  d
    a     s   t on       e
    a  t  re       a  d
    a  th  r    on       e
i       resurrect
                   a    life
i am              i n    life
i am    resurrection
i am the resurrection and
i am
i am the resurrection and the life⁶⁸
```

movement towards, elaboration of, and critical commentary upon, the phrase which is basic to the poem. It is as if the reader (and, by extension, the biblical or any other scribe) had been struggling to articulate or vocalise the mystical phrase (and in my terms here, this articulation means to make the phrase exist as a historical, voiced, reality, productive of meaning and consciousness), and only finally, perhaps breathlessly, manages to perform the verbalisation. Such a moment is a moment of clarity or revelation, in which all the parts of the text, literally, fall into place. But this is also, simultaneously, a return to the primal obscurity from which the critical poem began, for it reinstates the monumental text, 'i am the resurrection and the life', as fully written, and hence immediately in need of reinterpretation. But what is important is that the reading of the poem has been, fundamentally, an *act*, an act of some sort of revelation either theologically understood or, more generally, in terms of a 'betrayal' of some of the meanings that can be produced through a critical meditation on or reading of the scriptural ur-text. This poem, or rather, this reading, neatly fuses the two senses implicated and interfused in the Hebrew term, *dabar*. *Dabar* signifies both 'word' and 'event', and is thus useful in a theorisation of authority which strives to reconcile questions of textual authority, writing authority and historical authority. In oral discourse the word is clearly an event, instrumental in effecting a course of action. This is true both of so-called 'primitive' oral or illiterate society, and also of highly-technologised societies such as our own: when we ask for a hot pastrami sandwich in the appropriate context of the fast-food restaurant, generally this is what we get.[70] In printed discourse, while the word itself may not be an event in quite the same way, interpretation, the articulation or lending of a historical voice to the text, is a historical event, an action. This is axiomatic to a procedure which might be termed 'phenomenological hermeneutics'.

Theoretically, then, the notion that a printed text is some kind of self-erasing or self-consuming (in Fish's terms) artificial metaphor which facilitates quasi-oral communication between two individuated consciousnesses (identified as 'author' and 'reader'), is untenable. Instead, it might be theoretically more appropriate to 'save the text' (although perhaps not in precisely the same manner as Hartman reading Derrida). In this, I borrow from Ricoeur. According to Ricoeur, 'if we can no longer define hermeneutics in terms of the search for the psychological intentions of another person which are concealed *behind* the text, and if we do not want to reduce interpretation to the dismantling of structures, then what remains to be interpreted? I shall say: to interpret is to explicate the type of being-in-the-world unfolded *in front of* the text'.[71] This Heideggerian phrase, 'being-in-the-world' is itself derived from Husserl's *Lebenswelt* ('life-world'). When Ricoeur uses it here he is suggesting that the object of interpretation in a text is not another psychology, another consciousness; rather, it is another proposed or hypothetical world, a proposed 'state of affairs', a projected world 'which I could inhabit and wherein I could project one of my ownmost possibilities'.[72] This is of fundamental importance, for it replaces interpretation of another consciousness with interpretation as an activity, a mode of historical engagement, a manner of being-in-the-world, to which we can subscribe, and which we can thus authorise. One of the functions of writing, according to this stance, would be to erase the reference to the 'real' world and to use writing in order to propose a reference to another possible, hypothetical world, and another possible mode of consciousness in the appropriation or comprehension of such a world.

It follows, then, not that we as readers construct the meaning *of* a text, but rather we construct meaning *in* it (in literary terms) and *through* it (in historical terms). The text, as it were, once written, becomes 'an autonomous space of meaning'[73] awaiting animation or enactment through its critical reading. In Schleiermacher's favoured 'Romantic' notion of hermeneutics, 'the emphasis was placed on the ability of the reader or hearer to transfer himself into the spiritual life of a speaker or writer'. But, according to Ricoeur, in a shift of emphasis which I corroborate here,

> The emphasis, from now on, is less on the other as a spiritual entity than on the world which the work unfolds. To understand is to follow the dynamic of the work, its movement from what it says to that about

which it speaks. Beyond my situation as reader, beyond the situation of the author, I offer myself to the possible mode of being-in-the-world which the text opens up and discloses to me. That is what Gadamer calls the 'fusion of horizons' (*Horizontverschmelzung*) in historical knowledge.[74]

The objection might be raised that, as in much hermeneutical practice, there is a problem of subjectivism in this kind of procedure. A text comes to mean what we want or allow it to mean for us subjectively in our own limited historical perspective. But with the Heideggerian notion of the 'matter' of the text, Ricoeur's proposed 'world' of the work, there is a way out of the subjectivist vagaries of the hermeneutical circle. Ricoeur, accepting the inevitability of the circle, argues that it is misunderstood, nevertheless, if it is thought of as a circle between two subjectivities (author and reader) or as simple readerly projection of subjectivity into the text. He writes:

> What we make our own, what we appropriate for ourselves, is not an alien experience or a distant intention, but the horizon of a world towards which a work directs itself. The appropriation of the reference is no longer modelled on the fusion of consciousnesses, on empathy or sympathy. The emergence of the sense and the reference of a text in language is the coming to language of a world and not the recognition of another person. ... If appropriation is the counterpart of disclosure, then the role of subjectivity must not be described in terms of projection. I should prefer to say that the reader understands himself in front of the text, in front of the world of the work. To understand oneself in front of a text is quite the contrary of projecting oneself and one's own beliefs and prejudices; it is to let the work and its world enlarge the horizon of the understanding which I have of myself. ... Thus the hermeneutical circle is not repudiated but displaced from a subjective level to an ontological plane. The circle is between my mode of being—beyond the knowledge which I may have of it—and the mode opened up and disclosed by the text as the world of the work.[75]

In the Gadamerian fusion of horizons which results here, the effect is on the ontological or at least the historical plane. The reader is faced with the ethical choice of criticism of a present historical situation, or wilful corroboration of it. The text, as it were, 'lets be' a world,[76] at least as a hypothesis, and the reading subject has the ethical choice to make of

whether or not to 'authorise' such a world; but this authorisation, or this choice, is not a matter of mere literary
interest, it is also firmly entwined with questions of civil
(cultural) and political (historical) affiliations. The imagined
or hypothetical world can itself, if activated phen-
omenologically by a reading subject, work to change or
produce historical knowledge, historical meaning not simply
for a fragmentary subjectivity, but for a world. The task of
reading, according to this, or the function of criticism at the
present time, as we might phrase it, is to fulfil the hypothetical reference of the text, to enact meaning in such a way
as to give voice to the critical consciousness. That is, it is
the business of criticism to construct both knowledge and
meaning, producing, at least in the cultural sphere (Gramsci's
'civil' society) a dialogical consensus, orientated towards
truth and rationality, even if it has accepted the impossibility
of arriving at such a transcendental station. This may look
like a Rortean pragmatism, substituting 'what it is better for
us to believe' for Truth.[77] The modification which the critical
consciousness might want to make to this, of course, is to
ask 'better for whom'?; that is, it would want to historicise
such pragmatic self-justifications. In principle, however,
when such a modification is taken into account, the replacement of the epistemological quest for the anterior 'Truths'
of an authorial intention with a pragmatic pursuit of pleasure
for all people, seems to be admirable in terms of ethical
practice. It may also open up the way towards an explication
or theorisation of the notion of pleasure in reading or
interpretative criticism, a pleasure which comes from the
exercise of the conscious faculties themselves. It is towards
this 'therapeutic' philosophy, rooted in a fundamental de-
legation of authority among readers and listeners, that I hope
to make a contribution through the present text.

PART I
(Fe)male Authority

Chapter 1

Experiments in Living

> Writers are usually in the unfortunate predicament of having to speak the truth without having the authority to speak it.
>
> (W. H. Auden)

A Nostalgia for Utopia

Nostalgia: homesickness as a disease (from Greek: *nostos*, the return home; *algos*, pain);

Utopia: imaginary place with perfect social and political system (from Greek: *ou*, not; *topos*, place)

Present-day modes of thought stem, in some respects, from a crisis of authority at a very specific historical moment. Jeffrey Stout has argued the point that 'modern thought was born in a crisis of authority, took shape in flight from authority, and aspired from the start to autonomy from all traditional influence whatsoever'.[1] This 'modern thought' begins in the Renaissance and comes to fuller self-consciousness in the seventeenth century, when, in England at least, the crisis of authority realised itself in the Civil War. The roots of this crisis can be found in the divorce proceedings begun in 1527 by Henry VIII against Catherine. For this divorce was more than the personal separation of Henry from Catherine; it also precipitated the more radical divorce of England from Rome, and king from pope.

This is of crucial importance. 'Authority' at this time did not mean the personal initiative of individuals; an authority was rather a power, sanctioned by tradition, to which one submitted. Before 1527, the pope would have been such an

47

authority; but the Reformation, spurred on in England by Henry's divorce, multiplied and made problematic such authority. In theory, 'choice' of authority now begins to appear as a possibility: did one obey the pope, remaining Roman Catholic; or did one protest, as Henry had done, and obey the king? Further, the choice of submission to the king had complicating ramifications. To follow the path of Henry is to imitate his assertion of personal authority over any traditional authority whatever; thus a further dissemination of authority is made possible. In 'obeying' the king, the subject in England must do as the king did, imitate his choice, which involves, paradoxically, a degree of *dis*obedience to the authority of the king; the subject assumes herself or himself a measure of subjective power of initiation. The meaning of the word 'authority' undergoes transformation, coming closer to our understanding of it: to have authority now implies a power of instigation or innovation on the part of an individual capable of choice.

The semantic conflict over 'authority' problematises the issue of what it means to be an 'author' in literary, ethical and political terms. As Bate put it, describing eighteenth-century poetry, the question facing writers was 'the stark problem of what and how to write'.[2] But it is actually from the historical and cultural moment of the Renaissance and Reformation that English writing has had to face the issue of its own sources, provenance or authority. Clearly, not everyone actually did write as such; but this does not mean that they abnegated their authority or evaded the issue. The conditions of writing are themselves shaped by the kinds of authority which are available to a culture at a given historical moment. At the time of the Civil War there were at least two modes of authority in contention. On the one hand, there was an authority based upon a hierarchy of households and families in which the family of the king, the family royal, was paramount and understood as a microcosmic realisation of the archetypal holy family, from whom all authority is ultimately derived. On the other hand, there was the logical extension of the king's separation of himself from Rome; there was a mode of authority based on another 'house', a house of elected representatives who wished to assert their own powers of self-determination. Further, the Reformation's radical upheaval of religious authorities leads to a conflict between one mode of authority whose source is external, 'other-directed' (in Rome, say), and another mode which claims internal, self-directed authority (in England, or more fundamentally, in the 'self'). The fact that many people did not write does not alter the fact that many would still undergo the experience of the conflict of meaning over the word 'authority': Roman Catholic was in strife with Anglican, Parliamentarian with Royalist. This 'mere' semantic quibble, further, leads many people to experience very directly the changes of meaning in the word, in the deaths of the Civil War and in persecutions. But perhaps the arena in which the problem of authority was most immediately experienced, and the arena where it lends itself directly to theorisation, was in the organisation of the 'house' or family, which was itself in a period of transition and self-organisation at this historical conjuncture.[3] This affects a theorisation of writerly authority.

The 'experiment' with the so-called nuclear family unit leads to the postulation of other hypothetical social arrangements; and the safest place for such 'experiments in living' is in fiction. The growth of Utopian writings in this period is testimony to the fact that the organisation of social relations was in a state of turmoil, experiment and transition. Utopian writings stem from a contemporary interest in travel, in the discovery of other worlds and social systems different from those which are gaining dominance in England, 'at home'. A similar phase can be observed in the travel writings of the 1930s, when some politically disaffected writers took to this genre in ways similar to their Elizabethan forebears.

It might seem a paradox to suggest that people travel in search of stability, but this was precisely the reason for the travels of Amerigo Vespucci, as he wrote in 1505. As a merchant, he had discovered the whims of fortune, as he put it, and, losing money, went in search of a more stable fortune than trading afforded him.[4] His account of his first four voyages does not elaborate on different socio-political systems, though a great deal of attention is paid to alien customs, particularly that of cannibalism in the world outside

Spain. The second voyage describes a race of giants, making this 'factual' account look rather like Rabelais's *Gargantua* or *Pantagruel* or Swift's later Brobdingnagians. The basic point of similarity between Vespucci and Gulliver, however—travellers in fact and fiction alike—is the quest for stability, a search which can be said to have generated the conditions for what may be the archetypal poem of the whole post-Renaissance period, *Paradise Lost*. Travellers in hypothesised foreign parts were examining the possibilities of different social organisations in an effort to recapture a lost paradise, a stable station in life, a definitive and authoritative or 'natural' social organisation. Many such experiments in living were hypothesised. More's *Utopia* (1516), the Abbey of Thélème in Rabelais's *Gargantua* (1534), Philip Sidney's *Arcadia* (1593), the many 'green worlds' such as Arden or the forest near Athens in Shakespeare, the Ferrars' experiment at Little Gidding in the 1620s and 1630s, the 'experimental' parliament of the English Revolution, the interest in landscaped gardens as analogues of the social from Bacon through to Voltaire and Sterne, Candide's allotment and Toby's lawn, the interest in country-house architecture from Jonson's 'To Penshurst' through to Pope's 'Epistle to Burlington'; all of these writings bear witness to the fascination with discovering a new—or better, the original—state of Eden, the paradise lost which is the subject of Milton's poem. Both on the large scale, of imagining other worlds or societies, and on the smaller scale of an interest in cultivating gardens or institutionalising country-houses and domestic architecture, there was an abiding interest in rediscovering some mythic lost natural habitat, in which men and women would be more 'at home' than in their relativistic and contingent local situation.

The myth of paradise lost, then, is paradigmatic in the writing of this period; and that myth is essentially the myth of nature itself, understood as an originary 'pure' state from which our present position is an artificial deviation. The product of the myth is the experience of nostalgia; and these writings are conditioned by a belief in an uncontingent, a necessary, state of nature where every element will be 'at home' in its 'proper' assigned place. This state of nature, being the original pure condition of the world before

humanity, consciousness and theoretical curiosity
engendered the Fall, will be definitive and thus authoritative: its social order will be naturally, incontrovertibly,
given.

Such an ideology understands the present state of humanity
to be one of entropic decay or corruption; not only could
things be better arranged, they once were so. Utopian writing
is in one sense a manifestation of the desire for hygiene, for
the return to a world purged of the vagaries of the historical
human life-process, and purged, in fact, of the presence of
the material human body itself as a living organism. The
mythic unadulterated nature which Utopian fictions aim to
figure is that nature prior to its 'interruption' or rupture by
the presence of the human body. *Pace* Descartes, and the
contemporary dematerialist Lyotard, we are stuck with the
human body; and many writers from the sixteenth century
onwards have tried to deal with the fact of this adulterating
presence, the material body which is open to death and
decay and whose condition is primarily one of corruption.
Rabelais's Gargantua, experimenting with many different
substances, including animals, to find the best material for
wiping his arse, is simply one attempt to accept the body's
'decay', through comedy. 'Home', then, where we live or
where we are, becomes, through attempts like this to nor-
malise the body, even more intimate: 'home' is of interest
conceptually in these writings because it now encompasses
the question of the human body.

In the experimental writing which ensues, there is often
an understanding of the self or, more precisely, a self-construction (an 'autobiography') in metaphors of domesticity
and architecture. The body is conceived as a space, a space
to be explored, experienced and 'lived' in exactly the same
way as other geographical space. In some writings it has to
be purified to prepare it for habitation of that mythic space
of paradise lost from which we have entropically deviated.
The body becomes, then, a model for the whole organisation
of society. As space, the body can be experienced or lived
in several ways: as temple of the lord (religious and secular),
as a confluence of four fundamental humours, as a garden
whose inner sanctum requires careful cultivation, as a mere
'local habitation', and so on.

Thus the semantic conflict of authority as self- or other-directed is engaged most intimately in the sphere of the human body itself. Rather than being experienced as pure space, the body becomes understood as some kind of element which actually serves to demarcate the other spaces of nature, the space of nature which is 'interrupted' by the presence of the body itself. It is experienced, in other words, primarily as a boundary between inside and outside, as a tissue between an outside or 'other' and an inside or 'self': it thus constitutes or creates the very notion of a 'self' which is not itself identified with the materiality of the body. The physical body more and more becomes the medium through which experience is both constructed and controlled, and in some cases, provides that locus of 'selfhood' which becomes the centre of meaning for the world. Descartes, of course, made central use of this in his philosophical stance, granting an absolute primacy to the space demarcated as 'interior'. But one of Descartes' most recent 'commentators', Beckett, has reinstated the problematic anonymous body as medium, as unstable tissue between self and not-self:

> perhaps that's what I feel, an outside and an inside and me in the middle, perhaps that's what I am, the thing that divides the world in two, on the one side the outside, on the other the inside, that can be as thin as foil, I'm neither one side nor the other, I'm in the middle, I'm the partition, I've two surfaces and no thickness, perhaps that's what I feel, myself vibrating, I'm the tympanum, on the one hand the mind, on the other the world. I don't belong to either[5]

The family or 'house', together with this more intimate notion of the human body as proto-Heideggerian 'dwelling-place', will be of importance in a theory of authority. An examination of such space is necessary for a comprehension of the sources of authority which allowed seventeenth-century writers to write, to assume the modern sense of 'authority' for themselves. But cosmic space was also undergoing conceptual change at this time, of course. Mobility is the important factor to isolate here. The conception of the earth as static centre of the universe, the natural locus of a lost paradisal nature, is disturbed by the realisation that this 'home', understood as the earth and by extension even as the human body, is mobile: the human self need not occupy a 'given' position in the organisation of the world, but can change its state in discovering mobility and authority.

Pre-Reformation theology and astronomy placed men and women unproblematically at the centre of the universe: above animals but below angels, at the still centre of a turning cosmos. In this understanding of human space, people literally 'knew their place'; and it was this place, thought of as authoritative and unchangeable, that lent them stability and, more importantly, identity. Who one was equated with where one was; more precisely, identity was determined by the ownership of land.[6] The impetus of the new astronomy was to destroy such 'place-located' identity.[7] Rather than being the still point at the centre of a universe which derived its meaning from it, the earth itself, the 'human place' itself, became mobile, decentred and relocated in its own ever-moving peripheral ellipsis. The condition of humanity at the moment of this astronomical revelation becomes one of continual exile, with the human now paradigmatically understood as a traveller. That is to say, the mobility of the human body or self becomes operational in a very specific way once the discovery of its decentred loss of identity is made. Stable identity is gone; the human's 'rightful place' is open to debate, a 'debate' which becomes civil war. The human now has no 'home' in the universe, and exile from a paradisal state of transcendent certainty, authoritative identity, is now her or his lot: another 'fall' to match the mythic biblical Fall.

One of the main purposes of travel literature, then, is not simply to reflect the wonders of exploration of the expanding universe. Just as Vespucci went in search of stability, so the fictional travellers in writing go to explore 'outlandish' or foreign parts in order the better to identify and stabilise England, here and now, as a singular defined 'home'. The nostalgic desire for this return home is a desire for a return to a mythic originary nature, a state of given certitude and stable identity which the new astronomy, the divorce of England from Rome, and the problem of authority (as self- or other-directed) had all disturbed.

In the present chapter, I shall examine some of these experiments in living, both fictional and historical. One dominant concern of such writing is the organisation and conception of social space, most clearly seen in the proliferation of details about the domestic space of the house. The house, of course, is also the family, and its organisation is identified in the 'proper' familial name. Such familial nomination is especially important, for the simple reason that it aligns itself with the historical certainties of primogenitive rights. These notions of primogeniture, assuring as they are of the myth of origins, are vital to the construction of the authority model of the divine rights of popes, emperors and kings. They are no less important to the shaping of the modes of authority which are available for writing, at least in the period from the Reformation to Shakespeare.

Authority in Crisis: The Threat of Female Emancipation

In his study of Rabelais, M. A. Screech claims that 'Rabelais rejects monasticism outright. Nowhere in his novel does he have a good word for it'.[8] Bakhtin, on the other hand, would not corroborate such an assured and singular position; rather, he constantly stresses Rabelaisian ambiguity, comic irony and relativity of judgement.[9] The most famous monastery in his work is, of course, the Abbey of Thélème. This abbey seems difficult to locate or understand, even in fictional terms.

Thélème begins as a kind of anti-monastery, or more precisely, a monastery turned inside out. It is built in strict opposition to all conventional monasteries; but as each element of the conventional monastery is inverted, Thélème, paradoxically, begins to assume precisely the shape and form of the monastic life. Firstly, unlike other monasteries, it will have no walls. The problem with this is simply that it means that Thélème ceases to exist as a separately demarcated space. If it has no walls, then not only can we enter it without noticing that we are doing so, in theory at least; it can also be argued, more radically, that the removal of boundaries for the monastery serves to expand the space of the monastery, making the world in which we already find ourselves a kind of colonial expansion of Thélème. Unaware that we have crossed its boundary, we have already entered Thélème; since it has no walls, the world in which we locate ourselves becomes identified with Thélème. The eradication of the monastery's boundaries places us within the monastery.

The three vows of monastic life are to be reversed here:

> parce que ordinairement les religieux faisoient troys veuz, sçavoir est de chasteté, pauvreté et obedience, fut constitué que là honorablement on peult estre marié, que chascun feut riche et vesquit en liberté.[10]

This, together with the abolition of the regularities of the monastic clock which formed an exterior or objective source of authority for the recital of prayers and other duties, is meant to be in keeping with the 'natural' ordering of the place, as its inhabitants follow 'bon sens et entendement'.[11] Thélème appears, then, as an anti-monastery; more precisely, it appears like the world or state of mind in which we 'outside' the monastery already exist. But the important point is that Thélème is not postulated as an ideal. Rather, it is an ironic model which indicates the possibility of another ideal; and this implied ideal does in fact look more like a conventional kind of monastic life, but one which is not to be marginalised or institutionalised: a monastic life to be lived by those 'outside' the monastery.

Rabelais systematically excludes various classes of people from Thélème, notably ugly women, jealous or diseased people, hypocrites, bigots and scribes. Eventually, all we are left with are people supposedly in a pristine state of excellent perfection: aristocratic 'nobles chevaliers'. As Bakhtin says, 'Though this episode does present a popular Utopian element, it is fundamentally linked with the aristocratic movements of the Renaissance'.[12] Such aristocrats are often married, rich and 'free'; and the argument is that Thélème can be based on the dictates or authority of the internal subjective will of these inmates because such people of good birth and education will 'naturally' choose the path of virtue. This is why clocks and other external regulations are abolished, to be replaced by the authority of subjective will; and Thélème actually translates from the Greek as *volonté*. But the position adumbrated here, though perhaps seemingly admirable and desirable, is undercut by irony:

> En leur reigle n'estoit que ceste clause:
> FAY CE QUE VOULDRAS,
> parce que gens liberes, bien nez, bien instructz, conversans en compaignies honnestes, ont par nature un instinct et aguillon, qui tousjours les poulse à faictz vertueux et retire de vice, lequel ilz nommoient honneur. Iceulx, quand par vile subjection et contraincte sont deprimez et asserviz detournent la noble affection, par laquelle à vertuz franchement tendoient, à deposer et enfraindre ce joug de servitude; car nous entreprenons tousjours choses defendues et convoitons ce que nous est denié.[13]

There are important ambiguities here. Firstly, the aristocrats perform these virtuous deeds in adherence to a code of honour; that is, they look for a personal identity, as 'honourable', through conformity to an identity model of the ideal aristocrat. Further, they are like other people in that they react against anything which threatens to contradict their whims, envying what is denied them and doing that which has been forbidden: any order or law is regarded as 'ce joug de servitude', and they serve only themselves, accordingly. We 'outsiders', in fact, begin to look like these aristocrats: all corrupt, we are all aristocrats of the self, serving only ourselves. Further, is it the instinct for doing good that they call 'honour', or is there not rather an ambiguity in the phrasing here: it is unclear to which antecedent noun 'lequel' refers, and we may read this as 'vice, lequel ilz nommoient honneur'. These aristocrats, like us 'outside', may indeed call the pursuit of vice the pursuit of honour.

The system of values which results from this subjective choice is ridiculed by Rabelais as he indicates the greater degree of tyranny which selfish individualism brings about. The idea of the freedom of subjective choice is that everyone gets up when they feel like it, all drink and eat when they individually feel like it, and sleep when the impulse for rest comes on them. In fact, however, no such 'freedom' of choice ensues at all: rather, these aristocrats of the self all simply follow or imitate the choice of one other individual.

When one sleeps, they all do; when one rises, they all get up; when one suggests hunting, they all feel like it suddenly, and so on:

> Par ceste liberté entrerent en louable emulation de faire tous ce que à un seul voyaient plaire. Si quelqu'un ou quelqu'une disoit: 'Beuvons,' tous buvoient; si disoit: 'Jouons,' tous jouoient; si disoit: 'Allons à l'esbat es champs,' tous y alloient.[14]

The system looks to be freely democratic in principle, with everyone 'doing as they like', in Arnold's phrase; but what we see exemplified is the extreme tyranny which the notion of subjective individualist choice enables. The system lends itself to oppression, to loss of freedom. Based upon individualism, the result is the production of individualistic charismatic leaders, whose single choice is adopted, necessarily, by everyone: it is the democracy of 'one person, one vote'— and the leader has it. Only the loudest or most insistent speaker in such a situation has 'free' authority; everyone else is reduced to 'ce joug de servitude', slavish imitation and conformity. The irony is explicit: Thélème, free will based on individualist subjective choice, is not only undesirable but also an impossible, self-contradictory state of mind. If we are in Thélème, as aristocrats of selfish individualism, the irony invites us to abandon such a state of mind. But to leave Thélème is to sanction its opposite, which is here a more conventional kind of monastic life, with an 'other'-directed authority.

The irony does not leave the reader in a state of radical indeterminacy: some positive propositions seem to result. The abbey looks like a model for some later English country-houses, with a large central hall upon which all the 'private' apartments converge. There is, then, the possibility for some kind of balance between private and public construction of the self, between 'self'- and 'other'-directed authority; the self occupies a space here not entirely 'privatised' nor entirely 'publicised'. But Thélème seems to prioritise the private; and, more importantly, each private apartment looks like a domestic arrangement of the private familial house. There are 9,332 rooms, each with its own 'arriere chambre, cabinet, guarde robbe, chapelle': each is a kind of self-contained flat. The central hall in such an arrangement was usually constructed to be used as a communal dining area; but here such a space could be defunct. Bakhtin's suggestion that 'All the abbey's rooms are enumerated and described in great detail, but curiously enough no kitchen is mentioned',[15] is incorrect, for one contemporary meaning of 'cabinet' was precisely 'kitchen'. With kitchens privatised here, families eat alone and separately; there is no communal partaking of food and no ecclesiastical congregation around, for example, a Eucharistic kind of meal. The privatisation of eating here is tantamount to an abnegation of the ecclesiastical Eucharist, no less than a refusal of the church itself.

This all contributes to the line being pushed by the text, that privatisation causes social discord; Rabelais seems to favour the publicisation of the monastic regime, or at least a public-minded morality. One joke makes this especially clear. When talking of the abbey's lack of walls, Gargantua sets up a pointed, but jocular, remark by his companion:

> Premierement doncques (dist Gargantua) il n'y faldra jà bastir murailles au circuit, car toutes aultres abbayes sont fierement murées.
> —Voyre (dist le moyne), et non sans cause: où mur y a et davant et derriere, y a force murmur, envie et conspiration mutue.[16]

Walls and the privacy engendered by them produce 'murmur', secrecy and personalised intrigue, gossip and scandal, or in short, social discord and disaffection. The irony, then, seems, contra Screech, to favour the monastic life; but a monastic life which will be lived by those 'outside' the walls of the monastery. The heartiest welcome, in fact, is accorded the evangelists who will fight the enemies of the sacred Word; and notably, such people are those who are said to bear or contain the sacred Word in some sense.

This is tantamount to suggesting that for Rabelais the model of social behaviour becomes a female one; but this is not necessarily a liberating position for woman, for the female here is idealised as the type of Virgin Mary. Inside the abbey, the positive values are that:

> La parolle saincte
> Jà ne soit extainte
> En ce lieu très sainct

Chascun en soit ceinct;
Chascune ayt enceincte
La parolle saincte.[17]

Those who are 'in' the valued and valid state of mind, then, are those who, like Mary, 'contain' the Word of God. Insofar as this pregnancy is thought of as the birth of the Word, then it is also a further invitation to the public life or communicating the Word, or words, a life based not on the privacy of 'murmur' but rather on the evangelical publicising of the Word of God. The model for the good life, according to the Rabelaisian text, seems to be the female Virgin Mary's 'evangelical' position; objective authority, public speaking, is offered here as an antidote to the individualistic prison-house of Thélème.

Thomas More travelled while writing *Utopia*, and this condition of mobility is no less important here than in the work of Rabelais or in that of later, more clearly 'novelistic' and picaresque writings such as that of Cervantes. *Utopia* shares some of Rabelais's concerns but proceeds differently. Unlike Thélème, which is 'where we are', Utopia very definitely is a world apart, a world with little ease of access. Notably, it is 'like to the new mone',[18] and this early alignment of Utopia with the archetypically female moon is important. Further, though it begins as a world elsewhere, Utopia does have some clear similarities to England, being, for instance, an extremely well-garrisoned island. Though there is a boundary between Utopia and England, then, it is not primarily a boundary of physical space; rather, it is a distance between two ways of thinking, two ways of living.

One of More's central impulses is the attack on private separation, isolation as such, and the individualism which comes of the clear demarcations of private properties which are themselves fetishes of individualist identities. Theft, for instance, would not happen if there were no such concept as private property, which is a major cause of 'poverty and wretchedness'.[19] More proposes a muted kind of communist programme attacking the 'title' to property. By a none too devious etymology, Vico later explicitly linked 'property' to 'authority' and argued that '*Auctor* certainly comes from *autos* (= *proprius* or *suus ipsius*)'.[20] The OED finds an alternative root for 'author' in *augere*, with its suggestion of beginning or increasing. Both etymologies here bear fruit. Property certainly gives some kind of identity to its owner; the word itself does derive from *proprius*, 'related to one's self'. Property, then, does give the kind of 'title' name or identity at issue. But in order to retain such a name or identity, such an 'entitlement', the owner not only reifies herself or himself in the 'property' but also must by definition strive to solidify, increase or regenerate more of this property in order for the name or identity to remain stable. It is precisely this capitalistic 'title to property' that More is questioning, among other things, in *Utopia*.

The conflict between stable and mobile identity in *Utopia* is thus fairly crucial. The boundaries demarcating identifiable entities are shadowy, and social space is indeterminate in Utopia. There are houses whose doors, the logical demarcation or limit of outside and inside, are always open: the 'private' space of the house is undercut by the fact that its door is always open, and an *always* open door is no door at all. There is, further, no strict identification of self with house, since houses are changed by rote every ten years. The boundary between self and other, a boundary which houses and private property helps draw, is here being erased.

Furthermore, the family itself as private unit, a unit which gives authority, title and title to property, is drawn into question by More. The men in Utopia follow the craft of their fathers as a general rule, thus, we might think, strengthening notions of familial, patriarchal lineages and history. But although the family exists in some vestigial form still, it is not entirely true that a masculinist lineage necessarily results: 'For the mooste part every man is broughte up in his fathers crafte. For moste commonlye they be naturallie therto bent and inclined. But yf a mans minde stande to anye other, he is by adoption put into a familye of that occupation, which he doth most fantasy.'[21] The Utopian nuclear familial unit is open, and subject to permutation. The inhabitants, lacking a definitive familial identity, lack also the 'title to property', and thus also lack the kind of individualistic authority which was the object of Rabelais's attack in my analysis of the Abbey of Thélème.

It is a commonplace of feminist criticism that women are always in the position ascribed to the artisanal sons in Utopia. Women are, in a society based on patriarchal familial arrangements, the mobile tokens of exchange by definition. In *Utopia*, they are defined as 'weaker' than men by nature, and are relegated to the house and kitchen for the most part, where large amounts of unpaid work, and the preparation of food (a chore shared by the slaves and bondmen), are carried out by them.

But there is another aspect to this. Women are certainly in the position of oppression; but without ignoring that fact, it is important to note the further implications of the text. In marriage, the women are always 'exiles' or refugees, like the aberrant wilful artisanal sons, moving from one 'household' to another. The difference which must be borne in mind in what follows here is that the sons have some choice in this matter of movement; they are self-determining and authoritative in a way denied to the women. The women, however, are actually exiles by definition, and more so than any man, because in marriage it is they who always change abode. The ambivalence in this 'exiled' condition of woman is due to the fact that in *Utopia* it is precisely the kind of mobility of identity equated with the woman which the text seems to valorise and validate. The mobility of Utopians assures them of a wider social identity than that afforded by the local and private nuclear family; and the wider social or collective empathy which ensues gives them the real identity of social beings in a state where individuality is at a minimum. In real terms the text does subjugate woman, but the 'political unconscious' of the text permits a reading in which woman becomes the model for the kind of idealised society to which *Utopia* adverts us. Women give the ideal community its shape in a social sphere in which mobility of identity, multiplicity of identity, 'exile' and the refusal of individualistic acquisition of property are the most central factors. Given the contingency of the human in her or his 'mobile' home, mobile situation, More would seem, like Rabelais, to be proposing a mode of authority which is based on a transcendent, and therefore external source: these travelling people, who can always be assured of a home wherever they are 'on the road', find their authority in an objective source, if not collectivist then transcendent of their own contingent position. The twentieth-century figuration of this, of course, in Kerouac and others, claims to find authority in precisely the opposite realm, of the contingency of the subjective and temporary will of the individual. 'Exile' and mobility of themselves do not predict a specific political position with regard to authority.

In More, the motion of the body is itself celebrated. Vespucci has looked on in horror as some of the people he discovered on his travels urinated unreservedly before him; he regarded the body and its motions, especially defecation, as 'shameful'.[22] More, on the other hand, tried to reinstate the body as a locus of pleasure. It becomes, as the medium between 'inner' and 'outer', not only the site of a political struggle about authority, but also the locus, in More, of experience itself:

> The pleasure of the bodye they devide into ii. partes. The first is when delectation is sensibly felt and perceaved. Whiche many time chaunceth by the renewing and refreshing of those partes, which oure naturall heate drieth up. This commeth by meate and drynke. And sometymes whyles those thynges be expulsed, and voyded, wherof is in the body over great abundance. This pleasure is felt, when we do our natural easement, or when we be doying the acte of generation.[23]

This bears a remarkable similarity to the attributes generally thought to be favoured by Rabelais, of good cheer, the pleasures of food, drink and sex. In the case of both writers, this pleasure comes from material experience itself, and such experience is located in the body and identified as the relations between an external world and an internal sphere. The establishment of such relation, of inner with outer, in fact, is itself constitutive of the materialisation or realisation of the body. This body is generated as neither self nor other, but as the tissue in which the experience of self with other, that is, experience in the form of social and historical relation, is made.

In these experiments in living, or experimental organisations of space, three factors recur as important focal concerns. Firstly, there is the organisation of domestic space, as

the development and disposition of persons within identifiable 'houses' or families established the so-called nuclear
family as a socially normative unit. Secondly, there is the
space of the human body itself, understood as the locus of
experience of the wider social spaces of domesticity and
society at large. Thirdly, the question of the gender of such
bodies carries great importance, as masculine and feminine
positions within the organisation of space begin to determine
at least two different models of authority, of social and
authoritative relations.

The theorised societies which I have discussed remained
as fictions. But we are fortunate to have some of the records
of the real historical experiment in living carried out by
the Ferrars at Little Gidding. Little Gidding reveals the
problematic of authority in factual historical action. After
their involvement with the colonial experiment in Virginia,
the Ferrars retreated into a kind of 'counter-colony', where,
prefiguring Voltaire's Candide, they cultivated their own
garden. The establishment of the house is interesting, for it
seems to have been conceived not as a monastically institutional place of refuge and rest, but rather as a boundary
between earth and heaven. The first task to be performed
was the repair of the church, above whose door was placed
the inscription: 'This is none other than the house of God
and the gate of heaven'. The church, and the house at
Gidding, were thought of as gateways, 'tissues', between two
realms. Fairfax's inscription, at the entry to Appleton House,
offers the gloss on this:

> Think not, O man, that dwells herein,
> This house's a stay, but as an inn
> Which for convenience fitly stands
> In way to one not made with hands;
> But if a time here thou take rest,
> Yet think eternity the best.[24]

The house at Gidding, like Fairfax's abode at Nunappleton,
looks rather like the conception of the body, the human's
place, as I described that in More and Rabelais; the house as
the locus of validated experience, a location where normative

(religious) and hence 'authoritative' experience is to be generated and maintained.

Before 1936 at least, the image of the experiment at Gidding is one of a supremely harmonious, ordered, disciplined and austere life, which offered a return to the rediscovery of some primal unadulterated religious pleasure. Accounts of the place, such as those of the Rev. T. T. Carter, J. E. Acland and H. P. E. Skipton, present an idealised picture of complete harmony, tantamount to the real discovery of paradise.[25] This should have been disturbed by Bernard Blackstone's notice in the *Times Literary Supplement* of 1 August 1936, 'Discord at Little Gidding', in which he revealed the problematic relationship of Bathsheba Owen Ferrar to the rest of the community. When Blackstone gathered some documents in *The Ferrar Papers* (1938), the discordant nature of the place in at least one respect should have been noted; but at this time, Eliot was also making use of Gidding, and criticism began to mediate the place as harmonic once more. But Bathsheba, as Blackstone's edition of letters from Gidding helps show, was not at all 'at home' or in harmonious accord with the place.

Bathsheba was John Ferrar's second wife. We find her going away from Gidding sometime during the week of 12 April 1630; there was some debate about keeping her at the house 'agaynst her will' on 17 June 1631; she was extremely discontented, according to a letter of 16 July 1631 (or 1632), when she once more threatened to leave.[26] She seems to have found some aspects of life at Gidding intolerable, and her complaints made it difficult for the others in the community to maintain a condition of social accord.

John Ferrar was actually the elder brother to Nicholas. But he granted most, if not all, authority to this younger brother, who had been instrumental in rescuing him from his financial difficulties over the Virginia Company. Such a practice, of handing over authority in worldly affairs to a younger brother, was unusual in an age which adhered strongly to the social code of primogenitive rights. Bathsheba may simply have found the austerity of the regime at Gidding intolerable; or she may have objected to the monastic regularity and repetition of prayers and biblical readings which punctuated the day; or she may, of course, have worried about this relation between her husband John and his brother. If John continued to cede authority to Nicholas, then what would happen to the primogenitive rights of her husband over the family's material possessions?

When she was pregnant, Bathsheba wanted to have the child outside of Gidding; but John seems to have interpreted this as another manifestation of her dislike of the community, and stands uncomprehending at her desire to go away:

> it is Most vntrew that she is ill Since she Came to Gidding for she booth eates her meat well and Sleepes as well as ever she did I blesse me at Such impudency ... heer is noe want of meanes for her: heer are Ladys and other Gentlewomen [?] that doe well in these Cases good Midwifes to be had.[27]

If this was written in 1632, then another letter, of 30 July 1632, two weeks later, would confirm that she was most reluctant to stay. In that letter John tells Nicholas that his brother-in-law, Owen, had come to Gidding but could not stay. More pertinently, John also remarks that:

> I have received the day before he Came a letter from my wife the Effect is that god shall right her wrongs and for her [meate?] at the quarters End she must packe away
> I thought not good to Say any thing to my Brother Owine of any thing at all but shall Expect on an other opportunity[28]

What are the wrongs for which Bathsheba claimed God would revenge her? It might not be possible, on the documentary evidence we have here, to be certain; but some fairly clear hints emerge about the source of Bathsheba's wrongs. Two dominant themes recur: the care of children, and a question of property. On one occasion Nicholas sided with John against Bathsheba on the issue of which parent was to have the ultimate authority over their children. These comments, based on Pauline precepts, placed Bathsheba firmly in the wrong and in a position of inferiority, not only subservient to her husband but also to her younger brother-in-law. Nicholas advised John to pray and confess to God:

not onely of this but of all that in this kynde hath been committed by you touching Lofty or bitter Language promising the amendment by his Grace—And in a word resoluing neither to say nor doe any thing for strife nor Vayne-glory—

  And on the other syde her to doe nor suffer any thing to bee unduly doñ touching yr Children w^{th}out full Instruction [? fayre] reproof and yf that will not serue use lawfull restraynte— This exercize of y^r Authority for good is as needfull and will bee as acceptable to God as your patience and meekeness in bearing Iniuries and unkyndeness[29]

In another letter, Nicholas tells Bathsheba that she will be judged at the Last Day (as indeed, he judges her in her own day) by these Pauline precepts of subservience to the male partner. The rest of her complaints, he says, are quite simply wrong; and he argues that she is jeopardising her children's future and contravening the will of God in contesting the will or authority of her husband, a will which is actually Nicholas's, it seems. It is clear by this point in the proceedings, in 1636, that Bathsheba was thought of as a substantial threat to the community, and one which ought to be stifled. In a postscript to the letter in which Nicholas had delivered this 'advice', a letter which Bathsheba refused to accept and many times interrupted, Nicholas adds advice to John to make sure that his authority over Bathsheba is not wrested from his hands 'to y^r owne and all others destructioñ'[30]

  What are Bathsheba's 'other' complaints? A clue to the real basis of the threat posed by Bathsheba is to be found in the fact that she questions the male authority and domination in marriage and more precisely in the social or domestic space of the household or family. A letter, written to her brother Henry, which John intercepted, gives more details of the story. Bathsheba thanks Henry for writing to her, and for forwarding a letter from 'Cosen Smith'. Smith seems to have suggested in this letter that the Ferrars' house in London is due to fall to Bathsheba after the demise of Mrs Ferrar, the mother of Nicholas and John. Bathsheba feels cheated of this property by the assertions of these two sons, who reclaim the male lineage for themselves:

I did put him in many doubts and many feares in Soe much as he laughed at me And asked me why I did feare Soe much for he knew they were of great Estates Espetially as longe as the Old woman liveth you neede to feare not any thing. And he Said full true in that for She Stoode my freind in this to the last cast For I heard her Say to her Sonns looke to it Said Shee that none of you doe meddell wth my house at london upon noe termes for Saith She my daughter is the next woman after my disseise that must Inioye it I have vowed it and promised it Soe to her owne freinds[31]

She says that the letter from Smith disturbed the Ferrars; but they argue that the letter is a fake, written by Henry. Bathsheba goes on, however, to charge Nicholas with using gender, in the manner of Paul, to strip her of her rights and authority: 'For Saith Nicholas may not a man doe wth his owne what he listeth w^thout asking his wifes good will for what power hath the wife of any thinge whilest her husband doth Liue not the Cote of my Backe is not myne owne but my husbands he Saith.[32] What Bathsheba is struggling for, then, is quite simply the kind of title to property which would give her some measure of self-directed, autonomous authority in the man's world which constituted her contemporary situation. She wants some rights as a woman (though she sees these rights in terms of the male-centred notion of authority as a title to property); she wants to inherit the London home of another woman, her mother-in-law, but sees that inheritance stolen from her by the reassertion of male rights in Nicholas and John. Bathsheba is involved in a struggle for the power of her own voice, her own name, her own identity and authority.

The struggle for authority at Little Gidding, then, a struggle which seriously disturbed the harmony of the place, was finally a sexual struggle. A rising and rebellious female striving for her own authority came into conflict with a dominant masculinist mode of authority, one based on titles to property, primogeniture and the Pauline 'interpretation' of gender relations, all of which conspire to guarantee the historical continuity and stability of the male familial name and identity. This, in fact, is the core of the fictional texts examined in these pages; Rabelais and More both offered the possibility of some kind of female challenge to the dominant masculinist mode of authority in their contemporary cultural situations. The 'feminist' nature of this may not be clear; but at least the alternative female model for the organisation of bodily, domestic and social authority, posited here, relativises and thus questions the 'necessity' or naturalness of the male order. In Bathsheba Owen we see the beginnings of some kind of proto-feminist assumption of authority in historical action.

Chapter 2

The Female Landscape

O my America, my new found land,
My kingdom, safeliest when with one man manned
(John Donne, 'Elegy 19')

Though breasts become sombreros, groins goatees,
the beard of Conrad, or the King of Spain,
bosoms bikes or spectacles, vaginas psis,
they make some fannies Africa, and here it's plain,
though I wonder if the Vicar ever sees,
those landmass doodles show a boy's true bent
for adult exploration, the slow discovery
of cunt as coastline, then as continent.
(Tony Harrison, 'Doodlebugs')

Bodybuilders: Architectural Thought and the Experience of Human Space

The concept of 'home' or familial house is essentially one which is used by people to give a sense of centralisation to experience. The home not only gives a primary sense of identity, being the social space from which one comes; it also represents a hypothetical centre from which we may deviate but to which we can return. It thus guarantees a certain security in the possibility of dynamic action or movement from itself out into the flow of history. Christian Norberg-Schulz has written of this:

man since remote times has thought of the whole world as being centralized. In many legends the 'centre of the world' is concretized as a tree or a pillar symbolizing a vertical *axis mundi*. Mountains were

69

also looked upon as points where sky and earth meet. The ancient
Greeks placed the 'navel' of the world (*omphalos*) in Delphi, while the
Romans considered their Capitol as *caput mundi*. For Islam the Ka'aba
is still the centre of the world.[1]

Eliade's comment on the same phenomenon aligns home
with the myth of a paradise lost where the 'natural' self is
to be housed. Eliade's analysis, as Norberg-Schulz remarks,
points out that this 'centre' is usually thought to be difficult
of access, being an ideal goal whose attainment is only possible after a long and arduous journey. The simple 'house' is
more than it might at first seem.

Two more points emerge from Norberg-Schulz's
argument. Firstly, the 'centre' is not a conventional centre
at all, but rather, like the point between sky and earth, an
imaginary point or asymptotic boundary or medium between
two different elements. Secondly, the centre, conceived as
'navel' or 'head' implies an analogy with the human body.
These two ideas inform much post-Renaissance thought
about personal and social space.

Generally, there seems to be a development from the
allegorisation of the world as home and as body towards the
understanding of the body in its more dynamic relation to
its spatial environment. The body becomes conceived as a
tissue between two different realms, inside and outside; and
the realisation of a self is determined by the experience
located in this 'skinny' boundary position. The body, as this
boundary, is not strictly material, but is rather a discontinuous rupture in space, a no-person's-land between two
other, more material or substantial, spaces. The development
is illustrated by the difference between the Greek conception
of home as a body whose navel is at Delphi, and the concept
of home adopted by the Ferrars or Fairfax; for these latter
people, the 'dwelling'-place was merely a space to be traversed on their journey to some transcendent realm and was
thus characterised by kinesis, not stasis. There is, for the
male poets of the late Renaissance, a productive metaphorical
confusion of this 'home' with the (female) body.

Augustine offers many metaphors which clarify the allegorisation of body as house: 'My soul is like a house, small
for you to enter, but I pray you to enlarge it. It is in ruins,

but I ask you to remake it'.[2] Here the soul is not simply the house of the self but is also the house of God, the house which God is to inhabit and rehabilitate or inform. It is taken that since God occupied one human body in the figure of Christ, then God occupies the human body as such, making it a temple of the Lord, so to speak. It is such a temple that Herbert strove to build for himself; and the question for Herbert, as for Augustine, was whether the Lord was 'present' in such a human sphere, whether the writer could be 'in the presence' of God. The very notion of the *Civitas Dei* extends the house of God into the wider sphere of the city of God. Furthermore, the nostalgic desire to return home, which, in these terms is to rediscover the body as the house of God, is made explicit by Augustine:

> In you our good abides for ever, and when we turn away from it we turn to evil. Let us come home at last to you, O Lord, for fear that we be lost. For in you our good abides and it has no blemish, since it is yourself. Nor do we fear that there is no home to which we can return. We fell from it; but our home is your eternity and it does not fall because we are away.[3]

'Home' here is the realm of the necessary, the transcendent or eternal; in short, it is the self of God, domesticated in metaphors of 'abiding'.

In less specifically theological terms, Bachelard has theorised the space of the house. The material home, he argues, is the first place of self-identification, the first place through which we orientate ourselves to the rest of the world. As such, the family home lends us the myth of a stable, named identity from which we can come to terms with that which is foreign or other. Further, the conceptualisation of home engendered in these first stages of life remains with us, for our experience is itself intimately bound up, as in Heidegger, with a notion of 'dwelling'. Existence is spatial, and all experience is lived space, or a way of 'living in space', and the space which determines this experience, fundamentally, is that of the house: 'tout espace vraiment habité porte l'essence de la notion de maison'.[4] In Bachelard's theorising, this primary house, the house of our birth, emblematically resembles the womb in its spatial function; and the primary house becomes the archetype which delimits and conditions all subsequent experience. If we return to the *maison natale*, we find that 'la maison natale a inscrit en nous la hiérarchie des diverses fonctions d'habiter. Nous sommes le diagramme des fonctions d'habiter cette maison-là et toutes les autres maisons ne sont que des variations d'un thème fondamental.'[5] This corroborates the myth of an originary state from which we are in a constant process of entropic deviation. The house becomes the first experiential manifestation of the body, which is identified with it; accordingly, the body itself is here being conceived as a decaying, entropic entity. This theory, then, which tries basically to 'spatialise' the progress of time or history, can be understood as an apotropaic warding-off of the decay of the body: its writing is itself conditioned by our historical condition and by the fact of death. The fact of time, of history, is the tacit enemy here. Bachelard even locates memory in space, making it a spatial, not a temporal, category:

> On croit parfois se connaître dans le temps, alors qu'on ne connaît qu'une suite de fixations dans les espaces de la stabilité de l'être, d'un être qui ne veut pas s'écouler, qui, dans le passé même quand il s'en va à la recherche du temps perdu, veut 'suspendre' le vol du temps. Dans ses milles alvéoles, l'espace tient du temps comprimé. L'espace sert à ça.[6]

The example of Proust, of course, corroborates this. When the Narrator remembers, his text is actually the 'presentation' of an anterior topography. Here, for example, is the Narrator 'catching up with himself' in time, and more precisely in space, in his room at Balbec:

> Je restai seul dans la chambre, cette même chambre trop haute de plafond où j'avais été si malheureux à la première arrivée, où j'avais pensé avec tant de tendresse à Mlle de Stermaria, guetté le passage d'Albertine et de ses amies comme d'oiseaux migrateurs arrêtés sur la plage, où je l'avais possedée avec tant d'indifférence quand je l'avais fait chercher par le lift, où j'avais connu la bonté de ma grand'mère, puis appris qu'elle était morte; ces volets, au pied desquels tombait la lumière du matin, je les avais ouverts la première fois pour apperçevoir les premiers contreforts de la mer (ces volets qu'Albertine me faisait fermer pour qu'on ne nous vît pas nous embrasser). Je prenais con-

science de mes propres transformations en les confrontant à l'identité des choses.[7]

What is recovered here is not primarily a temporal experience but the spatial experience of the room at Balbec, which becomes the focus and centre to which or into which are drawn various anterior scenes. The 'sameness' of the room, the unchanging, quasi-transcendent condition of this space, becomes the centre in and through which the Narrator defines himself ('mes propres transformations'); that is, the identity of the space becomes the condition of the identity of the Narrator, who is steadily working towards the construction of a personal identity, a personal name. This room, like the myth of the Bachelardian *maison natale*, exists as a kind of transcendental focus not only localising the Narrator's experiences but also 'identifying' them, making them refer to the one basic personal identity; it thus works to 'authorise' those experiences and to grant the Narrator access to the realm of the transcendent, the realm of the authoritative. It is, of course, towards this that the Narrator strives. Moreover, there is, importantly, a real room behind this fictionalised room at Balbec, and that is the room in which Proust locked himself to write not only the novel but also, in a sense, to write himself as an author.

Proust's novel and Bachelard's philosophy both work at the level of allegory in a sense. By thinking time in terms of a quasi-transcendent space, they attempt to circumvent history and the contingency of change, a contingency which threatens the authority of the human caught in the circle between womb and tomb. Both render personal identity static and absolute, quasi-essential; but such a notion came into disrepute at a time in the sixteenth century when writers were discovering the mobility of the human home, the human body. A comparison of two passages of writing, from the fifteenth and sixteenth centuries, will illustrate the distance between this static notion of the human body or house and the more dynamic, contingent, historical self-conception against which Proust seemed to react in the twentieth century.

Journey into Foreign Parts

In his lyric 'Se Dieu plaist, briefment la nuee', Charles d'Orléans wrote of the gracious sunlight of a woman's beauty entering his consciousness 'Par les fenestres de mes yeux'. When this happens,

> Lors la chambre de ma pensee
> De grant plaisance reluira
> Et sera de joie paree.[8]

Charles begins to develop the allegorical relation between the space of the body and the 'room' or dwelling that is the house. The repeated refrain, 'Par les fenestres de mes yeux' is the starting-point for another poem, which extends the comparison into what is one of the first 'conceits' in lyric poetry. In that poem the poet imagines himself as a house, with windows, rooms, doors. The image is a static one, with the house working as conventional allegory. Growing old, the poet will keep his rooms (thought) cool by closing his windows (eyes) against the heat of love:

> Par les fenestres de mes yeux
> Le chaut d'Amour souloit passer;
> Mais maintenant que deviens vieux,
> Pour la chambre de mon penser
> En esté freschement garder,
> Fermees les ferai tenir.[9]

He will use the same protections against inclemencies of other seasons, other weathers. The image produced is that of the poet as empty, shuttered house, secure against the entry of love. The building here of self-assurance and self-confidence is precisely coterminous with the construction of a space, a house for the poet, and specifically a house which will withstand historical accident. As allegory, this works extremely well; but by definition, the house remains one which is alien to us, one which we do not enter. There is to be no access to the house, and thus no movement through its space. But this is tantamount to explaining, tautologically, the allegorical nature of this house: given that we can only appreciate it from the outside, it becomes a topography which is no space at all but rather a two-dimensional façade, or surface: a mask against the world.

Altogether different from this is another, later allegory on a similar theme. In Canto IX of Book II of Spenser's *Faerie Queene*, Guyon reaches the house of Temperance, Alma's house. To gain entry, Guyon has to perform some mighty tasks, defending himself and the house against its enemies ranged outside. This done, Guyon enters the house, whereupon he is taken on a fantastic voyage, which is basically a journey through Alma's body, allegorised as a stroll through her house. The first orientation followed is that of the digestion. Guyon goes through the mouth into the stomach (cauldron), passing the lungs (bellows). His voyage takes him to the private apartments, the 'private parts' of the body/house where Alma excretes. Once again, there is some kind of attempt to sanitise or render acceptable, through humour, the corporal and historical existence of the body as a medium through which the environment passes or is experienced:

> But all the liquor, which was fowle and wast,
> Not good nor seruiceable else for aught,
> They in another great round vessell plast,
> Till by a conduit pipe it thence were brought:
> And all the rest, that noyous was, and nought,
> By secret wayes, that none might it espy,
> Was close conuaid, and to the back-gate brought,
> That cleped was *Port Esquiline*, whereby
> It was auoided quite, and throwne out priuily.[10]

The body, then, is a medium in terms of space; it becomes the medium of Guyon's (euphemistically sexual) experience, the location of that experience and the body or space with whom it is identified.

It is also a medium in terms of time. The second direction on the journey is into the head, where Guyon discovers three chambers, of imagination (futurity), reason (the present) and memory (the past). Reason is in the middle here, but this 'present' is itself no more than a boundary between memory and imagination, past and future, and a boundary which is incessantly transgressed. It has itself no name, while the others are identified, as Phantastes and Eumnestes. The present, it seems clear from the text, is a medium through which history becomes fiction, where 'all that in the world was aye thought wittily' becomes 'Shewes, visions, sooth-sayes, and prophesies;/And all that fained is, as leasings, tales, and lies'. This movement, from history to fiction, is one which the text itself corroborates at this 'present' point. In the following Canto X, a prior text, *Briton Moniments*, and its companion volume, *Antiquity of Faerie Lond*, are translated into this work of fiction, *The Faerie Queene*.

In both these voyages the body is understood as a medium. It has undergone some radical changes from the house/body allegory of Charles. Where Charles's house was static, Alma's is a mobile home: it is experienced in the dynamic relations and choices of direction which Guyon and reader make on their progress through the body, their 'colonisation' of it. Everything inside the body is in motion, further: Diet manages a white rod, Appetite walks back and forth in the hall, cauldron burns and bellows stir, and so on. Alma's body is not experienced as a unified or whole surface; rather, it constitutes a series of spaces which define Guyon as he journeys through them. Our view is always partial in the house of Alma, and always self-modifying. One other major difference, of course, is the gender of the allegorised house: it is notable that Alma's experience of Guyon passing through her is consistently ignored, and that the narration is always taken from the male voyager's point of view.

In Spenser the human organism becomes a paradigm for our understanding of all social space, and its geometrical organisation is overladen with a morality which attaches to the aesthetics of mathematical numerology. Norberg-Schulz offers some argument on why the body is construed in this way at this time, as Renaissance architects rediscovered the classical notion of relating cosmic proportion, the organisation of cosmic space, with the proportions of the human body. This makes the body available for allegorisation as an entire cosmology; but with the new science, that cosmos begins to move at its centre in a very specific way, and the human body accordingly becomes allegorised as mobile. Norberg-Schulz locates this development in the understanding of space, from stasis to kinesis, in the architectural example of Raphael's Villa Madama. To perceive this house one has to progress through it, but there is no single straight-forward orientation for the journey: at various points we could turn either left or right. Two points arise from this 'open-form' of space: 'The static, symbolic space of Renaissance architecture ... has been transformed into a dynamic occupation of the environment', and 'Space is no longer simply a "container", but something which ought to be conquered by action'.[11] This describes accurately the distinctions I have drawn between the house/body of Charles d'Orléans and that of Alma in Spenser. Charles's house is static, making allegory of the symbolic equation of house and body, and it is a static 'container' for Charles within; Alma's is dynamic, occupying and being occupied in relation to a voluminous and changing spatial environment, and further, it is a space which is conquered by the actions of Guyon and even by those elements of Alma's body itself who control the space of the body in their regulatory motions. The 'mobile home/body' thus invites questions of control, power, conquering by action and hence colonisation—in short, the new conception of the human's place at this time invites questions of authority; and such authority, as is clear from these examples, is involved with the issue of gender. An examination of some specific 'homes' in writing will clarify these issues.

Home and Woman's Body

There exists a group of poems in the seventeenth century which confront the issue of social and domestic space directly. Usually referred to as 'country-house' poems, they include Jonson's 'To Penshurst' and 'To Sir Robert Wroth', Carew's 'To Saxham' and 'To G.N., from Wrest', Marvell's 'Upon Appleton House', Herrick's 'A Country Life: To his Brother, Mr Tho: Herrick'; and the tradition is thought to continue into the eighteenth century with Pope's 'Epistle to Burlington'.[12] These poems might equally well be described as 'poems of nostalgia', for they usually conceive of the present state of social architecture and space in terms of an anterior, more 'natural' and usually rural mode of organisation: a space which offers a more 'original' and hence authoritative social arrangement. In almost every case, a central concern is the possibility of return to such a pristine state of nature or 'home', together with reminders of our present corrupt deviations from this ideal centre, or source. Two of these poems, 'To Penshurst' and 'Upon Appleton House', are useful in revealing the issue of gender which is intimately bound up with this discovery of the authoritative source, the authoritative space.

Penshurst and Saxham are both described as having no clearly demarcated bounds. The gates at Saxham, we are told,

> Vntaught to shut, they do not feare
> To stand wide open all the yeare;
> Careless who enters[13]

Similarly, no one wants the walls around Penshurst to be dismantled, for they are supposedly ineffective anyway: the free entry of people is not impeded by them. Like the house at Little Gidding, these houses are written of as median spaces between earth and heaven, contingency and necessity. This is apposite in the case of Appleton House, which Marvell reminds us used to be a nunnery, though never a religious house until lived in by its present incumbent, Fairfax. The house is overtly aligned with the gate of heaven early in the poem, when the element of nostalgia, the return home, is written of as the return to heaven:

> But all things are composed here
> Like Nature, orderly and near:
> In which we the Dimensions find
> Of that more sober Age and Mind,
> When larger sized Men did stoop
> To enter at a narrow loop;
> As practising, in doors so strait,
> To strain themselves through *Heavens Gate*[14]

In a similar way, Jonson compares the resident of Penshurst, Sidney, with Christ, suggesting that to partake of a meal at

Penshurst is to celebrate a religious communion, as one
drinks the wine and eats the bread of 'the lord's own meat'.[15]
Penshurst, like Saxham and the other houses discussed here,
is a median space, and here that space is emblematised as the
ark, a symbolic boundary between a death of the world and
a rebirth, between the contingent and the transcendent.

At a time when the human space, the body as such, is
beginning to be understood as some kind of radical interruption into the plenum of nature, a kind of conservative
response sets in. Nature, in some of these poems, is depicted
as being entirely subservient to the masters of the house:
such 'colonisation' of the foreign spaces of the world is one
way of dealing with human alienation from nature, with the
fact of human historicity. Jonson begins this trend with the
assertion that in Penshurst not only do the animals know
their place, they also cheerfully accept their assigned role.
They come willingly to the slaughter, fulfilling their 'natural'
(hence authoritative) function in feeding other animals,
humanity. This, in fact, explains the presence of nature in
the poem at all:

> Each bank doth yield thee conies; and the tops
> Fertile of wood, Ashore, and Sidney's copse,
> To crown thy open table, doth provide
> The purpled pheasant, with the speckled side:
> The painted partridge lies in every field,
> And, for thy mess, is willing to be killed.
> And if the high-swoll'n Medway fail thy dish,
> Thou hast thy ponds, that pay thee tribute fish,
> Fat, agèd carps, that run into thy net.
> And pikes, now weary their own kind to eat,
> As loth, the second draught, or cast to stay,
> Officiously, at first, themselves betray.
> Bright eels, that emulate them, and leap on land,
> Before the fisher, or into his hand

The poet asserts that fish and beast accept their naturally
authorised role as meat for humans: the implication that
follows is that there is a natural place for the human as well,
a space which has been authoritatively designated as 'ours'.
Carew, describing Saxham, took on precisely the same argument and increased the element of 'pleasure' that the elements

of nature take in finding their place relative to the human, a place which can be identified as in the human stomach: 'The scalie herd, more pleasure tooke,/Bath'd in thy dish, then in the brooke'. The problematic relation of humanity to nature, the difficulty of finding the proper human space, begins to become apparent; as, indeed, do the relations between one human space and another, the relation between human material bodies. In Penshurst not only do the rural animals come to serve the master of the house, but also the local population assume a similar role: we may ask, according to the Jonsonian subtext here, whether the fate of the rural human population is akin to that of the beasts.

Penshurst is walled, but no one wants the walls destroyed, on the grounds that they are all allowed in anyway. This is suspicious: if the wall is so redundant, why is it worthy of mention? When the rural population do come in, they come almost dressed as food, prepared with offerings of capons, cakes, nuts, apples, cheeses and, equally ripe for the devouring, daughters. These women are written in precisely the same terms as the fruity offerings, that fruit which is 'naturally' the property of the master of Penshurst and which offers itself to him, tries to establish close spatial relation with his body. This appropriation of the natural world of fruit and animal, an appropriation which deals with the fact of the human's alienation from nature, is now uncomfortably extended towards the appropriation of those other rural animals, ripe young women. The daughters, as marital offerings to the male-centred house, contrive, through marriage, to increase the importance and centrality of their rural forebears by placing them nearer the centre of the house, the centre of meaning for this rural scene of the natural world. In other words, these women are instrumental in gaining the real access to the house, through its 'walls', for their forebears. There is a wall, after all, round Penshurst; and the way to transgress it is to offer daughters as 'natural' offerings, tokens of exchange which grant, if they are accepted, tasted and eaten, entry into the interior of Penshurst and the place or standing represented by that central space.

Entry into Penshurst is difficult after all; the interior space is reserved finally for the family which identifies itself through ownership of the place. To gain access to this 'house' or family, ripe women are necessary. Women provide the medium through whom power, centralised identity and authoritative influence are to be achieved. The real space marked by Penshurst is not architectural at all but is rather the metaphysical social space of the family; its boundaries are determined by who is in and who is excluded from that family, and by degrees of proximity to its name-giving centre. This becomes clearer in the final part of the poem. Assurance of identity is to be guaranteed by a continuous notion of temporal history, in which knowledge of one's parents will be the determining factor. This focuses upon the centrality of women:

> These, Penshurst, are thy praise, and yet not all.
> Thy lady's noble, fruitful, chaste withal.
> His children thy great lord may call his own:
> A fortune, in this age, but rarely known.

The religious connotation of lord here importantly blends into the material owner of land and the domestic ruler of the family. It is clear from these lines that Jonson sees the family in its 'nuclear' form, and the kind of society subtended by that arrangement, to be under threat, but worthy of preserving. The locus of threat is the ('fruity') woman who is theoretically in a position to disrupt the familial history and lineage which guarantees a child a certain kind of centralised identity, an identity given by the male family name. The woman, through a lack of chastity, could clearly disrupt this spatial arrangement of history. For, in the terms in which the argument is cast here, not to know one's parents implies a lack of identity, and the loss of the centralised (paradisal) space or place in the 'natural' house. Crucially, as the subtext makes clear, this whole system depends first and foremost on women 'knowing their place', and that place is to be the safely controlled position at the centre of a domestic arrangement. Even more radically, it is to be the centre (in the stomach or heart) of the male lord of the domain. The woman here, though seen as potentially mobile or promiscuous, is the character who, as fruit, is firmly placed at the centre of the circle of nature, the boundary, drawn by the husband.

Marvell repeats this strategy of 'domestication' of the woman in some ways in 'Upon Appleton House'. The house, once more, is a gateway to heaven, but a gateway which is itself a body. Unlike other houses, this one is built in perfect proportion to the space of its owner. It is in this way humanised to some extent, and the relation between body of owner and body of house is perfectly established as congruent. If Appleton House is built in 'perfect' proportion to its owner, however, it is in some sense identical with the body of that person: quite literally, Appleton House is mediated as an embodiment of Fairfax.

This is odd. At the start of the poem it is argued that humans take up too much space: the human's place is disproportionate in building dwellings on too large a scale and in too grand a manner. But Marvell expresses this in such a way that the implication is clear: the dead body, in the grave, is the most 'proportionate' human space:

> No Creature loves an empty space;
> Their Bodies measure out their Place.
>
> But He, superfluously spread,
> Demands more room alive then dead.

As the poem develops, the alignment of the house with the body of Fairfax, dead or alive, in fact becomes even more problematic; for the spirit of the place is more or less explicitly characterised as female.

As Marvell relates the history of the house, its space is conceived to be akin to some kind of female womb. It was, of course, a nunnery; the ambiguity of that word (meaning brothel as well as religious house) is made appropriate to Nunappleton (itself, as the text makes clear, a place for 'fruity' nuns in some sense). But there is more to this equation of the house with the nunnery; for insofar as it is a 'Virgin Building' which gives birth or brings forth, it is being aligned with a specific female body, that of the Virgin Mary. Mary, in the guise of Maria Fairfax, will later be acknowledged openly as some kind of *genia* of the place. But if the

building or home is Fairfax's body, then Fairfax must be,
according to the symbolism of the space, female. Fairfax is
identified with, even embodied as, Appleton House; but that
house is itself a female space. In other words, 'home' here
is a female landscape of sorts. It is also the arena within
which one of its elements, the one whose name seems to be
central to the text, defines itself as 'different' through the
difference between that name, Fairfax, and the name of the
house, Appleton. Fairfax, as identifiable man or male, actually depends upon the primacy of the existence of this female
space, this womb or female landscape called Appleton House,
in order to define himself, and to distinguish himself as
'different' from Appleton House, though 'identical' with its
space. This male name owes its existence to the female home;
but also differs from it in some fundamental way: 'he' is not
'at home' here, at the same time that it *is* 'his home'.

There is a further definition in this poem, this time of the
poet, and in terms of Englishness. As McClung has pointed
out, the myth of England as the 'garden of the world',
a kind of prelapsarian natural realm (and hence centre of
authority), came to prominence in the mid-seventeenth century. Marvell's sense of nostalgia, a desire to return to this
Edenic state of authority, now actually looks rather like a
desire to return to some female element in nature, perhaps
some female element in his own nature, or in 'his' body or
home.[16] The hortulan paradise, the countryside which is the
'real' England or a real home, is written of in this poem as
a specifically female abode. Nature itself, according to this
mediation of the garden of the world, is female; or, alternatively, the female is closer to nature than the male. If the
male wants identifiable authority, a name as a poet together
with the individual authority to control and organise social
space, the female landscape has first to be controlled or
'colonised'. The cultivation of England as nation, of the
garden itself as myth, and of the domesticated female all
seem to go together here.

The place of Appleton House, of course, is also instrumental in acquiring authority for Marvell. The identity and
authority which he assumes in the poem, moreover, is that
of Christ. This furthers the comparison of Appleton House

with the body of Mary (and of Maria), the Virgin Mother
of Christ; and this also contrives to lend the poet a greater
authority, a more primary authority, than his patron:

> Bind me ye *Woodbines* in your 'twines,
> Curle me about ye gadding *Vines*,
> And Oh so close your Circles lace,
> That I may never leave this Place:
> But, lest your Fetters prove too weak,
> Ere I your Silken Bondage break,
> Do you, O *Brambles*, chain me too,
> And courteous *Briars* nail me through.

These allusions to crucifixion are clear. Even while the social
space of the house is used to identify Fairfax as 'lord', this
order is subverted; for Fairfax is made to owe his being to
some primary female entity, and also to this poet, now in
the position of a more religious 'lord'. The poet contrives to
place himself above his patron not only in terms of authority,
but also in terms of his proportioned suitability to the place.

There is an element of sexuality in this equation of Marvell
with Christ. As I indicated, the real spirit of the place is
Maria, whose name recalls the identity of the house itself as
the womb of the Virgin Mary. Marvell identifies himself and
his authority through his being pinned into the house; but
he also identifies himself sexually through his relation to
Maria Fairfax, at thirteen years old, 'ripe' like Jonsonian fruit
and at the marriageable age of a Juliet in Shakespeare. The
'Silken Bondage' in the stanza cited above seems to be a
fairly clear reference to Maria's hymen, as well as to some
other unspecified 'knot' which ties Marvell to the place. If
we read the silken bondage in this way, Marvell seems to be
requesting an indulgence in permanent sexual activity with
the virginal Maria, in order to identify himself, located at
the neck of Maria's womb, both as male and as a representation of Christ, springing from this virgin womb. It is
thus a further play for the maintenance of a specifically male
mode of authority for the poet.

Maria is seen as a median stage between earth and heaven,
whose dialect she speaks, according to Marvell: she is thus
a space between Marvell and God. The equation of house,

woman and 'angel' (as this space between the historical and transcendent authorities) now complete, Marvell celebrates the family or name which is identified through the symbolic space of Appleton House. Maria Fairfax, moreover, is on yet another boundary, 'ripe' for marriage:

> Hence *She* with Graces more divine
> Supplies beyond her *Sex* the *Line*;
> And, like a *sprig* of *Misleto*,
> On the *Fairfacian Oak* does grow;
> Whence, for some universal good,
> The *Priest* shall cut the sacred Bud;
> While her *glad Parents* most rejoice,
> And make their *Destiny* their *Choice*.

There is a sense in which Marvell *is* the priest here, placed himself now in some median position, in the space identified as the body of Maria, the *genia loci*, the female landscape; and he is thereby identified as the author both *of* and *in* Appleton House.

The house, finally, is mediated as 'Heaven's Center, Nature's Lap./And Paradice's only Map'; it is thus a medium upon an originary and authoritative state of nature. But the medium afforded to Marvell by this house upon such an authority is nature itself in the form of the woman, Maria, in whose lap he has lain to map out this paradise. The way to map out paradise, then, and to acquire a transcendent authority, is by mapping out, colonising or appropriating Maria: the acquisition of poetic authority, through a hypothetical sexuality with the *genia loci*, is the result. This female spirit, in other words, has to be domesticated or stabilised within the 'home' of the male poet, in order that he produce a specifically male, identifiable, mode of authority.

Colonising Women

Fiedler has argued forcefully that one great 'other' which caused a problem for Shakespeare was woman:[17] woman was the terrifying unknowable other which was yet absolutely crucial to Shakespeare's personal and dramatic identity or authority. This should be widened into a dominant cultural phenomenon in our understanding of poetic authority at least in this period. The female space, or 'female landscape' as it is often mediated, is precisely the space or area in and through which the male poet defines himself as authority, and where he also constructs a mythic 'femininity' which can be domesticated, institutionalised and controlled. Women are not understood as women but are rather symbolic media upon nature, heaven, or are instrumental in the assurance of transcendence as the family name in a patriarchal lineage survives history.

In Donne's Elegies 18 and 19, the woman is described in almost straightforward geographical terminology. She is an other land, an alien social space which, like Raphael's Villa Madama, has to be traversed and conquered by the wandering unstable male in search of home, identity and authority. An interesting development of this colonisation of women is offered in Elegy 19. The woman here slowly peels off her clothes, revealing more and more of an essential nature, it is claimed:

> Your gown going off, such beautious state reveals,
> As when from flowry meads th'hills shadow steales.[18]

After seeing the woman in these 'landscape' terms, of hills and flowers, as a still life if not landscape, she is then to be understood as an angel of sorts, but one which will make flesh and not hair stand upright; that is, she is an angel who will identify the poet as male by producing his erect penis. Then comes the most quoted part of the text:

> Licence my roaving hands, and let them go,
> Before, behind, between, above, below.
> O my America! my new-found-land,
> My kingdome, safeliest when with one man man'd,
> My Myne of precious stones, My Emperie,
> How blest am I in this discovering thee!
> To enter in these bonds, is to be free;
> Then where my hand is set, my seal shall be.

The woman here is the geographical space through or in

which the male poet defines himself as priest, king, pilot and
author. He is also emperor, and the body of the woman as
his store of riches is a 'container' of his fetishised imperial
identity. All of this contributes to the notion of male control
of a passive female space; and yet the female is primary in
the sense that it is through the prior existence of this land,
a space which was there before the male author, that the
male gains any stabilised identity and authority whatsoever.
The passage cited recalls some lines from *Othello*, where
Cassio tells those awaiting the arrival of Othello in Cyprus
to greet Desdemona:

> O behold,
> The riches of the ship is come ashore!
> Ye men of Cyprus, let her have your knees.
> Hail to thee lady! and the grace of heaven,
> Before, behind thee, and on every hand,
> Enwheel thee round!
>
> (2, i, 82-7)

The woman here is fetish, as 'riches'; but the brief allusion
to the biblical Mary ('Hail to thee, lady') introduces a
religious note. As the men kneel to her, Cassio blesses her,
the movements of 'before, behind thee, and on every hand'
being a verbal elaboration of the motion of the priestly hand
in the act of blessing. In the Donne example, the woman is
blessed in the same way, but blessed as a new landscape to
be inhabited, controlled and named by the male, sanctioned
by the power of the male priest and by the authority vested
in the church itself. The male arrogance here is enormous,
as the act of sexual foreplay is written of as a male blessing
cast upon the female; and the masculinism of this is theistically approved. The woman, like England at this time, is a
kingdom, supposedly safest when controlled by one man, a
monarch who will unite and give specific identity to the land.
The act of colonisation here negates the authority of the new
land, or the woman herself; she is to have no separate identity
or authority but has to wait for the blessing of the male.
There is a pun on the word 'man'd', for besides meaning
'piloted', it also suggests 'gendered male'. As the poet progresses, he writes the female body in increasingly male terms:

she is thus 'man'd' as Donne presents his seal, his erect penis, to 'stamp' or coin her, and give her worth, indeed existence. There is a confusion of gender, as even the blessing of the new land or woman turns out to be a self-blessing ('How blest am I'); and the woman, *qua* woman, disappears. The discovery is a literal 'uncovering' as the woman undresses; but it is precisely at the moment when the woman is most naked that she disappears, and the real act of *male* self-revelation occurs; when she is naked, Donne 'produces' himself as a male, produces or reveals the phallus:

> To teach thee, I am naked first; why than
> What needst thou have more covering then a man.

As Donne lies on the woman, covering her up again, he discovers himself, through the erect penis, as male. It has been a *male* striptease, in fact, that the poem celebrates; but this male striptease, this revelation or production of the male body, is dependent upon the priority or anteriority of the female body, which has to be colonised, appropriated, 're-covered'.

Similar treatments of this theme are available in Cowley, Crashaw and Carew. Many poems were written in which the female is characterised as some kind of garden or landscape to be explored, traversed and colonised. Woman as woman disappears, and is reproduced as a symbol, often as a symbolic medium between corrupt humanity and an essentially pure primal nature. Nature, it is implied, can be seen, and thus authority gained, through the body of woman: thus breasts become 'snowy hills', curves become 'valleys', places of shelter or rest. The woman's body, in short, becomes 'home'. Women are severely domesticated or colonised in this poetry through this intimate equation of their material reality with a metaphysical conception of home: they *are* the home or locus of authority which the male poets nostalgically desire. This space of authority is often characterised specifically as the various spaces of a female body, and emblematic equations are enacted among elements of the house and body such as the room, the ark, the bed, the grotto, the grave, the tomb, the temple, the womb, the vagina, the eye, and so on. For the male writer, the female body *is* all these emblems, simultaneously. The relation of the poet to a theistically guaranteed locus of authority is linked to the question of this 'female landscape' or environment in and through which the would-be male poet moves. Woman is the social space in which the writer identifies himself as authority; and it is thus through the anteriority of woman that authority, in its modern sense of autonomous 'autobiography' is attained.

Crucial to these masculinist modes of authority is the domestication or colonisation of woman. But there is the problem: women, real historical women, can betray this system of authority, through divorce or adultery, both actions which question the individuated identity and power or authority of their male (dependent) 'authors'. Women, either as real or then as symbolic threat, form the very condition of authority which works to suppress them; but the namable, identifiable mode of authority or intentionality is only one mode of authority among many. It is becoming clear that the very idea of an identity-based authority, that is, authority as we most commonly and ideologically think it, is closely related to specifically masculinist modes of thought. The cost of maintaining such a specialised and delimiting mode of authority as normative requires detailed examination in the following chapters.

Chapter 3

Degenerate Bastards

But then, I must also confess, at the age of seven or eight, I can't exactly remember when, I came to realize that I wasn't, that I couldn't be, a Hargenau. ... I am a bastard. Perhaps an appropriate role for a writer

(Walter Abish, *How German Is It?*)

In his preface to his edition of Shakespeare's plays, Samuel Johnson praised Shakespeare, in the face of criticisms from Dennis, Rymer and Voltaire, for his 'adherence to general nature'.[1] But, quite apart from the theoretical difficulties of representation which this tends to evade, there would seem to have been a difficulty for Shakespeare in 'mirroring' innocently the state of sublunary nature, even given that this might have been what he was doing. This difficulty stems from the fact that Shakespeare spent most of his writing life trying to imagine what precisely would constitute a natural social order. Empirical evidence of the state of nature is lacking, given that Shakespeare's world had, at least since the discoveries of Copernicus, fallen from nature or from its 'natural' and central position. A naturally sanctioned ordering of the world in which men and women would fall, like the flowers in Eden, into their own proper allotted beds and places, seems to have been unavailable to Shakespeare. One of the areas in which he explored and experimented with such social formations was in the arrangement of the family as a social base.

He begins from the assumed centrality of the fact of biological blood. But although this is important to an idea of male lineages, in which the blood is somehow thought to flow not only in the bodies of individual men but also through them and into their first sons, and thus across history itself, Shakespeare discovers the most pressing issue of how to authenticate such blood. For example, as the history plays make clear, a present ruler or father may have sons who seem to be his natural heirs and are thus in line for the primogenitive inheritance of the position of throne or father. However, the present king or ruler may himself be a usurper, and so we may be tricked into furthering the wrong, inauthentic line of blood at any given moment. If we replace such a usurper with another whom we claim to be the 'authentic' carrier of some kind of originary blood, then we have already, by definition, demonstrated that such 'authenticity' is suspect; for we, and our interpretation of the validity of varying claims to the blood, are actually in some degree of control. A 'correct' or authentic line of blood would be, by definition, incapable of subjection at the hands of a usurper. Further, the plays also show that Shakespeare seems to doubt the worth of a social order which was based upon such notions: the continuous and uninterrupted flow of male blood is not necessarily conducive to the best or (pragmatically) 'correct' ordering of society. Blood, nonetheless, remains a potent symbol; but Shakespeare makes the flowing of material female blood more central than that of a transhistorical male lineage.

A Touchstone of Authority

Northrop Frye has put forward the suggestion that the 'argument of comedy' has primarily to do with re-birth, re-newal, and re-generation.[2] That is to say, in one sense at least, it has to do with the reproduction of the individuals who enact it. Raymond Williams has gone some way towards ridding us of the legacy of the Bradleian manner of understanding Shakespeare, in terms of individuated characters, by pointing out the ideological basis of such interpretation.[3] Although Frye's 'argument' may be shown ultimately to share that individualistic basis, it nonetheless is useful insofar as it offers at least one way of differentiating between those plays we

call tragic and those we call comic. For regeneration, reproduction or representation of an individual immediately begins
to problematise her or his individuality. As such, in comedy
as Frye mediates it, there arises the possibility of seeing
plot or the enactment of pattern to be central. Plot, in our
interpretive understanding, supersedes character here. On
the other hand, due to the ideologies to which Williams
adverts us, perhaps, we valorise individual character in tragedy at the cost of plot. The point is, however, that in these
terms, tragedy can be seen as a very specific and distinct form
of comedy, a form in which the reproduction of characters in
a regenerative process fails. But there are other difficulties
with Frye's thesis as applied to the texts of Shakespeare.

In relation to Shakespeare, Frye's argument may be
explained in the following way. The play opens by showing
a world, the putative 'real' world, in a state of some disarray:
perhaps brother is against brother, a familial disorder which
mirrors the civil disorder of a state in which a tyrant has
taken power. Put simply, the disarray, in comedy at least,
is of a familial or domestic nature: it refers us to our own
disarray at 'home', wherever we understand that home to
be, at a private address or in the state of England. Quite
rapidly, however, everyone of importance in the play leaves
this 'real' world and proceeds into an underworld of sorts,
a 'green world' as Frye calls it—where, in Arden, or the
forest near Athens, or on a desert isle, tests, trials and labours
are undergone. Sexual and social relationships are tested and
evaluated; sexual partners are tried, found wanting and
changed, and so on. In the green world, where the characters
have a glimpse of nature, of an ideal state or condition to
which the 'real' world could conceivably conform, they come
to some kind of self-knowledge and to a proper awareness
of social values. Thus they are able to return to the real
world and correct the disorder which was apparent at the
start of the play. They are ready to return, marry, procreate
and thus regenerate the flagging real world in an ameliorated
manner. Marriage is the proper symbol for this, it is argued,
because it is based upon order, forestalling sexual licence and
the chaos of bastardy and adultery; it is based on love, and
is thus positive; it promises rightful and natural procreation,

in which one knows one's own parents, knows one's identity, knows one's place in the universal natural order of things. Marriage also satisfies, in a Bergsonian manner, the mechanics of the plot. For such plots are constructed around a number of characters who could, due to their sexual difference or attraction to each other, be paired off into stable units.

This may all sound neat, but it is wrong. All Shakespearean marriages and domestic affairs have problems: getting people married is just the beginning of the troubles in Shakespeare. If the man is not murdering his wife (as in *Othello*), she is urging him to actions which will provoke his death and her madness (as in *Macbeth*), or the son is plotting against both of them (in *Hamlet*). And the alarming propensity to change partners, fall in love immediately or love people as well as money in the comedies make these 'loves' rather problematic. At a time in history when the premise of 'affective individualism' was becoming the basis on which to measure romantic love, Shakespeare's plays worry themselves about the viabilities of such sexual relation.

It is argued against this that the marriages are merely formal symbols, indicative of the new community's orientation in the direction of a society based upon care and affection. But in one of his earliest plays, Shakespeare had already refused this very 'convention'. In *Love's Labour's Lost*, there is a deliberate deferral of marriage. This, together with the death of the king of France which is partly responsible for it, introduces the possibility of tragedy into the play. Instead of the neat elaboration of a spatial pattern, or Bergsonian mechanism, of four pairs of lovers all finding the right partners, we have the possibility of change through time, and thus the chance that the prospective partners, primed for sexual activity, will disrupt the mechanical satisfaction of the marital pattern in one way or another. In short, the deferral of marriage produces the possibility that the men, in their 'labour' (which will last for approximately the same length of time it takes for a human child to gestate), may 'miscarry': the regeneration may go wrong, and love's labour may indeed be lost. The important point here, however, is in the very refusal of the formal contrivance of marriage as a symbolic closure of comedy.

As You Like It is a play which has been subjected to this kind of evasive critical approach, despite the fact that the marriages at the end form a clear focus for some of the play's most pressing problems. Anne Barton, among many others, has celebrated the festive spirit of this play, with its 'generous' and 'convincing' happy ending marked by the pleasant prospect of regeneration as implied in those symbolic formal marriages at the end. She comments:

> this ending still presents an image of reality. The classicism of the comedy declares itself both in the assurance with which it exacts belief for improbabilities so considerable, and in the unprecedented generosity and inclusiveness of the society which finally emerges from Arden. The cynicism of Touchstone, the unseemly postures of Audrey, may disturb the symmetry of the dance at the end. No society, not even this one, is perfect. Nevertheless, the fact that the fool and the goat-girl can form part of the pattern testifies to the flexibility of the new social order, its ability to accommodate deviation. More than any of its predecessors, *As You Like It* demonstrates Shakespeare's faith in comedy resolutions. It is a triumph of form.[4]

A triumph of form is most assuredly what this play is not. If it were so clearly and unambivalently triumphant in the phoney resolutions of marriage at the close, critics such as this one would perhaps not feel the need to try to justify the end in any way. Barton has to struggle to convince, and having implied the acquiescent acceptance of the discovery of a 'perfect' society, or one with no dissent, she has rapidly to point out that no society is perfect: some characters, some marriages, are more 'perfect' than others. The close of the play, as I shall show, is not even an amelioration of the society which was posited at its opening. The new society is simply one which can 'accommodate' more 'deviation'; that is, it can successfully neutralise any threat (from Touchstone's cynical criticisms or Audrey's body) to its triumphant formal order. (How in fact it will accommodate more people is difficult to see: at the start, one character is explicitly excluded, Duke Senior; at the close, Duke Frederick, Jaques and Adam are all explicitly excluded, and Touchstone and Audrey, according to this criticism, are marginalised.) The social order which, as a triumph of form, wins such admiration, is simply a more authoritarian one based or symbolised in the familial order of marriage. Shakespeare's critics may be happy with this; but the text which Shakespeare produced suggests some other possibilities, and works to problematise such critical conclusions.

A production of *As You Like It* might properly begin by making clear the moral choices with which the spectator/reader is presented. The strife between Orlando and Oliver is related to order in the family. The rule of primogeniture means that Oliver, by an accident of birth and time, succeeds his dead father in the continuance of the male family lineage, and he is the prime carrier of the familial blood and name. Supposedly closer, in time, to his origin (which is identified as his father), he is a 'purer' manifestation, realisation or reproduction of that father. Orlando is not content with this and makes a plea for meritocracy, but bases his claim on the same convention which suppresses him: he wants a share in the family name or identity, and looks for 'fairer' treatment from Oliver, since he too, Orlando, is also a son of his father. A moral decision has to be made here, or at least acknowledged, by the audience: with whom do we side? In fact, since we see Orlando first and hear his version of events first, he tends to win the audience's favour. The 'convention' of primogeniture then looks as arbitrary and unfair as it is when Oliver appears, upholding it.

This moral choice is immediately followed by another. Charles tells us the 'old news' that 'the old Duke is banished by his younger brother the new Duke', thus opening up the wider question of the choices we will make between Arden and court. It is important to note, however, that the two familial situations, that of the dukes and that of the de Boys boys, is *not* parallel. In the one case we are being asked, it seems, to support a rebelling younger brother, and in the other we are asked to support the overthrown elder brother. The problem, of 'artificially contrived' as oposed to 'natural' authority, is there right from the start, and it is focused on the social organisation of the family. It is a fundamental error to collapse the two moral choices and suggest that the court represents disorder; it is no less an error to suppose that there is some 'natural' social ordering, based upon marriage

and the privatised unit of the nuclear family, which is revealed
at the close of the play. In any case, the characters, just as
much as the critics, flee the angst of these questions and rush
into Arden, supposed scene of unadulterated nature.

Nature, however, is simply another problem. In this play
nature seems to be extremely hostile to the human characters
who exist under its dominion. The facts of nature surround
them, and look unpalatable: they consist of the broken ribs
of a wrestler, death to an old man, men bleeding as a result
of being attacked by other beasts, beasts bleeding as a result
of attacks by men. Jaques makes his eloquent speech on the
seven ages of man, and is silenced when he comes to describe
the final stage, for the nasty reality pierces the linguistic
ritualised eloquence and Jaques is presented with a real dying
old man, as Adam is carried on. Ganymede, similarly, is
silenced when confronted with the biological fact of
Orlando's blood. At court, Charles is silenced at the moment
when he is brutally hurt. Nature bursts through language,
artifice and ritual here, and looks harsh, cold, hostile.

Two responses are available to this harsh landscape. The
characters either retreat into silence or incoherent noise, or
they create and elaborate upon fictions, rituals, play, in
order to circumvent the confrontation with nature. Celia
and Rosalind, for instance, are 'banished' to the 'natural'
environment of Arden, whereupon Celia immediately
indulges in self-delusion. Like the later Coriolanus, who
when banished from Rome will turn and cry 'I banish you',
taking 'Rome' or *Romanitas* with him and leaving the
Romans defenceless, Celia will state what is a demonstrable
lie, in order to make nature or reality easier to bear.

> Now go we in content
> To liberty, and not to banishment.[5]

This is immediately followed, in Arden itself, by an equally
self-deluding speech made by Rosalind's father, Duke Senior:

> Here feel we not the penalty of Adam,
> The seasons' difference; as the icy fang
> and churlish chiding of the winter's wind,
> Which, when it bites and blows upon my body,

Even till I shrink with cold, I smile and say
'This is no flattery; these are counsellors
That feelingly persuade me what I am'.

(II. i. 5–11)

The penalty of Adam is thus precisely what he does feel; but
his elaborate rhetoric allows him to 'translate the stubborness
of fortune/Into so quiet and so sweet a style' (II. i. 19–20).
Linguistic ritual plays a crucial role in this drama. The play
is actually a network of such rituals, such linguistic fictions,
and 'nature' as such is rapidly lost from view, together with
any verifiable, naturally correct or self-legitimising social
orderings of human relations.

The play moves between two overt rituals. At the start
there is the court wrestling match. This necessitates a lot of
close carnal contact, and we call it a sport. Insofar as it is a
struggle, however, it is a sport based on power, or aggression,
and its movements determine an at least symbolic supremacy
of one of the partners in the match. At the end of the play
we have the ritual of marriage. This too implies a lot of close
carnal contact and is, in a certain sense, a kind of sport,
supposedly pleasant. The physical struggles of sexuality, we
say, are not symbolic of the hatred or supremacy or struggle
for power of the wrestlers but are, rather, symbolic of love.
The play presents the issue, however, of how to differentiate
between these two apparently similar signs or rituals.

The problem for Shakespeare was not how to make his
work mimetically adequate to a pre-existent, preconstituted
'reality' or nature, but rather one of how in fact to discover
or lay bare such a nature, if indeed it can exist for humanity
apart from its linguistic construction. If there were such
things as natural love, or naturally occurring hatred, then
the difference between them would be clear. But not only
would hypocrisy be impossible if we followed the theory
of clear, natural, non-arbitrary relations between signs and
referents through to its logical conclusion; more importantly
for Shakespeare, acting itself, the theatre, would be a manifest
impossibility: 'lovers' could never successfully act out a
hatred between themselves.[6] There would seem to be no such
nature available to Shakespeare, at least as dramatist. All he

has are a number of similar linguistic signs which construct
'love' or 'hatred', depending upon their interpretation and
historical incidence.

The courtiers, then, certainly do not speak a 'natural'
language, but cover nature through ritual. The rustics in this
play are open to the same charge. Corin and Silvius, stock
characters from the conventions of pastoral, speak in a highly
artificial conventionalised way. Silvius pleads his 'love' in a
rather peculiar manner; and his 'love', such as it is, is in fact
determined to some degree at least, by the language he has
at his disposal. This 'love' is experienced within the par-
ameters of emotion which the language itself, the language of
pastoral, affords. Silvius speaks and behaves 'inauthentically';
not only does the actor playing Silvius act, but the character
Silvius is also already acting:

> If thou rememb'rest not the slightest folly
> That ever love did make thee run into,
> Thou has not lov'd;
> Or if thou hast not sat as I do now,
> Wearing thy hearer in thy mistress' praise,
> Thou hast not lov'd;
> Or if thou hast not broke from company
> Abruptly, as my passion now makes me,
> Thou hast not lov'd.
> O, Phebe, Phebe, Phebe!
>
> (II. iv. 31–40)

It should be pointed out that it is not his passion but the
language in which it is expressed which provokes the physical
action of running off. Further, where is the difference
between this highly structured statement and Orlando's
poetry hanging all over Arden? Both, in fact, are euphemistic
evasions of desire. The play will not cure the characters of
such evasions but will simply offer them different euphemisms, most notably that of marriage.

Given that nature is unavailable, then, what happens to
the status of a supposedly 'natural' authority, gained either
from gender or the arbitrary accidents of time and space, as
in primogeniture? Authority, or its attainment, becomes a
question of power; and that power is gained through adept
linguistic rhetoric. Two scenes, both involving Touchstone,

corroborate this. In the first (III. ii), Touchstone debates the relative values of court and country with Corin. Touchstone is 'at home' in both places, proficient in both languages:

Corin: And how like you this shepherd's life, Master Touchstone?

Touchstone: Truly, shepherd, in respect of itself, it is a good life; but in respect that it is a shepherd's life, it is nought. In respect that it is solitary, I like it very well; but in respect that it is private, it is a very vile life. Now in respect it is in the fields, it pleaseth me well; but in respect it is not in the court, it is tedious. As it is a spare life, look you, it fits my humour well; but as there is no more plenty in it, it goes against my stomach.
(III. ii. 11–21)

Here, Touchstone claims both places as home, and he makes this claim in two forms, at least one of which (that favouring the country) speaks directly to Corin. In this same scene he also perfectly parodies the court language, as he 'extends' one of Orlando's poems, demonstrating his ease, thus, with courtly discourse. His mastery of both languages, his knowledge of the discursive conventions of both places, allows him to transcend and control them. He speaks neither language 'naturally', and uses whichever of them expediency demands. Both discourses are 'nostalgias for utopia', both equally deviations from an original language or source which is no longer available to speaker or writer.

The second scene (V. i) casts explicit light on the aspect of power in this. Touchstone has 'stolen' Audrey from William; but the entry of William poses a threat to Touchstone's pleasure. Once more this threat is defused through language. It has been noted that William has little to say here; but it has not been pointed out that this is for the simple reason that Touchstone steals his lines, strips him of authority through mimesis or parody and thus retains his own power and authority over the situation. William should tell Touchstone to 'leave the company of this woman'. But Touchstone gets there first and says this both in his own voice and also in that of William, in both discourses of court and country, thus rendering William's speech and authority redundant. He leaves William speechless:

> Therefore, you clown, abandon—which is in the vulgar leave—the
> society—which in the boorish is company—of this female—which in
> the common is woman—which together is: abandon the society of this
> female; or, clown, thou perishest; or, to thy better understanding,
> diest; or, to wit, I kill thee, make thee away, translate thy life into
> death, thy liberty into bondage.
>
> (V. i. 43–8)

It is precisely linguistic 'translation' such as this which allows
Touchstone to have the authority whereby he shapes the
world into his fiction; as he subdues William through
rhetoric, he repeats the basic impulse of all the characters
in this play (and perhaps that of Shakespeare himself), of
euphemistically translating the stubborness of nature into so
pleasant a form.

Language in this play is like a formal dance. One speaker
or partner leads and has authority; the others generally follow
this authority in *subservient*, non-parodic, imitation, an iter-
ation of the same 'steps' which merely serves to underline the
'correctness' or 'naturalness' of the first speaker's authority.
Towards the close of *As You Like It* (V. ii), there is just
such a formal verbal dance. The choice of marriage partner
on the grounds of affective individualism, the impetus which
has been a central organisational principle for the play, is
suddenly forgotten. Another social organisation enters, one
which will try to resolve the problem of desire and promiscuous sexuality and which will construct a certain type
of family. The play brings us to the point at which all the
'lovers' follow the pattern or steps danced out by Silvius:

Phebe:	Good shepherd, tell this youth what 'tis to love.
Silvius:	It is to be all made of sighs and tears;
	And so am I for Phebe.
Phebe:	And I for Ganymede.
Orlando:	And I for Rosalind.
Rosalind	And I for no woman.
Silvius:	It is to be all made of faith and service;
	And so am I for Phebe.
Phebe:	And I for Ganymede.
Orlando:	And I for Rosalind.
Rosalind:	And I for no woman.
Silvius:	It is to be all made of fantasy,
	All made of passion, and all made of wishes;

All adoration, duty, and observance,
All humbleness, all patience, and impatience,
All purity, all trial, all obedience;
And so am I for Phebe.

Phebe:	And so am I for Ganymede.
Orlando:	And so am I for Rosalind.
Rosalind:	And so am I for no woman.
Phebe:	If this be so, why blame you me to love you?
Silvius:	If this be so, why blame you me to love you?
Orlando:	If this be so, why blame you me to love you?
Rosalind:	Why do you speak too 'Why blame you me to love you?'
Orlando:	To her that is not here, nor doth not hear.

(V. ii. 76–101)

This dance in words constitutes, like any other formal dance, a self-enclosed, primarily self-referential ritual, with no explicit reference to history or to anything beyond its own artificial conventions. The dance, in fact, stops precisely at the moment when Orlando steps out of its frame and makes such a reference to history, speaking to someone who is not there, someone who cannot 'respond' within the steps of the dance.

This is the moment in the play when there seems to be most confusion. In terms of affective individualism, everyone is chasing the right person; but that meets with the difficulty of arranging these partners in self-enclosed, clearly demarcated social units. In order for the characters to pair off at all in a comprehensive way, it is necessary for Rosalind to reappear, Ganymede to vanish; and then everyone in the dance must 'change partners'. This is done with alacrity. The values of love based on affective individualism are sacrificed in favour of the generation of as many procreative family units as possible. In other words, the very values which the play has, in its romanticism, been celebrating are in stark contrast with the supposed final values of the play, marriage and the promise of the regeneration of a very specific kind of family. For the family which is regenerated at the end is precisely the same kind of nuclear unit which had caused the disarray of the play at the beginning. Contrary to the notion that these characters have attained some high degree of knowledge and awareness of the best social organisation of themselves in Arden, they have, in fact, learnt precisely nothing. They simply corroborate an ideology which had caused their problems in the first place. However, insofar as the play problematises this marital basis for society, it offers the critic a valuable question concerning the kinds of authority which seem to be available under two different systems. On the one hand, there is a system which pretends to be natural (because transhistorical), stressing the flow of male blood in the continuity of a male lineage; and on the other hand, there is the possibility of a different kind of authority, one which is avowedly 'unnatural', based upon rhetoric and ultimately the rejection, by women, of being no more than the vehicles through whom male authorities ('natural' authorities) are propagated. The problematic marriages highlight these issues.

Four couples enter the ark of marriage. Touchstone does not want to stay with Audrey forever; he would prefer to remain mobile, promiscuously flitting from one partner to the next, from one social relation to another, just as he floats in and out of languages. Silvius is stuck with a woman who does not love him, Phebe; and she has been fooled into marrying him against her better judgement and preference. The two central pairs seem to be no more promising.

The play begins with Celia asking Rosalind to cheer up, and Rosalind finally agrees, saying, 'From henceforth I will, coz, and devise sports. Let me see; what think you of falling in love?' (I. ii. 21–2). Practically the next available young man to appear is Orlando. He enters as a counter in Rosalind's 'sport' or game; and she proceeds to manipulate him and make a fool of him for the rest of the play. One reason for this might be that she has an interest in winning her game, an interest not in love for its own sake but rather in love as a means to power and sexual authority. The 'love' espoused between these two is in itself nothing (although there is certainly as much ado about nothing here as there is in *King Lear* and *Much Ado*). This 'love' is no more nor less than an alternative manifestation of the sport of wrestling.

The relation between Celia and Oliver, purportedly the purest love of all, makes explicit the equation of 'love' with wrestling. Rosalind tells us:

'tis true. There was never anything so sudden but the fight of two rams
and Caesar's thrasonical brag of 'I came, saw, and overcame'. For your
brother and my sister no sooner met but they look'd; no sooner look'd
but they lov'd; no sooner lov'd but they sigh'd; no sooner sigh'd but
they ask'd one another the reason; no sooner knew the reason but they
sought the remedy—and in these degrees have they made a pair of
stairs to marriage, which they will climb incontinent, or else be incontinent before marriage. They are in the very wrath of love, and they
will together. Clubs cannot part them.

(V. ii. 27–38)

The love of these two is expressly a fight, a power struggle,
an angry yoking together of their bodies. Here is perhaps
the most brutal affection in the play.

Behind all the human talk which circuitously strives to
evade the confrontation with nature, there does, finally, seem
to be a more 'natural' kind of language after all; but it looks
as brutal as the relation between Celia and Oliver. In Arden
the 'natural' inhabitants are not Corin, Silvius, Audrey and
William, but rather the inarticulate deer, for whom Jaques
has to speak, since 'The wretched animal heav'd forth such
groans' and no coherent words at all. It is important that
'nature' speaks in such a groaning. Apart from pain, a 'groaning' in Shakespeare can signify sexual intercourse; many
women pay their 'debts' with such a 'groaning'. Groaning,
then, can signify two basic facts of nature, birth and death;
or less abstractly, sex and pain which interfuse, perhaps, in
the notion of (female) labour. Here, if anywhere, is the
language of nature. As soon as the ritualised game of human
words intervenes to euphemistically remove nature in the
form of sexual activity and pain, 'nature' and language
become an arena of power, a power dependent on 'labour'
and its transformations. Touchstone, master parodist, committed to no 'natural' tongue, has power over all other
characters: linguistically promiscuous, he can cohabit with
any of the languages, and any of the characters in the play.
He is not named ironically; as 'Touchstone', he is our touchstone, our authority on values in the play. If we allow this,
then the possibility of an alternative mode of authority from
that of the masculinist primogenitive system appears. For the

sexual promiscuity, adultery and lack of familial fidelity which Touchstone advertises offers a more diffuse kind of authority. Rather than one individuated and identifiable man (the bearer of the name, blood and authority of the family history) having the sole authority to which all conform, there arises the possibility of others taking the power to establish their own alternatives to this authority. The *betrayal* of the kind of family which criticism celebrates in Shakespeare's comic resolutions is necessary for this. Touchstone, as mobile authority himself, is paradigmatically a model for a mode of female authority, if we accept, as the play's contemporary conventions seem to do, that women are the variable coins of exchange in society and ideologically identifiable with transformative labour.

To accept the marriages at the close of *As You Like It* in a celebratory manner evades the problem that the text presents them as contentious. To celebrate these marriages, rather than defer them as in *Love's Labour's Lost*, is to acquiesce in the regeneration of the kind of masculinist authority-relations, centred on this specific kind of family unit, which the play presents as the source of discord at its opening. In such an acquiescence, criticism has corroborated the values of marriage for civilisation (thus restricting sexual freedom, especially on the part of women), and for procreation (thus ensuring the continued centrality of the male lineage for social power and authority); this criticism further sanctions the value of sexual fidelity (making women the property of men), along with which goes the matter of faith or allegiance to Duke Senior (despite his inability to face nature without lies and self-deluding flattery) and the kind of court he runs, a court which the basic familial unit subtends and maintains. In what way has this criticism seen the play as progressive at all? What is regenerated is the strength of masculinist marriage, the source of the play's (and its society's) problems at the start. Unless we listen to Touchstone, and use him as a touchstone, things in this play merely get worse; Touchstone's promiscuity offers an alternative mode of authority, which may not win in the play, but which stands out against the blind repetition of the play's problems which a masculinist mode of authority effects.

Wounding the Family Name

Paul Valéry made a useful theoretical distinction between verse and prose. Verse, he argued, was like dancing: it wanders around, circuitously winding back on itself, repeating similar gestures, and, following these strictly formal lines, it is not directed towards any single definite end. Prose, on the other hand, is more like walking: a prose sentence has its own end always in view, and is often teleologically determined; it marches as straight as possible towards such an end, laying no great or overt emphases on the formal qualities of the language itself, which become relegated to secondary importance.[7] If we can accept the kind of distinction which I began to elaborate between comedy and tragedy earlier in this chapter, in which I suggested that comedy is about the establishment of plot or pattern above all else, including characters, who are subservient to such a pattern, then Shakespearean comedy becomes more closely like Valéry's definition of verse, while his tragedy is prosaic. This is of relevance to the problems of the different modes of authority, based upon the organisation of social space in the family, which dogged Shakespearean writing.

The family as we most immediately know it, in its nuclear form, is inherently comic. This is clearly not to say that it is funny, but rather to suggest that it is an effective euphemistic way of curing certain anxieties. Like the formal dance in words at the end of *As You Like It*, the family is an enclosed, hermetic, private and self-referential formation. Insofar as it is some kind of equivalent of such a formal dance, the play *As You Like It* subtends a rather problematic equation: hatred = wrestling = sport = dancing = family = marriage = love. This is one of the play's central concerns: how to differentiate between the signs for hatred and those for love, and how to discover a 'natural' condition in which such emotions will be pure and unadulterated. The question posed in such a way in Shakespeare's text opens the play to some of the society's contemporary anxieties. Lawrence Stone has argued that sixteenth- and seventeenth-century Europe:

saw a breakdown of old values of sense and order. The unity of Christendom had been irreparably shattered by the Reformation, and the pieces were never put together again. The result was that from henceforth there were various options in terms of religious ideology, faith and practice, and no one could be completely certain which was right and which was wrong. The first result of this uncertainty was extreme fanaticism. Internal doubts could only be appeased by the most ferocious treatment of those who disagreed. The authoritarian family and the authoritarian nation state were the solutions to an intolerable sense of anxiety, and a deep yearning for order.[8]

Shakespeare's contentious marriages in comedy simply work to reopen the question of how to organise a society, and refuse to evade the anxiety: here is part of the source of the 'negative capability' which attracted Keats.[9]

In the typical family, a male and a female parent are echoed by the formal repetitions or representations of themselves, and of their blood, in their mirror-images in male and female child. The formal symmetries and 'rhyming couplets' here are obvious. Such a family unit 'contains' time, tames its passage; it exists, formally, to forestall the death of the parents, whose blood is supposed to flow still in their children. As in a rhymed couplet, the secondary line (here the children) refer us not to any future time in the history of the family, for their identity is dependent upon the primary line (the parents) to which they immediately refer us. As the family seems to move forward into history, it actually retracts further into itself and its own 'stable' ahistorical identity. From the point of view of all concerned, then, there is no explicit reference outside this artistic familial arrangement to social history at all; and the threatening progress of history, which brings nature in the form of death, is metaphorically arrested. Here is one more basic anxiety which Stone's 'authoritarian family' exists to circumvent. Writing of Shakespeare's Sonnets, Jan Kott discovers a similar concern:

> The first theme of the Sonnets is the attempt to preserve beauty and love from the destructive action of time. A son is not only the heir of the family, not only a continuation, but above all a repetition of the same face and the same features; literally the way of making time stand still.[10]

The familial unit thus contrives to evade this flow of time, or history. And it is history itself, Kott argues, which constitutes, in its inexorable prosaic march forwards, the real tragic protagonist of Shakespeare's tragedies.[11]

Comedy, then, seems to be concerned with the establishment of an organised space, and the space in question is primarily the domestic space of the home as private unit. Hymen's song at the close of *As You Like It* points out that Hymen is the god of the town and of citied civilisation. The marriages at the end are aligned with the generation of the unified nation, a nation defined as single and secluded, isolated from the rest of the world, and a nation whose single ruler will be strictly authoritarian. The play could be seen to be 'about' the divorce of the state of England from the rest of Christendom, the establishment of a certain mode of authority, and its consequences. When Henry VIII established himself as 'authority' as against the traditional authorities of the church, he inadvertently also opened the theoretical path through which the demands for a greater dissemination of personal authority would come. But rather than having a radically different kind of authority, one which would be less 'authoritarian' (like Touchstone's, perhaps), Henry's manoeuvre contrived to arrest the flow of authority before it became too diffuse. The ruler of the state becomes a model for the rule of authority in the smaller microcosmic unit of the household. A 'unified' state, by paradoxical definition, requires a series of smaller 'sub-units', within which the mode of authority of the ruler of the state will be recapitulated, thus bolstering up that mode of authority. Lest the state's component families or parts become too fragmented, those component families must themselves offer the model of 'unity', singularity, private isolation from the rest of the world, to the ruler of the state. Thus, the authoritarian rule engendered by Henry, based upon masculinist notions of primogeniture and the primacy of male blood, works to forestall a radically different, perhaps female, mode of authority which would work to fragment the individuated 'unity' of the state and its components.

Stone writes of the shift of emphasis towards the nuclear family in the organisation of the state. He suggests that it is given added impetus by Reformation theology and practice, and points out that:

> Whether in Anglican or Puritan households, there was, in varying degrees, a new emphasis on the home and on domestic virtues, and this was perhaps the most far-reaching consequence of the Reformation in England. The household was the inheritor of many of the responsibilities of the parish and the Church; the family head was the inheritor of much of the authority and many of the powers of the priest. Thus the Word of God was to some degree removed from the parish church and transferred to the private home: the Holy Spirit was partly domesticated. [12]

Stone's metaphors of 'inheritance' here inadvertently give away the bias of such a diffusion of authority. As with primogeniture, authority is inherited from some pristine state, claimed as male and identified through the stability of the male familial name which identifies social place. This diffusion of authority, 'handed on' through the male heirs of a family or state, actually works to consolidate singular authority. Just as the family in its nuclear form 'guarantees' the continued presence and authority of the parents, so also the inherited authority here preserves its source (the king, the father) intact, as the ultimate and real source of authority: all other 'authorities' are mere failed representations of this originary authority, and must bow to its weight of tradition. In other words, Henry's move did not spark off a diffusion of authority at all. Having challenged the authority of tradition in the church, Henry's strategy then set himself up as precisely such an absolutising authority, an absolutist monarch or ruler whose authority had to be obeyed or conformed to, and which would brook no dissolution of itself.

These problematic paradoxes are repeated in more clearly literary terms in Shakespeare's writings. If the father is an author of sorts in Shakespeare's families, let us say a poet, since what he produces is 'rhyme' in the form of echoing representations of himself, then this very fact of the production of another potential couple, especially of a male son, creates anxiety through the presence of a possible 'rival poet'. Apart from the Freudian Oedipal situation thus invited, there are other sources of anxiety. The son, 'rival poet', may firstly step outside of the framework of the familial space or household, may leave such Valérian 'verse' and make a reference to the historical arena surrounding the house: such 'desire' as he is capable of imitating from his father may lead him to express an interest in the child of another household.

To model himself fully on his father (which gives both himself and his father existence), this rival poet, the son, must attempt to make an 'alternative' family, with himself as its author, or father. As a rival poet, he must take authority and begin to write. Such a move is heretical, in the sense of that word as etymologised by Said, in which heresy means 'to begin, to innovate' in an alternative tradition.[13] Given that the 'comic' familial unit is a microcosmic reflection of the arrangement of state, city, nation and universe, there is a huge amount at stake in the problematic familial authority which was establishing itself as normative in Shakespeare's time. A son must rebel against a father (in order, paradoxically, for both son and father to exist and define themselves); but that father is no less than totalitarian king or God.

If the son does manage to establish an alternative family, an alternative poem, then we have moved from one comic situation to another. However, it is precisely in the movement between 'two households', as in *Romeo and Juliet*, that Shakespeare discovers the arena of history and tragedy. In the movement out into the communal street, in obedience to his 'desire' to write or inaugurate, the son enters the realm of tragedy, inviting nature, in its basic form of sex and also death. As the son attempt to write, to act historically, which in these terms means to act sexually, there arises the concomitant possibility of death, of tragedy. If, on the other hand, this danger is circumvented and there is the new generation of another family unit, comedy returns. In the return of comedy, however, there is also apparent a maintenance of the importance of the continuance of male blood, a male lineage and identity or name. The son, reiterating the father's life, produces a son. The original father thus lives, in a metaphysical sense at least, in these repeated images of himself; or to put it another way, the line of blood from father to grandson is established as continuous, circumventing real historical accident.

It should be clear from this that the son's rebellion is strictly limited. All he can do is to set up an alternative domestic comedy which appears as a precise imitation of the familial authoritarian order which he has rejected in his own rebellion. His rebellion is forestalled in real terms because its success entails the continuance of his father's blood lineage and identity: in short, its success entails its failure. The son, 'making a name for himself', in fact concretises all the more the name of the father. It is perhaps for this reason that in Shakespeare the more interesting conflict aroused by the rebelling *daughter* forms the crux of many of the plays. If anyone is the agent of familial rebellion in Shakespeare, it is the wife or daughter. Desdemona betrays Brabantio (who dies as a result); Juliet betrays Capulet (and she dies); Jessica betrays Shylock (and the whole of Judaism) by marrying Lorenzo; Portia betrays the will of her father by loading the dice in favour of Bassanio when he comes to choose a casket; in *As You Like It* the situation between the families of Sir Rowland de Boys and Duke Frederick is precisely the same as that between Montagues and Capulets in *Romeo and Juliet*, and Celia betrays her father in marrying Oliver, at which point Frederick is converted 'from the world'.

In the characterisation of the comic family, the flow of male blood, through the primogenitive carrying of the family name, appears to be crucial. But in this family there is always the threat of the flowing of female blood, firstly in menstruation (marking sexual potency) and secondly in the transgression of the hymen (signifying sexual activity and loss of virginity). While attending to the continuance of the male line, the door of the household is left open for the possible intrusion of a foreign body, the son of another family, whose entry into the daughter marks a threat to the hermetically ordered, married family. The stricken father now has yet another 'rival poet' to contend with. But more importantly, the daughter may be seen as betraying the unadulterated integrity not only of herself but also of her family in permitting this 'rival poet' to write his name upon her and leave her pregnant. Thus pregnant, she is due to give birth to an element which does not fit the social order, having no clear identity, no name; and an element which, as a bastard, presents a threat to the hermetic household, for it is a free-floating agent held in check by no clear anterior model of parental authority. The spilling of female blood thus marks a possible end of the nuclear family and the authoritarian masculinist ethos which it subtends. The power the daughter has, then, is the power to be unfaithful to the father, to the authority within such a family. The daughter, unlike the son, can instigate a completely new order, based upon the diffusion of identifiable, namable individual authority. In such an order, the flow of female blood, rather than the name-carrying blood of the masculinist primogenitive lineage, will be central. The activity of 'illicit' sex will also invite history, tragedy and the more 'natural' arrangements of sexual promiscuity all in one. It is thus that a different kind of authority can be broached by Shakespeare; and this was one of his obsessive concerns. The question can be phrased in a more suggestive way by pointing out that what this amounts to is an attempt on Shakespeare's part to discover or construct a mode of authority in which women can actually speak or write. His response may be ambivalent, constructing such an authority in the very moment at which he most fears its threat; but the diffusion of his own writerly authority among so many interpreted meanings for his drama does suggest that he did manage in some way to instate the possibilities of a distinct kind of authority, based upon a Touchstone-like linguistic promiscuity, a promiscuity of meanings.

Catherine Belsey has suggested that the mode of linguistic existence for women in Elizabethan and Jacobean drama is actually a mode of silence.[14] Women, according to a contemporary cliché, are either overtly praised for their silence or low voices, or because they are women, they go unheard. In Shakespearean drama, as in a Platonic dialogue or Socratic argument, there is frequently a conflict between word and deed, *logos* and *ergon*.[15] If the thesis were correct that women are, by definition, silent, then Cordelia, saying 'Nothing', would be a manifestation of the perfect collocation of *logos* and *ergon*; but the case is not as straightforward as this. Cordelia is not at all silent in the opening scene of *King Lear*; on a strictly numerical basis, only Lear himself says

more than she does. In a scene of just over 300 lines, Cordelia
has forty-six, precisely twice as many as Goneril (twenty-
three), and substantially more than Regan (fourteen), and
more too than the other men present, France (thirty-two),
Burgundy (twelve) and Kent (forty-one). This in itself is no
proper basis for argument, however; it is important to ask
when she speaks and why.

King Lear asks for some signification of love from his
three daughters. Goneril begins by saying, or elaborating in
speech, the feeling which Cordelia claims to be proper to
her, a love which goes beyond the power of *logos*, words,
to express. Goneril loves 'more than word can weild the
matter', with 'A love that makes breath poor and speech
unable'.[16] This kind of love is extreme, to say the least; and
here Goneril's words are a kind of euphemism for the activity
or deed of love itself. She is urged into silence, or incoherent
noise, like the groaning of love in sexual activity, which
makes 'breath poor and speech unable' as orgasm approaches.
The audience is then informed that Cordelia will 'Love, and
be silent', which implies that she will in some way replace
logos with *ergon*, will perform an act of love without words.
Regan proceeds, and gets closer to the bone, and to Lear
himself. She firstly proclaims that her love for Lear is of
precisely the same kind as that of Goneril: 'In my true heart/
I find she names my very deed of love' (I. i. 69–70). So
Regan is clearly like this when making love; 'Only she comes
too short', says Regan, inviting a comparison between herself
and Goneril as physical, sexual lovers. The euphemisms then
become more transparent when she says, 'I profess/Myself
an enemy to all other joys/Which the most precious square
of sense possesses,/And find I am alone felicitate/In your
dear Highness' love (I. i. 71–4). In a speech which is clearly
attending to the physical prowess of Regan as lover, and in
which *ergon* constantly threatens to replace *logos*, it is apposite to suggest that 'the most precious square of sense' can
be productively read as referring to the clitoris. The tenor of
the speech then suggests that Regan is only happy when
actually physically making love with Lear. Cordelia still will
not say anything, it seems. However, the whole tendency of
the scene has been to refuse the euphemistic use of words

and to replace them with direct action. Cordelia, having said that she will 'Love, and be silent', need only do precisely this; that is, refuse words at all and make some gesture of love. Cordelia, who will do precisely this in Act 4 Scene 7, when she kisses Lear, would make this scene the neat little comedy which Lear perhaps wanted it to be if she offered the kiss now. Instead, she chooses to speak after all; but she utters such a word which publicly humiliates her father and gives him arguably his worst moment in the play, as the word 'Nothing' is hammered twice into his head by Cordelia, and repeated five times in all.

But why should Cordelia conform to this little comedy at all? Like Desdemona, she knows the difficulty of sharing affection between a father and a lover or husband. Part of the reason for the court-scene at the beginning of *King Lear* concerns the impending marriage of Cordelia. There are two suitors in the wings, and Cordelia knows it; this is the reason for her dismay when asked to profess love to someone else, her father: 'Sure I shall never marry like my sisters,/To love my father all' (I. i. 102–3). When France and Burgundy enter, Cordelia becomes positively loquacious, urging Lear to assure the suitors that she possesses the virtue of silence, and urging him to assure them of her faithful disposition, lacking a 'still-soliciting eye'. As Burgundy begins to excuse himself, Cordelia actually interrupts and sends him away, saying she will not be his wife. With France, she acquiesces. It is not cynical to point out that she demonstrates her 'silence' by talking at great length about it; and she demonstrates her lack of a 'soliciting eye' by more or less overtly choosing France as a husband. At the moment of inception of her sexuality, then, Cordelia prefers another man to her father (and even seems to prefer France to her father's 'first' choice for her, Burgundy); this propels the play into tragedy, as Lear, no less than Brabantio, ponders the dissolution of his familial authority. Lear then has to face the trials of nature, unprotected by the ritualistic artifice of the family.

Thrown out of the house of his daughters, Lear then faces nature; the play has seen the steady stripping of Lear's clothes and retinue, leaving him, finally, naked, a grotesque parody of the 'naïf abroad'. As Lear comes to this trial, the play's central issue, the relation between the human and nature, is raised. On the heath, is he in control of nature, or is nature in control of him? Can there be a human ritual, such as the family, which will allow the successful manipulation or control of nature, or does nature inexorably exert its force indiscriminately through the human body? Towards the end of Act 2 Lear is on the point of exclusion from the house of Regan. He rages against his daughters, and his words fail him, but are supplanted by deeds in a sense:

>   —I will do such things—
> What they are yet I know not; but they shall be
> The terrors of the earth. You think I'll weep.
> No, I'll not weep.
>   [*Storm and tempest*;]
>   (II. iv. 279–82)

As his words fail, the terrors of the earth, as *ergon* rather than *logos*, appear: the storm begins. Further, when we next see Lear on the heath, is the storm something which exists independently of Lear, or is it generated by him, and thus, quite literally, a manifestation of him?

> Blow, winds, and crack your cheeks; rage, blow.
> You cataracts and hurricanoes, spout
> Till you have drenched our steeples, drown'd the cocks.
>   (III. ii. 1–3)

Is this speech made in response to a storm; or is it a kind of prayer, or even order, command, to nature to begin to storm? And is Lear's final 'O, ho! 'tis foul!' (III. ii. 24) not a note of triumph, as nature has still obeyed? The ambiguity of such a reading is there. And this is partly the point. Lear moves from a position in which he is in control of nature, even in the juridical control of sexuality and labour, to a position in which nature has begun to speak through him, through his very body and without his conscious informing or controlling will. This is one of the fundamental conflicts in the play.

There is more, then, to Shakespeare's 'doctrine of nature' than Danby's criticism clarified.[17] One of the questions to which Danby drew attention concerned the question of 'natural' offspring, bastards. This is of vital importance, and I can add to Danby's argument by posing the questions he asks in a more theoretical or abstract manner. In terms of sexuality, the debate becomes a conflict between an opinion which holds that marriage can control or harness nature, and one which argues, on the contrary, that in the act of sex, the brutal facts of nature ('groaning': birth and death, transformative labour) simply and coldly act through or across the body, controlling humanity. Broadly speaking, we watch Lear move from the first position here towards the second. But the problems merely begin here, at this latter pole where we find Edmund already standing.

Edmund, we say, is a 'natural' child or bastard; but Cordelia, in another sense of the word, is also 'natural' to Lear at the close of the play, when she begins to be kind to him, like a daughter should be in one ideological version of 'nature'. Edmund and Cordelia are actually quite close in some respects. The first insistent repetition of the word 'Nothing', five times in ten words, hammers it into our heads as much as into Lear's. It is difficult to ignore it then when it next occurs, after the confusion and rage of the first scene. In our introduction to Edmund (I. ii), we have a precise repetition of the situation in which we were introduced to Cordelia. A father asks a child for information and is met with the word 'Nothing':

> Gloucester: What paper were you reading?
> Edmund: Nothing, my lord.
>
> (I. ii. 30–31)

Edmund repeats Cordelia's lines, and she is aligned with him already in language. By this point she has been disowned, bastardised by Lear, who told France, 'Thou hast her, France: let her be thine; for we/Have no such daughter' (I. i. 262–3). Shortly after this, of course, Lear disowns Goneril too, as she refuses to allow him his full retinue of knights: 'Degenerate bastard! I'll not trouble thee;/Yet have I left a daughter' (I. iv. 253–4). That final daughter is Regan, who receives similar treatment, becoming, with Goneril, an 'unnatural hag'.

If these daughters are bastards, then, where is their mother? Where is Lear's queen in the play? Notably, the one reference made to Lear's wife is one in which the word 'adulteress' is used. We hear of her, and Lear thinks of her, within the terms of the parametric range of possibilities between 'adultery' and 'fidelity', in other words, in terms of sexuality and marriage. Lear, of course, tries to imply that his wife was not, could not be, an adulteress. Not only does that offer the possibility of thinking that she was, but also the evidence unfortunately seems to work against Lear. When he runs to Regan after Goneril has begun to strip him of his knights, Regan is not at all pleased to see him, nor disposed to care for any of his knights. However, she says:

Regan: I am glad to see your highness.
Lear: Regan, I think you are; I know what reason
I have to think so. If thou shouldst not be glad,
I would divorce me from thy mother's tomb,
Sepulchring an adulteress.

(II. iv. 126–30)

The fact that Regan is not glad to see him places Lear in the invidious position of having implied that his wife was indeed adulterous.

There is a sense in which this is true. There is in fact a queen in the play: Cordelia is queen of France. When she returns to Lear at the end, great stress is laid upon their domestic, almost connubial, bliss. She returns to fulfil the function which Lear had outlined for her, to take care of him in his old age and become a kind of surrogate wife to him. The household of Lear's family, and of the nation, having been disrupted at the start, is now re-established for Cordelia and Lear. Cordelia, having performed the action which was deferred from the first scene, having kissed Lear, reinstates the situation of domestic and connubial bliss, the situation of comedy. Lear says:

Come, let's away to prison.
We two alone will sing like birds i'th'cage;
When thou dost ask me blessing, I'll kneel down
And ask of thee forgiveness; so we'll live,

And pray, and sing, and tell old tales, and laugh
At gilded butterflies, and hear poor rogues
Talk of court news
...
He that parts us shall bring a brand from heaven
And fire us hence like foxes.

(V. iii. 8–23)

The metaphysical meanings, the play's subtexts, now seem clear. Cordelia is in a kind of female Oedipal situation. Coming back as a queen, and now Lear's household queen at that, she is, in a sense, satisfying a desire to be the mother of herself. Lear's wife was, and is (insofar as she is Cordelia), an adulteress; and all the children are 'natural', bastards. Cordelia, in order to re-establish familial order at home, has adulterously left France for her father, whom she can now kiss. She has thus, and this is the most crucial point, attained a measure of authority not only from France, whom she betrays in marital terms, but she has also managed to attain an authority over her own familial presence and historical existence. She is now not simply the echo of an anterior mother, bound in duty to obey a father; for she is, in one sense at least, the mother of herself, both Lear's daughter and Cordelia's mother (being Lear's adulterous queen). Having authority, she can in the end not only speak at last but can also physically, sexually act, and in this attaining of authority she stands on equal terms with Lear. Lear's absolutist authority is only now, when Cordelia returns, successfully challenged and dissolved. Cordelia, as bastard and as mother of herself, now has the authority to inaugurate a heretical familial or social order. But to reach such a position, she has had to betray a male authority; infidelity to authority has been crucial;[18] and infidelity has been crucial to the establishment of female authority.

Like Edmund, then, Cordelia at this point is subscribing to the notion that nature speaks through the human, and she becomes a kind of evidence of the futility of marriage as an authoritarian base from which to control or harness nature. However, the other pole of nature, apart from bastardised birth and sexual activity, beyond that pleasure principle, is pain and death. To subscribe fully to the passage of nature through the body, the possibility of death must be entertained. In Cordelia, death is realised; the model of authority which she proffers is refused. The play has, however, addressed itself to the possiblity of such a female challenge to the authority model proposed by the primogenitive family.[19] Dissolution of such authority is seen here to be intimately related to questions of gender and infidelity.

Hymenal Transgressions

> entre le dehors et le dedans, faisant entrer le dehors dans le dedans et retournant l'antre ou l'autre en sa surface, l'hymen n'est jamais pur ou propre, il n'a pas de vie propre, de nom propre. Ouvert par son anagramme, il semble toujours déchiré, déjà, dans le pli dont il s'affecte et s'assassine.
>
> (Jacques Derrida, La Dissémination)

The appearance of Hymen at the close of As You Like It has disturbed many commentators, but Hymen is there for an explicable and specific purpose. That purpose is symbolic, for Hymen or the hymen symbolises the difference between virginity and sexuality.[20] In terms of the monogamous order of marriage which organises the play, the hymen is a wall which has to be transgressed to cement or mark the marriage and inaugurate the new familial line. The appearance of Hymen as a character marks this play not as a celebration of marriage but rather of the intact hymen; the play stops before the transgression of the hymen, before the endorsement of the masculinist authority which depends upon that transgression. The lovers are as yet virginal; indeed, Rosalind, who has been 'gestating' as the ambiguous Ganymede, has only just discovered her sexuality, literally 'dis-covering' it at the significant moment when she sees a blood-stained napkin. Similarly, Celia and Oliver have not yet been incontinent. The play has taken us to the point before the ritual transgression of the hymen, before the instant of heterosexual differentiation.

The hymen as a symbolic wall occurs in a number of plays. In A Midsummer-Night's Dream we even have a character called Wall, significantly enough a wall with a little space in it, through which Pyramus and Thisby commune. In *Romeo and Juliet* there is another real wall, the wall which separates Juliet from the street, which keeps her in the Capulet household and maintains her virginity. This wall, then, like the untransgressed symbolic hymen, works to maintain Juliet's identity as the property of a certain household. The maintenance of the 'house' of Capulet itself, as with any other house, is a ritualised means of dealing with the fear of nature. The house is first and foremost a shelter against the hostile elements. The family or house such as we have it in *Romeo and Juliet* is established in reaction to the fear of nature, which brings with it sexuality and death. Thus, in this nature or history, the authoritative identifiable father loses control over his own life, destiny and lineal name. More pertinently, then, this fear of death in nature can be aligned to a fear, on the part of such father-authors, of acknowledging the flowing of female blood in sexuality; for to acknowledge that entails an endorsement or at least risk of the kind of socio-sexual order which radically challenges individuated singular male authority. The free flow of female blood might inaugurate an order based upon bastardy, promiscuity and a public life, a life or experience outside the 'home' and its private values; the consequence, clearly, is a loss of individuated and privatised identity and a loss of paternal control of possessions (the house) and of nature.

The wall around the Capulet household, being a wall which for Romeo it is death to transgress, can be equated, symbolically at least, with Juliet's hymen.[21] Most of the time, Romeo stands at the base of this wall and is refused entry to Juliet's private chamber. On many occasions, when he clambers over the wall itself he is still only in the garden or forecourt to Juliet's chamber: this is a kind of sexual foreplay. The question is, do they actually consummate their marriage? It may seem that they do, on the occasion when Friar Lawrence sends Romeo to 'comfort' Juliet in her chamber, after the news of his banishment. But if they do make love on this occasion, it must be a very hurried affair; and more importantly, it is a sexual intercourse which is explicitly interrupted by the approach of Juliet's mother, coming to tell Juliet to marry Paris. This intercourse is explicitly *coitus interruptus*.

This love-affair and marriage looks precisely like that between Othello and Desdemona, especially in this respect that the question of consummation of a marriage becomes central through its constant deferral. Othello and Desdemona also suffer from many nocturnal interruptions. Firstly, there is the war to which they must proceed 'this night'.[22] Then when the war is won the nuptials can be celebrated properly: Othello stresses the fact that the marriage has not yet been consummated as he says 'The purchase made, the fruits are to ensue;/That profit's yet to come 'twixt me and you' (II. iii. 9–10). However, this is the very night when there is a civil brawl, and they are disturbed again. After this, verbal communication falters, as they argue about the significance of a handkerchief, and any kind of intercourse is forestalled. Othello is next reduced to being the voyeur of an imagined or fantasised sexual activity from which he is barred. And when we finally see Othello and Desdemona in a bedroom together, all that happens is that Othello assaults and be-whores Desdemona. All of this, together with the fact that Desdemona pointedly asks Emilia to lay out the still unstained marriage sheets on her bed on this fatal night, lends weight to the argument that the marriage is not consummated before this point.[23] When they do finally 'come together' on this final night, blood is finally spilt on the marriage sheets; but it is the blood of the onanistic Othello, who turns his weapon on himself. Othello echoes the dying words of Romeo in this sex-death:

> I kiss'd thee ere I kill'd thee. No way but this—
> Killing my self, to die upon a kiss.
> > (*Othello* V. ii. 361–2)
> Thus with a kiss I die.
> > (*Romeo and Juliet* V. ii. 120)

Romeo and Juliet come to their moment of sexuality only at the moment of death in precisely the same way as Othello and Desdemona. There is a recurrent alignment of the sword or dagger with the penis all the way through the play, even from the opening lines. The sword is the 'naked weapon'

with which Samson, at the start, will not only fight the
Montagues, but with which, as his 'tool', he will also cut off
the maidenheads of the women of that family, pushing
against a wall:

> *Samson:* A dog of that house shall move me to stand. I will take the
> wall of any man or maid of Montague's.
>
> *Gregory:* That shows thee a weak slave; for the weakest goes to the
> wall.
>
> *Samson:* 'Tis true; and therefore women, being the weaker vessels,
> are ever thrust to the wall; therefore I will push Montague's
> men from the wall and thrust his maids to the wall.
>
> *Gregory:* The quarrel is between our masters and us their men.
>
> *Samson:* 'Tis all one; I will show myself a tyrant. When I have fought
> with the men, I will be civil with the maids—I will cut off
> their heads.
>
> *Gregory:* The heads of the maids?
>
> *Samson:* Ay, the heads of the maids, or their maidenheads; take it
> in what sense thou wilt.
>
> *Gregory:* They must take it in sense that feel it.
>
> *Samson:* Me they shall feel while I am able to stand; and 'tis known
> I am a pretty piece of flesh.
>
> *Gregory:* 'Tis well thou art not fish; if thou hadst, thou hadst been
> poor-John. Draw thy tool; here comes two of the house of
> Montague.
>
> *Samson:* My naked weapon is out.
>
> (I. i. 11–33)

These puns continue in the play right through to the end.
Romeo approaches the tomb of the Capulets towards the
close of the play, where the sleeping Juliet lies, in familial
privacy, and in what she herself had called her 'bridal bed'
(III. v. 201). Romeo, like Paris who is also there, wishes to
lie with Juliet and to kiss her undisturbed. But firstly he
must cut through this 'womb of death' (V. iii. 45); the tomb
collapses in metaphorical imagination into the womb which
is his ultimate goal. Both Romeo and Paris aspire to the
condition of paternity with Juliet here; they aspire to the
condition of 'authors' or 'poets' of the family in the manner
I outlined earlier. But Romeo is now interrupted by Paris,
and so he kills this 'rival poet', leaving blood at the entrance
to the tomb/womb. Friar Lawrence will later draw explicit
attention to this blood as he recoils from it in horror seeing
it as a 'stain' in this 'place of peace' (V. iii. 140). It is here,

if anywhere, that Romeo and Juliet consummate their union; and their sexuality brings death. When Romeo prefigures Othello's orgasmic death by killing himself here, Juliet responds by taking Romeo's 'tool' into her own hands and sheathing it in her body, thus finally spilling her own blood through the agency of Romeo's 'naked weapon'. This aligns the blood at the entrance to the tomb, which is Juliet's own familial blood (being that of her kinsman Paris) with her own blood at the entrance of the womb towards which Romeo has approached. Three things interlink at this moment. Firstly, Juliet has had to seize the authority for this sexual activity herself; she guides Romeo's 'tool' into her body; secondly, this sexual activity is itself a betrayal of her family and more particularly of the paternal authority, which makes of it an act of infidelity by definition; and thirdly, the movement out of the paternal house into an identification of herself with her womb not only invites nature which brings death in its historical wake but also permits the linguistic slippage between womb and tomb, equating this faithless seizure of female authority, this dissolution of the Capulet name and singular identity, with death itself. Tragedy ensues.

The tenor of this argument, then, is to suggest that in Shakespeare, *coitus interruptus* equates somehow with comedy, while full coition invites the tragic. This requires more careful and precise elucidation: it might be more correct to argue that a kind of primal scene of sexuality, the female genitalia themselves, equate with the arena of tragedy for Shakespeare.

I drew attention earlier in the present chapter to Frye's comments on the formal construction of the Shakespearean stage. In many plays there is a play-within-a-play, or an arena cut off or isolated from the 'real' world of historical event, or from the flow of history. Arden, where everyone is sheltered from the passage of time ('There is no clock in the forest'), or Prospero's isle or the forest near Athens can be some such areas. In general this framed-off sphere is highly artificial, an area of wit and witchcraft, art and poetry, books and writings: they are, in short, very often areas of ritual, and the ritual which they are most frequently used to construct is that of the nuclear family. There is another aspect of this 'green world' to which Frye draws attention. He argues that the rhythmical movement from 'normal' world to 'green' world and back again has something to do with mythical sacrifice, death and rebirth.[24] The characters who are usually thus sacrificed and reborn tend to be women:

> In the Hero of *Much Ado About Nothing* and the Helena of *All's Well That Ends Well*, the theme of the withdrawal and return of the heroine comes as close to a death and revival as Elizabethan conventions will allow. ... The fact that the dying and reviving character is usually female strengthens the feeling that there is something maternal about the green world, in which the new order of the comic resolution is nourished and brought to birth.[25]

This suggests the possibility of viewing the green world of which Frye writes as some sort of womb, and the rhythmic movement thus becomes one of entry to and exit from a womb. The gender-orientation of the audience becomes important at this juncture, for it seems to be integral to the very comprehension of the play as a staged performance.

These green worlds are not the sole province of comedy. *Hamlet*, for instance, has at least one play-within-the-play; and more strikingly, *Othello* takes place for the most part in the 'green world' of Cyprus, where Iago, like Rosalind in Arden, controls and 'writes' the plot of the action. Shakespeare's attitude to the green world varies from its use in tragedy to its use in comedy. But one thing seems to be fairly constant: insofar as the green world is the female womb and a place of nature, it is hostile to men. King Lear makes a judgement on both nature and female sexuality. Nature for Lear seems to be licentious, full of bastardy and adultery:

> I pardon that man's life. What was thy cause?
> Adultery?
> Thou shalt not die. Die for adultery? No.
> The wren goes to't, and the small gilded fly
> Does lecher in my sight.
> Let copulation thrive.
>
>   (IV. vi. 107–14)

And for Lear, woman's sexual nature is the nastiest of all:

> Behold yond simp'ring dame
> Whose face between her forks presages snow,
> That minces virtue and does shake the head
> To hear of pleasure's name—
> The fitchew nor the soiled horse goes to't
> With a more riotous appetite.
> Down from the waist they are centaurs,
> Though women all above;
> But to the girdle do the gods inherit,
> Beneath is all the fiends';
> There's hell, there's darkness, there is the sulphurous pit—
> Burning, scalding, stench, consumption.
>
> (IV. vi. 118–30)

This equation of the vagina with a sulphurous pit or even with hell itself, is not uncommon; 'hell' often works in both Shakespeare and in contemporary poetry as a euphemism for 'vagina', as Fiedler, for instance, has pointed out.[26]

Lest it be thought that this is merely a local comment of relevance simply to Lear's disgust with his daughters (or wife) we can look at a much earlier but more developed use of the symbol of vagina as hell in *Titus Andronicus*. After the initial intrigue of this play, which once more centres upon authority and primogenitive rights within the family, there is a hunt. Bassianus and his new wife Lavinia, daughter to Titus, are accosted on this hunt by Demetrius and Chiron, who plan to kill Bassianus and rape Lavinia. They stab Bassianus and throw him into a pit on stage, where he bleeds and dies. Demetrius and Chiron then announce that they will use his dead body as a pillow upon which they will rape Lavinia. In fact, they take Lavinia off-stage to rape her, attending perhaps to theatrical *bienséances* and propriety; but the equation of the pit with the scene of the rape still operates, at least symbolically. All through Act 2 Scene 3 of the play, this pit is described as something dark, usually unseen, into which some men fall; it is a 'blood-stained hole' or 'blood-drinking pit'. Titus's sons appear and fall into the pit, which certainly now is all bloody with the carcass of a dead man in it. Martius's words at this point, however, are particularly suggestive:

> So pale did shine the moon on Pyramus
> When he by night lay bathed in maiden blood
>
> (II. iii. 231–2)

This makes explicit the equation of this pit with the scene of
the play's rape, or sexual intercourse; but the real scene of
such a rape, of course, is Lavinia's vagina. Here, in fact, the
whole stage, the green world of the hunt, has become a kind
of huge parallel not simply for Lavinia's womb but more
precisely for her vagina. Shakespeare reveals this 'hell' as the
locus of tragedy itself. When Lavinia, speechless, manages
to communicate to Titus and Marcus that she has been raped
like Philomel in Ovid, Marcus says, in reference to the pit/
vagina:

> O, why should nature build so foul a den,
> Unless the gods delight in tragedies?
> (IV. i. 60–61)

The vagina itself, then, or perhaps more abstractly female
sexuality, is the locus of Shakespearean tragedy. But insofar
as every play has such a pit at its centre (if not a 'green
world', then at least an *orchestra*, a 'dancing' area) insofar as
nearly every play focuses on questions of authority-rights,
familial primogeniture, infidelity and bastardy in one way or
another, there is an implicit invitation to tragedy in every
Shakespearean play.

Shakespeare, then, was clearly not entirely content with
the socio-sexual formation of familial domesticity as his contemporary society was beginning to constitute and consolidate it. Nor was he altogether content with the obvious
alternative, for it was based upon female sexuality and promiscuity, which he seemed to fear more than anything else;
that 'state of nature' leaves no defences against the natural
facts of sex and pain, birth and death. This 'alternative' also
serves, then, to invite the passage of history, which attacks
the desire for immortality. Such a desire is primarily the
desire for the stability and continuity of a singular identity,
and it is this single authoritative (familial) namability which
the alternative 'female' mode of social organisation threatens.
Women in Shakespeare are, as Fiedler says, the 'other' which
is necessary to Shakespeare's identity; but more than this,
these women are the 'other' who are vital to guarantee the
very possibility of the identity of Shakespeare as an author—
without the woman-problem, Shakespeare would literally

not be able to write, or not to write as 'William Shakespeare', the signature which editions of his work celebrate.

In a play such as *Titus Andronicus*, the invitation to tragedy is, temporarily at least, realised. In this play the audience's movement in and out of the stage's green world, in and out of Lavinia's vagina, does in fact draw blood: the locus of tragedy is *realised* as more than a simple unseen abstraction, and the audience is placed in a position which explicitly genders them as 'male'. This is further corroborated in the fact that Lavinia, having no tongue, has no ability to speak, no 'authority': she becomes, according to the play's workings, entirely dependent upon both anterior authority (in the form of Ovid, through whom she manages to reveal the tale of her rape), and upon another male mediation or interpretation of her hieroglyphics, that made by Titus and Marcus. The interpretation of the audience, similarly, is precisely such an 'obedience' to, or imitation of an anterior, 'male', authority.

Entirely different is the procedure in *As You Like It*. In that play the entry to and exit from the womb has not (yet) drawn blood. The epilogue to the play genders the audience, moreover, in a radically ambiguous way. The play has finally established heterosexuality as normative; and then Rosalind says:

> If I were a woman, I would kiss as many of you as had beards that pleased me, complexions that lik'd me, and breaths that I defied not.
> (Epilogue)

Having told the men that she perceives that none of them hate women, this places them in the position of liking/loving Rosalind, who is in fact a boy. And insofar as Rosalind/Ganymede is a boy, those who have beards in the audience which please her/him are precisely those who in fact have no beards at all. In short, the audience here is placed in the gender position of either the female or the 'unsexed' boy. For this audience, then, there is established a position of pleasure which flies directly in the face of the 'pleasant' ending of the play; for the audience's position of pleasure is one which is avowedly homosexual, and it depends primarily upon female homosexuality.

A somewhat different version of Frye's sacrificial death and rebirth of the woman in many of Shakespeare's plays is available. The withdrawal and return of the woman, as Frye puts it, looks somewhat like Freud's 'fort-da' game. In Lacan this game is translated into the terms of the formation of the 'I' in the mirror-stage. In such a stage the child performs an activity rather akin to the movement into and from a green world, only this green world is the surface of the mirror itself. The child learns to control its appearance and disappearance, perhaps, but this is already an advanced stage of the 'play'. The child begins to recognise itself, begins to identify itself when it performs a kind of Lacanian *suture*, a stitching together of the perceiver and the body in the mirror. It is precisely through such a manoeuvre that self-recognition can come about: implicit to it is an identity, a self-identity of perceiver and image through the movement into and out of the mirror. Before such singular identity is attained, however, the child is still in a stage of ungendered dissolute non-separation from the environment. This child has no identity, has no name, and is to that degree precisely a manifestation of the female mobility, or bastardy, both of which obsessed Shakespeare. The non-identified child, who has not yet made the journey in and out of the womb/mirror/green world, is in the position of the audience of *As You Like It*; as such, this play works to dissolve authority. Shakespeare's own development, from the early comedies through to the 'mature' tragedies, comes aligned with an audience-orientation in which the audience is at the less primal stage of development and has mutated into the position of singular identity, male namable authority. The fact that Shakespeare makes a return to the romantic kind of comedy of *As You Like It*, with all the problems of authority which that involves, is testimony to the fact that he was unhappy with the kinds of singular 'male' authority which his tragedy constructed.

Shakespeare, then, was able to outline the possibilities of the feminist threat to the masculinist blood-lineage and patriarchal order of family, state and universe. But this was also a threat to his own authority and cannot be allowed to become dominant if 'William Shakespeare', as individual male, is to write at all. However, in some of the comedies he was also able to retain his own singular authority by positioning the audience in the gender-orientation of femininity, a position from which they could not arrest his writing or authority. Insofar as this feminine position is in fact more 'originary', a state of indiscriminateness or a condition which is primary to sexuality itself (and in relation to which masculinity is secondary, a 'special kind' of femininity, an entropic deviation from it), Shakespeare is thus offering some kind of liberation from what Stephen Heath has called the 'whole sexual fix'.[27] Some of these comedies can be seen to offer an escape from sexual difference and biological sexual identity; they thus indicate, although in terms of content they refuse to sanction, an alternative mode of authority, one based upon the degenerate bastards which most of the daughters become, one based upon no singular namable identity.

Far from there being an anterior given sexual nature which Shakespeare accurately imitates, sexuality itself is part of the very conditioning of the writing, of the authority in the plays. The theoretical equation of his own artistic growth with the question of gender-identity which I have made does bear out at least one of Samuel Johnson's comments in his preface. We may now disagree that the value of Shakespeare's writing lies in the very notion of a fidelity to 'general nature'; however, both Johnson and Rymer agree that the comedy seems to be something more primal, more fundamental to Shakespeare. As Johnson put it, 'His tragedy seems to be skill, his comedy to be instinct'.[28] The theoretical differences underpinning this statement are part of the value of Shakespeare's texts, for through that differentiation Shakespeare managed to question the very activity, writing and authority, which literally gave him identity, gave him existence and identifiable being.

Chapter 4

Blood and Suicide: The Death of the Author?

> writing is the destruction of every voice, of every point of origin.
> Writing is that neutral, composite, oblique space where our subject
> slips away, the negative where all identity is lost, starting with the very
> identity of the body writing.
> No doubt it has always been that way.
>
> (Barthes, 'The Death of the Author')
>
> L'accomplissement normal du processus biologique et, en lui, du pro-
> cessus générique, c'est la mort. La mort est naturelle. Violente du même
> coup
>
> (Derrida, *Glas*)

The Civil War of 1642 was, among other things, a struggle
about authority, and made overt the problems concerning
social authority which had conditioned Shakespeare's texts.
The fact that the conflict breaks into physical violence in
1642 should not blind us to the more or less covert forms
of violence which operated before that date, in the forms of
the two authoritarian structures of church and state.
E. D. Watt's distinction between *auctoritas* and *potestas* is
useful at this point. *Potestas* is equivalent to the authority of
the past which demands our subservient conformity, for it
suggests the power to issue commands; *auctoritas*, less strin-
gent, is merely a counsel to be respected, thus leaving room
for a notion of the autonomous 'author' who breaks with
tradition in order to inaugurate an action, or a writing. The
seventeenth-century poet, as *auctor*, is faced with the two
massive 'rival authorities' in the *potestates* of church and
state; and, to remain alive, the author must conform to these
in some measure. What, then is the condition of authority
for these writers?

129

The idea of God as archetypal poet, dating at least from Plotinus, was a commonplace way of understanding both the divinity and the world in the seventeenth century. The everyday world of gardening and agriculture could be used to explain, by parabolic analogy, the natural world as deific art, structured text; and nature was seen as a realisation of Scripture. God's 'writing', then, was the original and thus the only possible valid one. The elements of the writing, the words of God, were supposedly precisely commensurate with the objects or nature they designated (or, even, brought into being): God's word was the essence of the object which matched it.[1] Such a totalising authority makes it impossible to write anything new, and problematic to authorise any human, ungodly, proposition. The anterior authority of God 'prevents' or makes redundant any notion of autonomous human authority. How, then, to write 'in one's own voice'; how to avoid mere reiteration of Scripture? Further, if the self is identified with its spontaneous, autonomous statements, if it is linguistically constructed as an independent self-determining authority, how can the poet even assure herself or himself of such autonomous existence: all poetic statement is mere repetition of an anterior authority, that of God. This problem affected the projects in self-construction, 'autobiography', of writers such as Montaigne and Descartes in France; but it also conditioned the writing of poets in England.

If the church was Scylla, the powers of the state were Charybdis. On the divorce of Henry viii, allegiance in England had to be sworn to the king rather than the pope. All writing had to conform to state-ideology, or be censored; in some instances an author's life would really be at stake. Most writers of the period suffered directly from direct censorship.[2] More fundamentally, there was a form of self-censorship at work among the poets; there were manoeuvres, metaphysical and rhetorical twists and turns, by which the 'anxieties of influence' of church and state could be circumvented, allowing the poets to write 'authoritatively'.

This struggle for authority, for self-determination, puts all lyric poetry of the seventeenth century into the mode of a kind of 'autobiography'. For male writers, woman remains, as she was in Shakespeare, the 'other' against whom he constructs an authoritative, poetic self. Woman exists as a kind of 'boundary', at the margins or extremes of the male self; yet she is also construed as central, not peripheral at all, in a poem like Donne's 'Valediction: forbidding mourning'. In fact, rather than being simply peripheral or simply central to these lyric autobiographies or constructions of male authority, she becomes, more basically, the medium of the writing itself. In some cases woman is construed as angelic medium between earthly male human and transcendent source of all authority, God, thus facilitating an equation between woman and Christ. In other texts she is regarded as a locus of death, a Cartesian *malin génie*, demonic rather than angelic, and is thus symbolised as archetype of betrayal. Although slighted and oppressed in terms of the content of the writing, woman remains one of the primary conditions of seventeenth-century male authority. Another condition, and one which is related at least emblematically to woman and sexual difference, is death.

Imagination of Women: Angels, Women, Poets

Death is one margin against which humanity defines itself, unpalatable though it may be. Augustine tried, in the *Civitas Dei*, to remove death from the sphere of reality of experience:

> there are three situations: 'before death', 'in death', and 'after death'.
> ... It is evident that as long as the soul is in the body, especially if sensibility remains, a man is alive, his constituent parts being soul and body. Consequently he must be described as being still 'before death', not 'in death'. But when the soul has departed and has withdrawn all bodily sensation, a man is said to be 'after death', and dead.
> Thus between these two situations the period in which a man is dying or 'in death' disappears. For if he is still alive, he is 'before death'; if he has stopped living, he is by now 'after death'. Therefore he is never detected in the situation of dying, or 'in death'. The same thing happens in the passage of time; we try to find the present moment, but without success, because the future changes into the past without interval.[3]

This sophistry contrives to reduce the present moment of

death to an imaginary point, a disappearing asymptote. In removing the fact of death from historical living experience, however, this argument simply relocates death as a potent force in the imagination, all the more trenchant in an age when untimely death was prevalent, like the seventeenth century.

The male imagination operates an equation between this 'imaginary' point of death and that other boundary or limit of male selfhood, the woman, or more precisely the female hymen. Both points operate symbolically as 'median' spaces between two different realms of existence, between the contingent and the necessary. In transgressing both these 'boundary' points, of death and of the hymen, the male imagination constructs its authoritative identity of selfhood: either 'after death' and authorised by a transcendent God, or after sex and identified as a specific male. Emblematically, of course, the womb, if not the hymen itself, equates with the tomb in which Christ lies.[4] Importantly, the female boundary of the hymen allows the imaginative equation of an act of sex with a Christian model of resurrection: the male 'dies' to be reborn as an authoritative selfhood. The woman's body, thus, is construed purely as a medium upon a transcendent, or at least more 'necessary' realm of authority than that contingent historical realm in which the poet happens to exist.

A more conventional understanding of woman as this kind of limit is to be found in the Thomist conception of angels: angels here were precisely a medium upon deific authority, poetic 'concord'. As Kermode writes:

> The concords of past, present and future towards which the soul extends itself are out of time, and belong to the duration which was invented for angels when it seemed difficult to deny that the world in which men suffer their ends is dissonant in being eternal. To close that great gap we use fictions of complementarity. They may now be novels or philosophical poems, as they once were tragedies, and before that, angels.[5]

One such fiction of complementarity in the seventeenth-century male imagination is woman, woman as 'angelic' boundary or medium upon a 'necessary' authority. This logically places the woman in a position of anterior or more originary authority than the male poet: the imagination, or imagining, of woman, is the condition of such male writing and authority.

There is, however, an ambivalence towards this angel/woman who acts as a medium for authoritative poetry. One important earlier locus of this male uncertainty occurs in Dante's *La Divina Commedia*. In the *Inferno*, Virgil foretells Dante of the supervention of Beatrice as his medium, the woman who, seeing all, will complement the Dantesque fiction and offer an originary mode of authority:

> ... 'quando sarai dinanzi al dolce raggio
> di quella il cui bell'occhio tutto vede,
> da lei saprai di tua vita il viaggio' ...[6]

But before meeting Beatrice at the end of the *Purgatorio*, Dante hallucinates an alternative female medium, a kind of rival poet to Beatrice who threatens to lead Dante away into dream and discord, utter contingency, through her own version of poetry: '"Io son" cantava, "io son dolce sirena/che i marinari in mezzo mar dismago,/tanto son di piacere a sentir piena"'.[7] This Siren threatens to lead astray, away from 'true' deific authority and poetry into merely 'pleasant' but contingent sounds.

Both images of women shape seventeenth-century poetry. On one hand, woman is idealised as medium upon authoritative, true poetry; on the other, as alien to men, she is construed as a siren leading men astray from their 'proper' path, and thus from their authoritative selfhood. To resolve this discrepancy, the male poets tend to imagine woman as such a medium upon truth, while simultaneously appropriating and controlling or, in short, sacrificing this woman-medium in their quest for autobiographical authority. Woman thus becomes typically a sacrificial symbol in much seventeenth-century writing, from Shakespeare's Cordelia right the way through to Racine's Iphigénie or Ériphile. This also facilitates the identification of this woman as some kind of Christ figure.

Male poets, then, tend to appropriate the position of medium, finally, for themselves, adopting an image of the

poet derived from neoplatonic sources. A scale of authority
is elaborated from the originary source (God or Muse),
through furious inspired authors to mad rhapsodists and
enthusiastic readers. Cowley uses this in his praise 'On the
Death of Mr Crashaw', where he addresses Crashaw as '*Poet*
and *Saint*! to thee alone are given/The two most sacred
Names of *Earth* and Heaven'.[8] Poet equates with saint here,
as mediator between earth and heaven, accident and poetic
necessity. Further, this achievement is as great as, and similar
to, Christ's: 'The hard and rarest *Union* which can be/Next
that of *Godhead* with *Humanitie*'. A confusion between two
models of authority, that of Christ as exemplary suicide or
sacrifice and that of woman as mediating angel, is rife in
seventeenth-century poetry.

Cowley's 'Maidenhead' links the boundary of the hymen
with the Augustinian moment 'in death', thus contriving to
make the hymen purely imaginary, and eradicating woman
at the very moment when he most makes use of her in his
autobiographical self-construction or assumption of autonomous authority. He laments that it is impossible to find a
virginal woman; the boundary he wishes to transgress is
unavailable, cannot be dis-covered. Maidenhead is thus
imaginary, since no maidens are to be found. On one level
this is conventional 'libertine' maltreatment of women. On
a more important level there is a suggestion that the hymen,
and women, are important precisely as symbol rather than
as reality. As symbol, the hymen is an imaginary point, like
Augustine's moment of 'dying':

> Slight, outward *Curtain* to the *Nuptial Bed*!
> Thou *Case* to buildings not yet finished!
> Who like the *Center* of the Earth,
> Does heaviest things attract to thee,
> Though Thou a *point imaginary* be.[9]

When is this hymeneal point transgressed? As in the Augustinian analysis, there is a time prior to transgression and a
time after it; but the present moment of transgression is
unavailable to the poet, who hints that virginity has been
lost during masturbation. The actuality of transgression is
unavailable to experience; which is precisely the compaint of

the poem. But the tenor of this is to suggest that women do not exist. The poem defines woman in terms of her identification with the hymeneal boundary; if that is imaginary, then, logically, women are also purely imaginary and are made so precisely at the moment when Cowley has made use of them to construct an autobiographically authorised male selfhood.

This takes a more religious cast in Donne's 'Aire and Angels', where Donne starts from the proposition that women affect him in the same way as angels; and further, that their mode of existence is invisibility, or the purely imaginary. He starts from an abstract love, from loving without an object of desire; and argues that such an object must be carnally realised. But this makes the realisation, the historical existence, of the woman dependent upon Donne's prior existence as desiring subject; and once again, this is at the moment when Donne is constructing an autonomous authority and selfhood through the medium of the angelic woman. The final comparison of the poem has proved problematic for commentary:

> Then as an Angell, face, and wings
> Of aire, not pure as it, yet pure doth weare,
> So thy love may be my loves spheare;
>   Just such disparitie
> As is twixt Aire and Angells puritie,
> 'Twixt womens love, and mens will ever bee.[10]

The ambiguity written into these lines, where it is unclear which gender is being compared to which element, air or angel, is productive. The ambiguity eases a reading which makes it appear that female and male change places and status in their carnal meeting. This carnal meeting is also their realisation through sexuality; that is, thanks to Donne's sexuality, his sexual desire and activity, not only does the woman come into existence but she also finds herself relegated to the position of material existence: she moves from pure to less pure, from ethereal medium to material reality. Meanwhile, Donne moves in the opposite direction, contriving to place himself in the position of the hymen, the imaginary female medium between 'man' and 'God': he himself assumes the authority of the angelic medium. As angel, the woman was the purer medium between Donne's historical contingency and his authoritative being; as materialised lover, she loses that purity and mingles with the lesser air as a condition of both the existence of the sexual encounter and the existence of the poem. The transgression of the median boundary, in sex and in the woman/angel's displacement, has reversed the positions, purities and priorities of male and female participants. Donne thus contrives to prove the logical anteriority of the male consciousness, and the dependence of women upon the male for her very being. She is supposed to be imaginary without his desire, and unrealised until his assumption of autobiographical authority. The phallocentricity of this mode of authority is clear, and illustrates the strategy of the 'death' of *female* authority as a precondition of male writings in this period.

Authorisation of Christian Men

The collocation of sex with death was not entirely new. Augustine suggested that the pleasure of lust was so intense 'that when it reaches its climax there is an almost total extinction of mental alertness';[11] and there had been a strong cultural attachment of sex and death in myths and tales such as that of Tristan and Iseult. What is new about the link in the seventeenth century is its instrumentality in establishing modes of authority based on gender. Much seventeenth-century poetry focuses on images of the grave or of the self engraved or shrouded, in an attempt to construct a necessary, authoritative (and complete) biography or identity. But that space of death is frequently associated with woman.

In Crashaw's 'The Weeper' Magdalene is identified purely in terms of her weeping; her tears are her essence. But this sorrow incarnate is equated with the moment of death in the poem:

> Not in the Evenings Eyes
> When they red with weeping are,
>   For the Sun that dyes,
> Sits sorrow with a face so faire.[12]

Magdalene's proper place, once more, is that of a boundary, a hymenal space between life and death, light and dark, day and night. It is on the point of the 'death' of the Sun that we have the most precise realisation of Magdalene here. But the omnipresent pun on 'Sun/Son' clarifies the religious context of this boundary, identifying Magdalene with the point of Christ's dying, a dying which is itself an 'imaginary' point between contingent secular history and necessary sacred transcendence, between Eliade's 'profane' and 'sacred' temporal organisations.[13]

The religious tenor of such a collocation as this is often modified by the presence of sexual connotations which render the 'boundary' more explicitly as a hymen. The place of death is often identified with the womb. Crashaw's 'Easter day', for instance, identifies Christ's tomb as a 'Virgin Tombe', aligning Christ's death and Mary's body. As this tomb mutates into a womb, the celebration is of a rising 'manly' sun:

> Rise, Heire of Fresh Eternity,
> From thy Virgin Tombe:
> Rise mighty man of wonders, and thy world with thee
> Thy Tombe, the universall East,
> Natures new Wombe.[14]

Cowley alludes to the same idea in his paraphrase of the angel's address to Mary in Book 2 of the *Davideis*, where the idea of God 'shrouded' in the womb firmly identifies that womb as a tomb or space of death. Emblematically, this idea is reworked in a number of ways: the tomb in Crashaw and the shroud in Cowley, the sepulchre or heart in Herbert, the grave itself in Marvell, even the wrinkles in Magdalene Herbert's face in Donne's 'The Autumnall'; all these identify the female body as a space of death, the medium of 'dying'. In more precise emblematic terms, the strongest equation is between womb and tomb. For Christian poets, Christ's entry into the womb was an acceptance of secular history, and this impulse to 'autobiography' on Christ's part, this incarnation, brings with it the inevitability of the tomb or death. That quasi-sexual meeting between Christ and the Virgin Mary, then, is like a suicide of sorts; and this Christian model of dying makes death itself not only acceptable but also desirable, for it is now a doorway or boundary to a deific source of authority. It is through such a death (such an orgasmic 'little death') that the ultimate autobiography can be written, according to the subtext of the Christian myth. The Christian 'suicide' becomes the very condition of authority for male poets. As in the *Imitatio Christi* of Thomas à Kempis, 'Happy is he that always hath the hour of his death before his eyes, and daily prepareth himself to die';[15] and, we might add, happy is he who attains an autobiographical authority, the illusion of control of his own moment of death, thereby. The Donnean interest in suicide, attested to by Carey, is not unique to him; rather, it conditions the very fact of writing on the part of male poets in this period.[16] Gender thus complicates the basic strategy of the imitatio Christi, the suicide as a means of attaining authority.

Sometime around 1617 Carew contracted syphilis. This, it seems clear, affected his attitude to women and sexuality. 'A cruell Mistris' looks to be about the contraction of this disease, and the mistress in question is deemed to be cruel because she 'burns' him in the very place and moment of his desire for her (tantamount, in this masculinist culture, to the moment of his creation of her, as in Donne above). Crucially, the woman in the poem becomes an archetype of the traitor: promising authority (being the poet's medium upon authority and autobiography), she actually denies authority in a specific way. Other deities are satisfied by sacrifices, but not this cruel mistress who 'disdaines the spotlesse sacrifice/Of a pure heart that at her altar lyes'.[17] Her disdain of Carew kills the 'poet' in him. Paradoxically, though there is a poem here, it is not the poem promised by the title, because the woman has left the poet unable to remember her in verse. Instead, not surprisingly, the poem turns out to be about Carew himself, and about the impossibility of writing 'A Cruell Mistris':

> With bended knees J daily worship her,
> Yet she consumes her own Idolater.
> Of such a Goddesse no times leave record,
> That burnt the temple where she was ador'd.

In Donne's 'Aire and Angels', I indicated the dominant manoeuvre by which these poets contrive to make the female appear to be dependent upon the priority of the male, and specifically the primacy of male phallic desire. In this poem by Carew, the poetic quill, the phallus which 'writes' or authorises both woman and poem, is corrupted by the woman in her treacherous act of contaminating the author with syphilis, producing a different kind of 'burning' from the passion desired. The temple of love in the text is the genitals; and it is upon this altar that the poet lies, burning in sacrifice himself. His genitals are on fire, not consumed by passion but corrupted by disease; his 'autobiographical' ability, his ability to produce a (biographical) issue is forestalled. Thus the female 'betrayal' here brings about his death as an author, as he fails to write the poem which his title promised. 'A cruell Mistris' cannot be written, paradoxically; the condition of betrayal which occasioned its genesis infects its execution as well, and the poet betrays his audience in arguing in the poem of the 'cruell Mistris' that she cannot be remembered or written in verse. It is more common for the woman, as female authority or medium of authority, to be sacrificed; and Carew does extract such revenge here. In burning the poet, she burns, concomitantly, the place where she is adored, and that place is the temple of her own body. It is this which Carew celebrates here: her 'betrayal' of him turns out to be a suicidal act of self-immolation. The final paradox here, of course, is that this suicidal act allows the woman to remain close to the Christian model of authority, making the male poet's death a mere contingent accident resulting from her primary identification with authority.

The fundamental point in this is to show that writing is not only linked to death; but authoritative writing, and especially that act of authoritative self-construction or biography which is crucial to the poets of this period, also involves the issue of gender and notions of betrayal. This 'female suicide', as well as betrayal, is important, for in many of these poems there is a dual system of authority at work. Firstly, the poet is pre-empted, prevented from authority, by Christ, and tries to circumvent this by imitating Christ to the point of domesticating or assimilating his own death.

But the means of effecting this mode of authority depends on the second aspect or system, in which the male is dependent upon the female in order to construct himself autobiographically as an authoritative imitatio Christi. The problem of female anteriority thus remains and conditions whatever male writing or male authority there is.

Authority and Infidelity: Writing as (Male) Therapy

'Celia bleeding' is a title whose ambiguity is not resolved merely by addressing the poem to a surgeon, as Carew does. He argues that Celia will not bleed, which is a curious thing to suggest, unless he means to suggest that she will not bleed in a sexual activity with him, will not lose her maidenhead:

> Fond man, that canst beleeve her blood
> Will from those purple chanels flow;
> Or that the pure untainted flood
> Can any foule distemper know;
> Or that thy weake steele can incize
> The Crystall Case, wherein it lies.[18]

Her virginity is being attested to here, not only through the claim that she does not bleed, but also in the statement that her blood is pure and unadulterated. The surgeon is thought of as a rival to the poet, having greater ease of access to more intimate knowledge of Celia's body. But there is a jibe at the surgeon's imputed impotence, his 'weake steele' which cannot pierce Celia. Both poet and surgeon, then, desire access to Celia's body, and more importantly to her blood, for their identities as poet/lover or surgeon. Celia's body is then itself construed in an odd image, as a 'Crystall Case'. This image does, in some sense, adulterate the purity of her blood, for there is a pun on Christ/Crystall.[19] This pun facilitates the understanding of Celia as container or bearer of Christ, or emblematically, as the tomb/womb within which Christ lies. This is tantamount to suggesting that the female blood (inside Celia) is equated with Christ (also 'inside' Celia). Once more, then, the flow of female blood becomes crucial to the constitution of authority; and, as I am arguing throughout this section, it is tacitly mediated as prior to male blood and masculinist lineages.

Celia becomes Virgin Mary and rock, and then, more precisely, the sepulchre wherein Christ, now as a *female* authority, lies: 'And the hard rock wherein it dwells,/The keenest darts of love repels'. As the narrative situation, of Celia being bled by a surgeon and Carew being pained by this, is recuperated, there comes the productive confusion of gender in the construction of an authority in the poem. Carew argues that it is not Celia's blood which flows at all, but rather it is he himself who is bleeding, pierced in the heart:

> But thou reply'st, behold she bleeds;
>   Foole, thou'rt deceivd; and dost not know
> The mystique knot whence this proceeds,
>   How Lovers in each other grow;
> Thou struckst her arme, but 'twas my heart
> Shed all the blood, felt all the smart.

Carew, lover of Celia (the autobiographical position which the poem tries to effect) 'grows in her', like the Christ already alluded to in the text; and it is his blood which flows. Carew, then, assumes the position of the 'Crystall' in the 'case' of Celia, the womb/tomb/virgin/rock. This 'Crystall' bleeds or dies in order that the poem become one celebrating Carew's own male authority (over the surgeon and over the writing of the poem) at the expense of the female blood of Celia, which is now passed over in silence. It is Carew who bleeds from the heart, like an iconic Christ, and he, therefore, who has been pierced in the side. The confusion of the female suicide (Christ) and its assumption in male terms by the poet, is crucial to the construction of a male authority which informs this poem.

When writing of blood in seventeenth-century poetry, one cannot avoid Crashaw, who wrote of blood with obvious relish and obsessiveness. More importantly, however, for Crashaw writing was in some sense actually done in blood. Authoritative writing was dependent upon the act of violence which made Christ's blood flow, and writing itself is stained with the mark of this originary violence. Writing is violence for this poet:

> What ever story of their crueltie,
> Or Naile, or Thorne, or Speare have writ in Thee,
> Are in another Sence
> Still legible;
> Sweet is the difference:
> Once I did spell
> Every red letter
> A wound of thine,
> Now, (what is better)
> Balsome for mine.[20]

According to this, writing involves a sacrifice of a divine authority, drawing blood, quite literally, from the body of Christ; and this 'death of the author', or sacrifice of originary authority, is therapeutic. Crashaw is healed by the act of writing, an act akin to the piercing of Christ's side, and an act which, in sacrificing Christ as originary authority, grants the possibility of autobiography or the writing of his own healthy life, to Crashaw.

Crashaw thought of Christ's blood, it seems clear, in an explicitly erotic way. Drooling over the wounds of Christ, naked and bloody, he frequently effects an equivalence between certain recurrent elements: Christ's red wounds mutate into red roses, which then, associatively, become women and more specifically women who 'bleed' in certain ways. 'The Teare', for instance, makes a comparison between Mary's tear and the dew drop on the rose or vine. But the collocation becomes explicitly erotic, and hints at other kinds of sexual 'dew':

> Such a pearl as this is
> (Slipp'd from Aurora's dewy breast)
> The rose-bud's sweet lip kisses,
> And such the Rose it selfe when vext
> With ungentle flames, does shed,
> Sweating in too warme a Bed.[21]

This refers at one level to the flower-bed. But the linguistic sexual overtones of kissing, sweating, the luxury of heat, and so on, construct another sense which makes the rose into a woman, weeping after sexual ravishment, 'vext/With ungentle flames'. This weeping tear itself becomes even more explicitly sexual, and is reddened, taking the colour of the rose, at precisely a moment of *de*-flowering:

> Such the Maiden Gemme
>   By the wanton Spring put on,
> Peeps from her Parent stemme,
>   And blushes on the Manly Sun.

This tear, reddened on the blushing face, begins to equate with maiden-blood. The rosy woman, deflowered, sweats not roses, but dew, and such dew is written of as a red or bleeding wound. Crashaw thus effects an ambiguity between this maiden-blood, female blood and the blood of Christ's wounds, 'authoritative' blood. The first two stanzas of 'On the Wounds of our Crucified Lord' clarify these connections and, further, make these wounds into mouths; they thus become the condition of Crashaw's speech/writing or authority.

The confusion or ambiguity of gender in this source of authorisation for Crashaw is elaborated in his confounding the martyrological Christ with another, female, martyr, St Teresa. In 'On our Crucified Lord, Naked and Bloody', blood is construed as the most appropriate garment for Christ because, for Crashaw, Christ *is* blood and exists only in terms of the sacrificial spilling of blood. It is this which makes it possible for Crashaw to inflict the violence of writing, for he writes not only *of* but also *in* Christ's blood. But there is a great iconographic resemblance between this conception of Christ and the image of St Teresa, who:

> never undertooke to know,
> What death with love should have to doe
> Nor hath shee ere yet understood
> Why to show love she should shed blood[22]

This death, however, becomes a more erotic spilling of blood, the repeatable 'little death' of a sexual ectasy. Teresa, seeking death, finds it in her 'dying' with Christ as spouse; in their commingling, the spilling of Teresa's blood is an analogue or faithful witness to the originary spilling of (male) authoritative blood in Christ. Again, however, there is a reiteration of the collocation of an originary source of authority (here, male Christian blood) with some kind of female source (here, Teresa as witness). Two kinds of 'betrayal' are necessary to reprioritise the male author as himself an originary authority. Insofar as the source of authority, the medium of authority, is female, she has to be eradicated or appropriated, usually sexually, by some male figure. Insofar as the origin of authority is Christ, an imitatio Christi, involving a metaphysical suicide, is necessary for the poet to establish a transcendent or absolute authority replacing the merely contingent authority of his secular existence. Firstly, then, the woman is 'betrayed': the male poet does not bear faithful witness to her priority. Secondly, the strategy of suicide represents a fundamental betrayal of the authorities of both church and state: as criminal and sinful act, it challenges the *potestas* of tradition and grants a theoretical autonomous authority to the individual writer.

The graphocentric link between writing and death is made explicit in Cowley's 'Written in Juice of Lemmon', a text which reflects what Ellrodt regards as Cowley's obsession with reading and writing.[23] The letter in the poem (perhaps the poem itself) appears to be blank and requires the assistance of a reader to articulate its message. A specific kind of reader is demanded: firstly, she must be female; secondly, she must 'heat' the letter by reading in a spirit of love in order to make the message reveal or discover itself. To read this letter, written in invisible ink, a more material heat is needed; and this materialisation of the metaphorical heat threatens both to bring the letter to existence or articulation, and at the same moment to destroy it. For Cowley, reading and writing are no trivial pursuits of pleasure, but matters of life and death, as Foucault would have it. The writing here exists only at the boundary-moment of the instant of death itself. It is revealed, written, at the very instant of its destruction:

> Alas, thou think'st thy self secure,
> Because thy form is *Innocent* and *Pure*:
> Like *Hypocrites*, which seem unspotted here;

> But when they sadly come to dye,
> And the last *Fire* their Truth must try,
> *Scrauld* o're like thee, and *blotted* they appear.[24]

There are two ways of dying by fire: either as martyr or as heretic. This dichotomy is central, for it focuses the issue of fidelity: the martyr is a faithful witness, the heretic an infidel. Cowley hopes he may die as martyr and '*enjoy* the *Flame*'; but this seems impossible. He advocates the rereading of the letter and argues that in this action there is an 'alternative' authority to his own at work, in the 'heretical' authority of the reader. The reader, beginning the text anew, constructs her heretical version, an alternative to the 'authorised version'.[25] But the crucial question now appears: where might there be an originary 'unheretical' version of this text, since the reader is presented with precisely the same blank sheet of paper which faced the writer when he began to write the poem. Cowley's 'original' text, 'Written in Juice of Lemmon', is itself heretical, a 'reading' of itself. Both writing and reading are inherently heretical, according to this, involving their subjects in infidelity as a very condition of their authority. The religious aspect of such heresy deserves attention.

Herbert as Heretic

That Herbert, like Donne, 'challenges' God in his poetry is a commonplace; but the degree, the enormity, of the challenge goes unremarked. Most criticism seems to suggest that even as Herbert questions God, his faith reasserts itself almost immediately in a mode of resignation, or reassumption of faith. But Herbert is too intellectual for this Browneian pursuit of reason to the '*o altitudo*'.[26] It bears repetition that Herbert was worldly-wise, having served as Member of Parliament for Montgomery borough in 1623–4, and that he was too much of a dabbler in sophistical words, having been University Orator and Praelector in Rhetoric at Cambridge University. The problems of faith and logical reason, both complicated by words and rhetoric, were important determinants shaping the writing of *The Temple*. Herbert, perhaps more than any other contemporary poet, was concerned fundamentally with the relation of religious authority to literary authority; and that relation posed many difficulties.

In a celebrated article and book, Colie drew attention to the centrality of Herbert's conception of God as Word, *logos*. She argued that, in Herbert, '"verse" and "rhyme" are noticeably consistent metaphors for divine creation, for bringing order from chaos, for fitting, for balancing, for satisfying and for making content'.[27] Using this precept, together with the notion of God as primal poet, she inaugurated a reading of 'Deniall' which has become almost the standard understanding of the poem, in which God answers Herbert's questioning prayer even at the very moment he asks it:

> Herbert has succeeded in making his Creator show himself (as He has always been in Greek) a poet, has persuaded his Creator into collaboration on this poem. ... The last minute solution, in which order is restored to poet and poem, exhibits and recapitulates the abruptness of God's original act of creation.[28]

Thus began a series of ingenious interpretations of Herbert as self-conscious *rhétoriqueur*, endlessly performing the trick of matching *logos* with *ergon*.

There are difficulties with this. According to this kind of reading, seemingly different or discordant elements in the world are revealed to be in a state of underlying harmony, and not in dissonance and strife at all; the optimism of this suggests that the poetry, the accords and rhymes, has already been written. Human poetry is thus made redundant; there is no necessity for Herbert to write at all, since the poetry has been written already: whatever is, is poetry, according to this. Herbert does pare his writing down, making it seem merely a record of what is;[29] but, as he plays a seventeenth-century Beckett to Donne's Joyce, he finds that the more language is pared down, the more it says. The puritanism of the enterprise leads to a situation in which all language is to be mistrusted, and he must fall into silence. Theologically, this silence or 'end' of writing is necessary, since any writing, according to the notion of God as originary poet, is inherently an insult to God, an attempt to rewrite the universe.

Such rewriting is not only implicitly critical; it is also an attempt to write 'the thing which is not', as Swift's Houyhnhnms would later put it. Herbert was aware of this theological notion that writing is, in this way, sinful. If God wrote all there is, any human writing offers a supposed addition to the universe (and therefore is purely imaginary, unreal, unauthorised by God), or it offers a deformation of that universe in a revisionary writing of it. Human writing must be seen as the devil's work, the creation of evil or of that which does not exist (a definition, in theological terms, of sin):

> O that I could a sinne once see!
> We paint the devil foul, yet he
> Hath some good in him, all agree.
> Sinne is flat opposite to th'Almighty, seeing
> It wants the good of *vertue*, and of *being*.[30]

Clearly, this is a fundamental problem for a devotional writer: the project to write has been negated, or prevented, by the theological premises from which the writer operates. And yet Herbert does still write.

In the face of this, various attempts have been made to rehabilitate the myth of 'gentle', 'humble' Herbert, despite the enormity of his ambition. Fish argues that he suppresses his own first-personal voice to let that of God come through him; he makes the action of writing '"not mine" by making the experience of his poems the discovery of their true authorship'.[31] Nuttall adopts a simlar stance, arguing that God, not Herbert, wrote the poems. But this leads critics of such a persuasion into two extreme positions. Firstly, they place themselves in the position of the very heresy which they are trying to avoid, for they are now criticising not the poetry of Herbert but that of God. Secondly, they are forced to make the bizarre, not to say utterly unverifiable, proposition that *The Temple* 'is not a mimetic performance but is a recorded conversation which once took place between Herbert and God. ... the very authorship of *The Temple* now becomes a dual affair. Herbert wrote most of it, but God wrote quite a lot'.[32] The notion that God wrote this poetry is extreme; but if Herbert did write 'most' of it, then the problem of critical heresy as a founding principle of Herbert's authority remains.

Both poems on 'The H. Scriptures' are relevant here. The first of these describes the Scriptures as a therapeutic balm and the source of health and eternal life. Herbert advises woman to look on the holy book, transforming the text into a mirror or reflection of the image of woman: 'Ladies, look here; this is the thankfull glasse,/That mends the lookers eyes'.[33] As Herbert reads or looks at the Bible now, interestingly, he is faced with a *female* image. The sexuality of the act of reading (recalling Cowley's 'Written in Juice of Lemmon'), and the quasi-sexual pleasure which prayer in front of the Bible offers Herbert comes clear in the punning final couplet:

> Thou art joyes handsell: heav'n lies flat in thee,
> Subject to ev'ry mounters bended knee.

This describes the book as open and laid flat to be read by one in an attitude of prayer, hoping to rise to heaven. But is is odd that heaven, in the book, should lie flat before Herbert, subject to him. But recalling the book as an image of woman, 'mounters bended knee' becomes sexual innuendo. Herbert's reading here is like a sexual relation with female authority akin to that established by his contemporaries. Prayer, for Herbert, is like sex for the libertine poet, bringing pleasure at the moment when he transgresses the boundary between his contingent historical existence and the transcendent necessity of sacred time, divine authority.[34] If such prayer goes unheard, of course, it offers the possibility of repeating the pleasure, of praying again. Denial, actually, is fundamental in a sense to the continuance of Herbert's writing.[35]

'The H. Scriptures (II)', though a description of the poetic (dis)organisation of the Bible, also happens to be a fairly accurate description of the organisation of *The Temple*, in which 'This verse marks that, and both do make a motion/ Unto a third, that ten leaves off doth lie'.[36] Herbert's text mimics the intertextuality and autoreferentiality of the Bible. The implication of this is even more radical, in fact, than the untenable positions of Fish and Nuttall. Herbert, dissatisfied with the organisation of the world, God's poem, feels he can better it, and opens himself to comparison with his 'precursor', purporting now to offer a radical rewrite of Scripture. *The Temple*, then, must be seen as an alternative to the King James *Authorized Version*. It is thus no less than a fundamental challenge to the *potestas* or authority of both church and state. The text is, fundamentally, a heretical act of criticism, but a mode of criticism which is itself secular poetry. Only one critic seems to have commented on the ambition of this. Chana Bloch, discussing Herbert's use of the sacred text, writes:

> where we might expect to find the self humbled and subordinated, we find it instead vigorously at work and conscious of its own motions in bringing the text to life. Herbert paraphrases or adapts the text to suit his purpose and clearly enjoys taking such liberties with the sacred Word. The delighted play of the mind ... belies Fish's picture of Herbert, martyr-like[37]

Herbert's ambition should make that of Donne pale into insignificance.

If denial is a condition of Herbert's continuing to write, then it is not surprising to find a poem celebrating such denial in its title. Colie's argument, that as Herbert articulates his request for order, he finds it already answered, would make the prayer itself in some sense redundant and the title ironic. But the poem supports a contrary reading to this. It has been noted that there is hardly a single repetition of verse form or rhyme scheme in *The Temple*; the invention of yet another such regular scheme in 'Deniall' should come as no surprise in this context. The surprise should come later, with the interruption of a different kind of 'accord' in the final rhymed couplet. Herbert tries to establish an autonomous rhyme scheme or pattern, one which is identifiably 'his own', and no mere reiteration of deific orders and concords. But he is, finally, denied such authority, with the supervention of God's 'style' at the close of the poem. It is precisely the final stanza which is aberrant, looking from the point of view of Herbert's striving for authority, and it is those closing lines that deny him such autonomous authority. Here, he goes unheard, exactly as the poem says; but it is also precisely because of that denial that he can have reparation to prayer once more, can write or try to establish an autonomous authority, again.

Much of the poetry is written in an attempt to escape from the *potestas* of God, so that Herbert can demonstrate, through his own autonomous prayer and style, a love which is genuinely, 'authoritatively', his own, based on his spontaneous *auctoritas*, a love for which he himself will be responsible. God's 'prevention' or supervention, though necessary to the continued prayer of Herbert, is, paradoxically, the thing Herbert must try to evade in order to construct his own authority, to write his own prayer, not the 'Lord's Prayer' or that of 'Our Father'. 'Coloss. 3.3' demonstrates the struggle for autonomous authority, independent of God. The poem has a 'double motion', for we can read it, thanks to its typography, either line by line, straightforwardly, or acrostically, to reveal the phrase adapted from Colossians 3:3, 'My Life Is Hid In Him, That Is My Treasure'. There are two ways of approaching this, depending on which motion is privileged. On the one hand, Herbert is again denied his own authority, for the words of God not only determine the shape of the poem but also relegate Herbert's words to the status of the merest critical marginalia around the core of Scripture. Herbert's poem exists, then, merely as a vessel or medium allowing the voice of God to be heard by those who flee sermons, the projected audience of *The Temple*. Herbert is not 'author' but vehicle or medium. Alternatively, Herbert's writing might be seen as a fundamentally critical revision of Scripture, a revision offered by the 'marginalia', which now become central. The verse from the Bible, according to this point of view, is written only by the grace of Herbert's authority. Moreover, it is his version, his heretical mediation or critical reading of the biblical phrase, which we have to read in order to discover the meaning of the Scriptural phrase. It is important, in this respect, to note that Herbert has indeed modified the words of God. In the *Authorized Version*, the verse reads, 'For ye are dead, and your life is hid with Christ in God'. In Hooker's terms, Herbert is the unfaithful witness of his source; not so much a martyr, more an authoritative heretic.

Herbert often contrives to locate himself in the mediating, angelic, female, Christian position outlined in the present chapter as a source for authority. There is a prevalent notion of writing in blood, and the demand for a superior authority, God, to impress itself or stamp its image on Herbert to validate him as angel/coin. Herbert asks God to write in his heart, where blood/ink will be found; or, recalling that his heart is made of stone and hard, he asks for the fundamental deifi: kind of writing in stone as a means of acquiring authority.[38] This is similar to the contrivance, available to libertine poetry, whereby male poets stamp or impress their image on that *tabula rasa* which they understand as the female body or female landscape. Herbert adapts this and makes himself the female upon which an authority much greater than the temporal, historical, contingent or 'autobiographical', the authority of God's originary word, writes itself. 'Jesu', for instance, is more than the conventional praise of a name: the poem conspires to turn Herbert into precisely the female medium or poet which is the real condition of authority in this cultural moment. There is more than one pun in the poem, and an important one is that which plays between 'engraving' and 'burying in a grave':

> JESU is in my heart, his sacred name
> Is deeply carved there: but th'other week
> A great affliction broke the little frame,
> Ev'n all to pieces: which I went to seek:
> And first I found the corner, where was *J*,
> After, where *ES*, and next where *U* was graved,[39]

As in other poems, Herbert contrives to place Christ in his heart; like the libertine male phallocentrically stamping or entering the female, God 'impresses' an image or name on Herbert's heart. But Herbert thinks of his body here as the place where '*U* was graved'; that is, where Christ was buried, where the literal word or name of God was placed. Through the emblem of the tomb/womb, Herbert has autobiographically made himself into a model of his own conception of Mary, of the woman both as mediating angel and as bearer of the authoritative Word of God. Like the Donne of Divine Sonnet XIV, Herbert wants to be ravished by

God, to become a woman labouring to utter the truth or the whole authoritative name of JESU. Thus Herbert here performs no mere imitatio Christi; he tries to suggest that by looking into his heart to write in the most innocent, sincere and authoritative manner possible, he will find Christ there. That is to say, the realisation of the name of Christ, the Word of God, is dependent on Herbert's correct arrangement of the letters or writing he finds in his heart. But if he utters his inmost self in the name of JESU, then, in some sense the imitatio Christi is complete; for he utters himself, brings himself to being, as Christ. The suggestion is that Herbert, as author, pretends to the position of actually being Christ.

Such an assertion requires exemplification; but there is no shortage of evidence. In those poems, for instance, where God writes upon Herbert's heart, the body of Herbert becomes in a sense the Word of God made flesh. Such a poem is 'Easter', where Christ stretched on the cross is compared to Herbert's own poetic instrument, the lute, such that Christ crucified becomes the condition of writing the poem at all. Herbert, or his heart, bearing or holding the lute, is exactly equivalent to Christ carrying the cross, the poem argues. The possibility of music or poetry is now dependent upon the authority of the body carrying this wood (cross or lute), and upon the tension of the sinewy strings; and the poem confuses the bearer of this 'wood', making it unclear or unspecific whether it is Christ or Herbert. In 'The Temper (I)' Herbert actually completes this by placing himself in precisely the position imagined for the strings or for the sinews of Christ's body in 'Easter'. The confusion carries on in 'Love (III)', where the roles of Christ and Herbert are reversed, and where Herbert prepares to ingest the body of Christ thus becoming a 'host' himself: the ambiguity of the word 'host' focuses the confusion of poet and author, Herbert and Christ here. Herbert 'speaks' 'The Sacrifice' entirely in a hypothesised dramatisation of Christ's voice, performing the perfect parody, an imitation so complete that it supersedes its original. The final line of 'Miserie', 'My God, I mean my self', might identify Herbert with the unnamed man in the poem; but it could also be construed

as Herbert actually writing down a slip of the pen, writing
'My God' when he means 'my self'. 'Artillerie' confuses what
is God's with what is Herbert's, a confusion of 'mine' and
'thine' or of proper identities which is realised more completely in 'Clasping of Hands'.

Perhaps the most glaring example of this heretical pre-
sumption is in 'The Crosse'. Herbert takes the commonplace
idiom of being 'crossed' or frustrated by God, and materialises the metaphor; but construes its realisation in the sense
of God putting him on the cross. The verbal play, and its
implication, becomes explicit in the final stanza after the
elaboration of the various ways in which God 'crosses'
Herbert:

> Ah my deare Father, ease my smart!
> These contrarieties crush me: these crosse actions
> Doe winde a rope about, and cut my heart:
> And yet since these thy contradictions
> Are properly a crosse felt by thy sonne,
> With but foure words, my words, *Thy will be done*.[40]

Here, the conventional domestication of religion, with God
called 'Father', allows Herbert to insinuate himself more
closely with God, identifying himself as the 'son'. When he
refers to 'thy sonne' in the poem, then, he comes close to
referring, actually, to himself ('My God, I mean my self',
once again). This is more tenable when it is recalled that
it is he, Herbert, who has been feeling the crosses and
contradictions of the father here. These 'crosse actions' are
now realised as the cross on which Christ was crucified: they
were nothing more or less than metaphors of their 'proper'
condition, the real cross. But Herbert is the one who feels
the pains of crossing or crucifixion now. In the position of
the son, on the cross, Herbert can now appropriate the words
or text of Christ, 'Thy will be done', and can claim these
words as his own. He stresses that the authority for these
words is his own; but they are his insofar as he has realised
himself, through rhetoric and metaphor, as Christ. Herbert
thus *is* the Word of God, and thus an incontrovertible authority as this Word incarnate. Here, if the words are indeed
Herbert's, he has attained some measure of his own

autonomous, 'autobiographical' authority; but it is only through the heresy of pretending to be Christ.

There is more than a tenuous link between the image of the rope wound about Herbert's heart here and the organisation of another poem, 'The Collar', which has a close intertextual relation with 'The Crosse'. In 'The Collar' there is some admission of Herbert's real position, which is one of betrayal or heresy; and hence there is a sense of guilt in the poem which a critical reading can produce. The heart and the rope are central to this poem, and form at least some emblematic organisation of images around which the poem is constructed. In the fourth line we are told that 'My lines and life are free';[41] and this is an accurate description of these verse-lines at least. The poem moves from this kind of 'free verse' towards the final four lines, which establish a different order once more (as in 'Deniall'). The standard mode of reading would suggest that this final order is a marker of resignation, a concordance between poet and God. But this is untenable in the face of the symbolic ordering of the text.

Following the notion that writing is done in blood, and from the heart, the complaint at the lack of 'cordiall fruit' here suggests that there is a problem with writing or with authority for Herbert. The 'freedom' of the lines, perhaps, should be construed as a reflection of Herbert's inability to harness them into poetry. Further, argues Herbert, the year itself has produced no positive harvest or flowers. Flowers would allow the creation of a garland, a crown or 'corona' of sorts which, like the bays, would surround the head and heart of authority, and at the same time be a symbol, in that crowning, of a positive victory as well as authority. There would thus be available a paradoxical emblematic comparison between this crown and the crown of thorns adorning the head of another authority, the dying Christ. A reading which follows Colie's insights might want to suggest the movement towards identification of these two crowns, and their wearers, an identification which the poetic concords of the final lines would clarify; thus, the poem would become an expression of Herbert's humility and resignation once more. But this ignores the development of the central images of line and rope in the text; and insofar as the line is the line of verse or of writing, the line which 'turns', it ignores the questions of writing and authority, crucial issues in the poem, completely.

These lines initially are 'free as the rode'; that is, they are directional, but leading in a myriad unspecified directions at once. They then mutate into 'rope', but firstly a 'rope of sands', which conveys no greater degree of fixity and purpose. This rope, however, is immediately instrumental in providing 'good cable'. This image gives the notion of intertwining of strings or clasping of hands which Herbert equates with textuality, poetry, good verse and the word of God on the cross or lute. It appears that this is approaching the condition of authoritative poetry. But then the development of the image turns, literally. The fixity and strength of purpose in the verse is transferred from the image of linear verse to a winding hang-man's noose: 'Call in thy deaths head there: tie up thy fears'. Suddenly, the link between the garland, the crown which is a crown of praise and a crown of thorns, is made explicit: the collar itself links these two. But this collar is one promising death, creating the 'deaths head'. The image of the line has become the extreme of the 'winding stair', the verse which winds back on itself so much that it constitutes the circle, the collar itself: it is thus that we have the kind of verse, rhyming and winding back on itself in a circular manner, in the final lines. The poem is quite literally the construction of itself, 'autobiographical' in the sense of that word elaborated here; it constructs 'The Collar' and the collar. Once more, then, the poem is about authority and Herbert's struggle to attain it, to write (from) himself. There is the attempt to gain authority from Christ, but the poem focuses on the betrayal of Christ which gives such authority. The parallel implied by the poem is of the poet with Judas, a parallel made clear by the notion of hanging in the collar. The striking of the board at the start of the poem now takes on further sense: it is not just Herbert striking the altar-table in church but is also Judas leaving the table at the Last Supper, betraying Christ in his saying 'No more' to him. 'The Collar' is not only about itself and about the creation of a garland of praise; it is also, fundamentally, about the betrayal of Christ which grants autonomous authority to the Christian poet. The idea is, then, that the mediation of God's word always inherently involves betrayal, a heretical paraphrasing or (mis)interpretation of the word. Such a self-judgement, on Herbert's part, is made explicit, of course, in 'Self-condemnation', where he makes of himself a 'Judas-Jew'.

Herbert, more than any other seventeenth-century poet, seems fully aware of the enormous criminality of his assumption of authority. Not only writing but also reading itself become heretical acts of self-authorisation, of inaugurating one's own (mis)interpretative meanings. As a reader of Scripture, even, Herbert is an infidel; for reading must always be deviant interpretation or mediation of the Word. But this is the very condition of authority, and is what allows him subsequently to write. Herbert's 'betrayal' of Christ is double-edged. On the one hand, it is heretical paraphrase, misrepresentation of the Word; on the other hand, it can create the conditions for the 'betrayal' (in the sense of revelation) of the Word, as his subtexts become themselves informed by the Word of God, which supplants Herbert's own words. That is to say, Herbert's activity of writing, his assumption of authority, generates faith, or so the logic of his position suggests, through the 'revelation' of Christ as the Word under the words, the authority in front of the poems. The assumption of authority, further, goes hand in hand with Herbert's own 'death' as individuated identifiable singular authority. His own singular meanings or intentions become irrelevant; the poetry, and the poet, become media revealing/betraying Christ or the Word as ultimate originary authority.

PART II
~~Natural~~ Authority

Chapter 5

The Theatre of Indeterminacy

A clear and transparent medium is admirable, when we love what we have to say; but when what we have to say is nothing previously definite, expressiveness depends on stirring the waters deeply, suggesting a thousand half-thoughts and letting the very unutterableness of our passion become manifest in our disjointed words. The medium then becomes dominant

(George Santayana, 'Tragic Philosophy')

Nature: Tragedy. Comedy: Language

The experimental writings of the first part of the seventeenth century could be thought of as conditioned by an idea of nostalgia. Existence in a prelapsarian state of paradise would absolutely guarantee self-assuredness and truth in authoritative pronouncements: the world itself would be poetry, and a mode of poetry written, authorised and thus sanctioned as incontrovertibly true, by God, or by the nature within which we too would have our 'true' place and identity. It is the loss of stable identity, itself a result of the loss of a stable home, with the realisation of the relativity of the position of England and even of the earth, which was partly responsible for the conflicts of modes of authority which condition the writing of the early seventeenth century. By the time of Milton's epic in 1667, paradise had most definitely been lost. According to one cultural mediation of the loss of paradise, woman was almost entirely to blame. However, this woman, instrument of human downfall, could also be thought of as a potential instrument of human rediscovery of paradise. This was one of the important determinants of writerly authority in the first half of the century.

159

The exclusion from paradise brings with it an even more fundamental problem. It may be the case that woman can be appropriated and controlled in such a way as to subtend the kind of male authority which I indicated in the first section of this study; but can the historical fact of death be circumvented by the same sleights-of-hand? In the quest for a natural source of authority, which is actually a nostalgic quest for nature itself, the writers of the seventeenth century come up against the most 'natural' event of all, the fact of death. This fact was extremely obvious to the writers of the latter part of the century, in the deaths which occurred as a result of the Civil War.[1] Death comes to supplant woman as a more fundamental 'other' which restricts, delimits and defines the possibilities of human autonomy. According to Blanchot, Rilke faced a similar kind of realisation in the face of another war in 1914. Blanchot writes:

> Ainsi s'affirme le souci qui va peu à peu déplacer le centre des pensées de Rilke: continuerons-nous à regarder la mort comme l'étrangeté incompréhensible ou n'apprendrons-nous pas à l'attirer dans la vie, à faire d'elle l'autre nom, l'autre côté de la vie? Ce souci est rendu plus pressant et plus tourmenté par la guerre. L'horreur de la guerre éclaire sombrement ce qu'il y a d'inhumain pour l'homme dans cet abîme: oui, la mort est la partie adverse, l'opposée invisible qui blesse en nous le meilleur, par quoi toutes nos joies périssent.[2]

The problem of autonomous authority which faced the writers of the Restoration period in England had still not, it seems, been entirely solved by the time Rilke was writing in 1914. With respect to the fact of death, the problem of human authority is transhistorical. Different kinds of authority will be available, clearly, at different historical and social 'moments'; but the fundamental theoretical difficulty of death as a determinant of human possibility transcends these local concerns. The theory which I shall elaborate more fully here, although perhaps focused upon seventeenth- and eighteenth-century texts in the main, is of relevance in a consideration of present-day writing.

In the philosophy of Hobbes, life is characterised as a constant motion, a perpetual change; it is, therefore, always in a condition of indeterminacy until the culminating moment of death: 'I put for a general inclination of all mankind, a perpetual and restless desire of power after power, that ceaseth only in death'.[3] Hobbes in fact made a virtue of this, and argued forcefully for a joyful acquiescence in the loss of a stable paradise:

> the felicity of this life, consisteth not in the repose of a mind satisfied. For there is no such *finis ultimus*, utmost aim, nor *summum bonum*, greatest good, as is spoken of in the books of the old moral philosophers. Nor can a man any more live, whose desires are at an end, than he, whose senses and imaginations are at a stand. Felicity is a continual progress of the desire, from one object to another; the attaining of the former, being still but the way to the latter.[4]

Some forty years later than this, Locke was to put forward a contrary view, in one part of his *Essay Concerning Human Understanding*. As an ironic counter to this Hobbesian position, he asserted that:

> I confess myself to have one of those dull souls, that doth not perceive itself always to contemplate ideas; nor can conceive it any more necessary for the soul always to think, than for the body always to move; the perception of ideas being (as I conceive) to the soul, what motion is to the body, not its essence, but one of its operations.[5]

This could be seen, however, as another attempt to discover stability in philosophical terms. The fact of the matter seems to be that instability was a dominant conditioning element in human self-understanding in the mid-seventeenth century. At the beginning of the century, Harvey had contributed to a destabilisation of one of the most fundamental, biological certainties in human social organisation. He had proved that the motion within the human body was precisely its essence and not a mere operation, as Locke has it in the quotation above. The human body was discovered to be not a mere stagnant pool but was precisely kept alive through activity, through the circulation of the blood. The biological certainties from which Shakespeare, for instance, began in his examinations of authority were no longer certain by mid-century.

At any given moment during a life, then, we cannot define that life, for subsequent change will modify or controvert the definition. According to the materia medica of Harvey and the philosophy of Hobbes, it is only the moment of arrest, the moment of death itself, which can ultimately define and determine a life correctly. Attempts at discovering the nature of a life from a point within that life, in the middest, to adapt that Kermodian phrase, would be fictions or writings analogous to a linguistic stutter: they could never be regarded as final, but would always be conditioned by the indeterminacy of what is to follow. Death, on the other hand, is more like the completely enunciated linguistic utterance, in which all the possibilities of the speech or life are given a non-deferred, determinate meaning.[6] This analogy, perhaps rather crudely developed in the contemporary culture, serves the functions of aligning authority (the enunciated utterance) with death (the determinate phrase) in some way, and of indicating indeterminacy as an important concern for the writing of the latter half of the seventeenth century.

Neoclassical tragedy is organised around the moment of death. By this I mean not the simple truism that the death of central characters is an important threat of actuality in tragedy. Rather I mean that the play itself is temporally organised at the moment which Augustine called the moment 'in death', a moment which asymptotically disappears between the two time-sequences of 'before death' and 'after death'. This moment 'in death', as I indicated earlier, equates precisely with the moment of the present, disappearing continually between the past and the future. A scepticism must then arise over the very possibility of existing 'in the present': more precisely, can we ever be 'present' to ourselves (in full self-consciousness, as it were) in the moment of the present? Can we be 'self-conscious' in the present, or is not the self of which we are 'conscious' different from the self we 'are'? The self of which we are conscious, then, might appear as always being deferred, displaced onto a future or past, either unrealised or an abstraction.

In the same way that the present or actual in space has become relativised as a result of the new astronomy and the decentering of the earth or 'home' or self, so also the present self in time is also displaced and relativised. At least two possible reactions to this are available. On the one hand, there can continue a belief in the stability of identity and in the possibility of being fully self-conscious or 'self-present'. In this case there will arise what might be regarded as a kind of 'essentialist' conception of the world, of nature and of the language we use to describe that nature. From this point of view, nature is accessible to the human, directly through the language which describes and circumscribes it. On the other hand, such a belief can be given up entirely in the acceptance of the notion that full self-presence is an impossibility; the self has always 'moved on' whenever we try to come to present consciousness of it. In this case there is the concomitant result that there can no longer be a belief in the 'essential' existence of a world of nature prior to our codification of it in language. In this latter case there will be a hesitancy to identify the self (selfhood will be deferred until the moment of death), and concomitantly there will be a similar hesitancy regarding our ability to use language to describe or circumscribe nature, for nature too will never be entirely 'present' to our consciousness. The confidence of the essentialist 'utterance' which controls the world of nature gives way here to the hesitancy of the deferred activity of stuttering with regard to the world: piecemeal descriptions are all that is available, and the world of nature essentially remains alien to the human, always 'not quite' where the language wants to locate it. Some explication and exemplifications of these abstract points is required. In this section, I shall be differentiating between a 'tragic' and 'comic' approach to existence, as it appears in the writings for the stage in England and France roughly between 1660 and 1700. In tragedy, there seems to be a belief that language is somehow intimately tied up with the natural world, and that, although this world of nature exists prior to its codification in language, a 'correct' use of language will help us to re-attain the natural world. In tragedy, the world of essentials and nature is available in and through a 'correct' (or essentialist) usage of the language that we speak. In comedy, on the other hand, this belief has been given up and has been replaced with the notion that there is no such thing as a 'natural' world prior to our language about the world; this language actually goes towards the construction not of an essential nature (for that paradise is lost) but towards the construction of an artificial, pragmatic, fictional 'nature', a rhetorical construction through which a speaker aims to win power over other speakers.

The Crisis in Tragedy Averted

It is a truism to suggest that the moment 'in death' is a moment of crisis, a moment which could proceed in either of two directions: in material terms, into continued life after all, or into the state of being dead; and in spiritual terms, a moment of salvation (continued 'life') or damnation (an equivalent of extinction). This moment, then, is a moment of great indeterminacy. This being the case, the question is whether such a moment can ever in fact be a determinate moment at all: can the moment of death ever actually, that is, presently, take place? For a writer such as Corneille, this conditioned the question of the logical as well as moral propriety of death itself ever being seen actually on stage. Corneille and others had to ponder the question of whether such a presentation or re-presentation of a 'realised death' was ever in fact logically even a *possibility*. Is there a temporal mode in which such a death can 'actually', 'presently', occur? The question is, of course, of relevance to the concern with the supposedly desirable 'unity of time'.

In the desire to make the action of a tragedy single and unified, according to the neo-Aristotelian precept, there was much debate about whether the action should be one which took place in twelve hours, twenty-four hours or the rather extravagant thirty hours. Similar debates, instigated largely by Dryden, although under the influence of the French, Spanish and Italians, were also taking place in England. But it was Corneille who, after almost thirty years of writing for the theatre, published his theoretical and critical thoughts on the matter, and began to isolate the real problem. When he published his plays in the three-volume edition of 1660, he prefaced each of the three volumes with a *Discours*, a theoretical and critical statement on the nature of drama, and especially on the nature of tragedy. In the *Discours des trois unités*, he wrote on the current debate on the unity of time in a thoughtful and thought-provoking way. He shifted attention from the mere counting of hours taken for the supposed action and directed attention instead to the more theoretical understanding of the temporal mode in which the play existed for the audience. Personal reasons perhaps account for this. *Le Cid* had been attacked for its *invraisemblable* nature on account of its severe, and clearly artificial, compression of events into the 'specified' duration of the neoclassical day. Corneille felt that had he left out the temporal indices which mark the passage of time during this 'day', then the play would have been better, and better-received.[7] These temporal indices, he then argues, are simply an irrelevant nuisance. His argument proceeds on the assumption that the play will be more perfect the closer its duration approximates to the time of the action and the time the audience spends in the theatre. This leads to a prescription of a great compression of time which, in theory at least, should lead ultimately to the extreme compression of time into the moment of the present, a moment which is, of course, evanescent, transitory to the point of disappearance or non-existence. There is still, he argues, a rationale at work here:

> Beaucoup déclament contre cette règle qu'ils nomment tyrannique et auraient raison, si elle n'était fondée que sur l'autorité d'Aristote; mais ce qui la doit faire accepter, c'est la raison naturelle qui lui sert d'appui. Le poème dramatique est une imitation, ou pour en mieux parler, un portrait des actions des hommes, et il est hors de doute que les portraits sont d'autant plus excellents qu'ils ressemblent mieux à l'original. La représentation dure deux heures et ressemblerait parfaitement, si l'action qu'elle représente n'en demanderait pas davantage pour sa réalité. Ainsi ne nous arrêtons point ni aux douze ni aux vingt-quatre heures, mais resserons l'action du poème dans la moindre durée qu'il nous sera possible, afin que la représentation ressemble mieux et soit plus parfaite.[8]

Theoretically at least, then, tragedy takes place, ideally, in the critical moment of the present, a moment whose temporal modality is problematic, for it is like the moment of death which is irretrievably linked to it, a moment without real duration.

Cornelian tragedy is usually set at the moment when there
is some 'péril de vie',[9] a moment of great doubt and uncertainty, indeterminacy. Insofar as the plays are set at the
boundary of the present, they are the setting for some kind
of 'conversion',[10] most clearly in a play such as *Polyeucte*;
or they are the setting for the moment of death and its
reverberations, as in *La mort de Pompée*; or they are the
setting for some crisis, as in the struggle between two bloods,
two households or two nations, those of Alba and Rome, in
Horace. But the single most striking thing about Corneille,
and something which serves to distinguish his work fundamentally from that of Racine, say, is that these indeterminacies are always resolved finally into certainty. Determinacy arrives, often in the form of death, and always
revealing the 'essential' truth or 'essential' nature of the universe, a nature whose character is beyond doubt and beyond
discussion.

Polyeucte is useful for demonstrating this. The play opens
with a foreboding of death, or more precisely with a death
which has, in some sense, already happened. We hear, in the
opening lines of the play, about Pauline's dream of the death
of Polyeucte; for her, the fiction has already been enacted,
as it were, and Polyeucte is dead already. The dream forces
the first moment of crisis or decision in the play, as Polyeucte
wonders whether to step outside today or not:

> *Néarque:*   Quoi? vous vous arrêtez aux songes d'une femme!
> ...
> *Polyeucte:*   Je sais ce qu'est un songe, et le peu de croyance
>   Qu'un homme doit donner à son extravagance
>
>   ...
>
>   Mais vous ne savez pas ce que c'est qu'une femme,
>   Vous ignorez quels droits elle a sur toute l'âme
>
>   ...
>
>   Pauline, sans raison dans la douleur plongée,
>   Craint et croit déjá voir ma mort qu'elle a songée.[11]

Polyeucte takes place, then, between the moment of
Polyeucte's (feigned) death in this dream related at the start,
and the moment of his (implied) death after Act 5 Scene 3,
when he goes off to die. The whole play occurs at the
moment 'in death'.

Symbolically, too, the play is an exercise in this pure 'presence of death'. The reason Polyeucte wants to go out in the passage just quoted is that he is to be secretly baptised. He wants to convert himself from a past life, identified as pagan, through a revolutionary but ritualised moment of conversion, into a future, identified as Christian. The baptism itself is a revolutionary moment, sandwiched between a past of the old dispensation and a future of being 'born again'; but this is a moment characterised by death as well as by birth or regeneration. As soon as Polyeucte is baptised, he seeks, and attains, martyrdom. The conversion is defined itself by death. As soon as Polyeucte becomes a Christian, he begins to speak with Christian authority, an authority which institutes his 'autonomous' authority as a Christian. From the point of view of everyone else in the play, except perhaps Néarque, he has been an infidel, a traitor to the old 'pagan' dispensation; again, authority is linked to the betrayal of tradition. It is also here explicitly linked to death; for Polyeucte compares himself with Christ, in persuading Néarque to join him in a suicidal death, or martyrdom. In short, then, Polyeucte here is attempting to convert his heretical act into a martyrological one. Néarque is hesitant, and advises Polyeucte:

Néarque: Fuyez donc leurs autels.
Polyeucte: Je les veux renverser,
Et mourir dans leur temple, ou les y terrasser.
Allons, mon cher Néarque, allons aux yeux des hommes
Braver l'idolâtrie, et montrer qui nous sommes.
                                                    (lines 643–6)

Néarque is finally persuaded to partake in the martyrological act. He reasons that Polyeucte is fired with a lust for death because, having just been baptised, he is closer to the divine source of authority for such a suicidal act. The act itself is divinely sanctioned, and in fact constitutes the model for the Christian 'life':

Néarque: Vous sortez du baptême, et ce qui vous anime,
C'est sa grâce qu'en vous n'affaiblit aucun crime.

Comme encor toute entière, elle agit pleinement,
Et tout semble possible à son feu véhément.

(lines 693–6)

Here, interestingly, Néarque indicates that what is motiv-
ating Polyeucte is the presence of grace; this operates as a
kind of analogue to the blood-lineage in Shakespeare, which
was supposed to guarantee authenticity, 'originality', to the
present carrier of the blood. It is further of note that when
Néarque does finally decide to join Polyeucte in death, he
echoes Polyeucte's lines, agreeing that they should go to
'montrer qui nous sommes' (line 706). Here the suicidal
moment is thought of as a moment of literal self-discovery,
a revelation of the presence of an essential nature, sanctioned
and authorised by the grace of God, within the self. Polyeucte believes in some such nature, and also believes that it is
present, flowing like blood or grace, within himself. It thus
need only be 'uttered', that is 'outered' or revealed: his
authoritative act is precisely one which reveals the single
undeniable fact of human nature, death.

It is clear, in the scene in which Pauline comes to visit
Polyeucte in prison, that he believes in an essential, unchanging state of nature, a state to which he believes he
has finally acceded in his conversion to Christianity. When
Pauline visits him, her aim is to defer the moment of his
death, to retain the death purely in the realm of fantasy,
dream or metaphor. Her advice is to refuse the revelation of
nature: she advises Polyeucte to dissemble, to play a part.
That is to say, she advises him to refuse the authority of the
Christian, essentialised, utterance, and to defer that utterance
(to 'stutter', in fact). Polyeucte will have none of this, saying
that dissembling is impossible, because the truth of nature,
Christianity, is clear and clearly self-revelatory:

Polyeucte: C'est le Dieu des chrétiens, c'est le mien, c'est le vôtre,
               Et la terre et le ciel n'en connaissent point d'autre.
Pauline: Adorez-le dans l'âme, et n'en témoignez rien.
Polyeucte: Que je sois tout ensemble idolâtre et chrétien!
Pauline: Ne feignez qu'un moment, laissez partir Sévère,

Polyeucte:
> Et donnez lieu d'agir aux bontés de mon père.
> Les bontés de mon Dieu sont bien plus à chérir:
> Il m'ôte des périls que j'aurais pu courir,
> Et sans me laisser lieu de tourner en arrière,
> Sa faveur me couronne entrant dans la carrière;
> Du premier coup de vent il me conduit au port,
> Et sortant du baptême, il m'envoie à la mort.

                                        (lines 1219–30)

The belief that there can be such a thing as a hypocritical utterance here marks Polyeucte off as a tragic figure. But the refusal to dissemble, to 'act', and the preference for suffering, for 'passive mediation' as it were of the grace of God articulating itself through the body of Polyeucte, is not all that there is to this tragic moment. The refusal to 'act' does mark Polyeucte's credence in the inevitability or truth of a revelation of essential nature, one which simply cannot be disguised. His death, as the fact of that nature, is certain; there is a movement from indeterminacy in the play towards the determinacy of this death, a movement from vague dream to actualised reality. If, however, the play was not set at this moment of death itself, then his position might begin to appear slightly comic. The refusal to 'act' is the integral component of the character of Alceste in Molière's Le Misanthrope. But this latter play avoids tragedy because there is no longer any currency, in Molière's theatre, for the belief that there is such a thing as one essential nature which can ever be fully revealed to us. Molière moves away from the religiosity of revelation towards the philosophy of reason. His comedy is set in a world where the full experience of death is absent, as it is in the philosophies of Augustine, Camus, Wittgenstein and others. Hypocrisy may be exposed in Molière; but, as in many English Restoration comedies, such an exposure reveals not an unquestionable state of essential nature but rather merely the next layer of deception.

The notion of the revelation of nature appears, however, in critical theories of both tragedy and comedy. It is perhaps a measure of how close these two theatrical experiences are that Boileau can argue that the revelation of nature is essentially a comic trait, while Nietzsche could later argue that it was precisely in the Dionysiac rites of tragedy that nature was revealed. Boileau wrote:

> Que la nature donc soit votre étude unique,
> Auteurs qui prétendez aux honneurs du comique.
> Quiconque voit bien l'homme, et d'un esprit profond,
> De tant de cœurs cachés a pénétré le fond;
> Qui sait bien ce que c'est qu'un prodigue, un avare,
> Un honnête homme, un fat, un jaloux, un bizarre,
> Sur une scène heureuse il peut les étaler,
> Et les faire à nos yeux vivre, agir et parler.
> Présentez-en partout les images naïves;
> Que chacun y soit peint des couleurs les plus vives.
> La nature, féconde en bizarres portraits,
> Dans chaque âme est marquée à de différents traits;
> Un geste la découvre, un rien la fait paraître:
> Mais tout esprit n'a pas des yeux pour la connaître.[12]

And later Nietzsche was to argue that the Dionysiac state of universal harmony and oneness was possible precisely because of the rediscovery of nature within or through this tragic state: 'Not only does the bond between man and man come to be forged once more by the magic of the Dionysiac rite, but nature itself, long alienated or subjugated, rises again to celebrate the reconciliation with her prodigal son, man'[13]

The quotation from Boileau, however, far from negating my own argument here, serves in fact to corroborate it. According to Boileau, the author of comedy will find in 'nature' many 'bizarres portraits'; this author will discover not the essence at the kernel of the self, but merely a work of art, a portrait, a contrived creation which skirts the natural fact of living, the fact of death. On the other hand, the Nietzschean precept here, perhaps without the presence of Apollo and Dionysus, is fulfilled in the tragedy of Corneille, in which there is a revelation of an essential nature. This kind of revelation occurs primarily because of the temporal modality of the play, its location in the point of the present, death. This moment of self-presence is a moment of literal self-discovery, the discovery of an identity; and with this discovery of identity goes not only an autonomous authority but also a death. The discovery of identity implies the defi-nition of the authority (i.e. the stable proper 'name') discovered or revealed; hence it implies a lack of a future for the character whose essence is thus revealed. Polyeucte, as a character, has no future.[14]

Robert McBride has tried to instate doubt as a mode of existence for the Cornelian hero, and thus to show, in my terms, that the hero lives (or dies) in a state of radical indeterminacy: 'Doubt, far from being alien to the Cornelian hero, is on the contrary a permanent attribute. It is the reflex which stimulates him continually to question his worth and his capacity to perform the heroic deed'.[15] But this argument is countered by McBride's own concession that although such doubt may characterise the hero at the start of the play, the play progresses at all only through the dissolution of such doubts and the discovery of certitude. This certainty comes from a supposed discovery of nature, and, as in *Polyeucte*, it leads to some sort of death or downfall:

> Once deprived of this interrogative and creative doubt, he is helpless, for only in the action to which it goads him does he perceive the possibility of emerging from its miasma into the serenity of heroic self-fulfilment. ... The hero can only act to good effect if he rediscovers in his action the certainty of his superiority which is both the objective and the motive of his quest, dispelling all his doubts. In its initial stages heroism emanates from doubt, but of course transcends it as it is spurred on by self and others to commit action of a unique kind, capable of securing *gloire*. But the deep paradox of *gloire* is that it implies in itself the death of heroism. Once *gloire* has been achieved by the hero, he is obliged by his own and by its nature not to fall below its supreme standard.[16]

The play moves from uncertainty to clearly defined certitudes through, in conventional Cornelian terms, the acquisition of *gloire*, the making of a 'name' for the hero; and in my terms here, through the discovering of an essential nature, which fundamentally is the revelation of the presence of death within the character.

In *Polyeucte*, then, the dream of Pauline is to be interpreted in the most seemingly naïve manner possible. Corneille and the play itself seem to demand that the dream be interpreted as a transparent 'pre-presentation' of an essential nature or reality to which it unproblematically refers us. The dream becomes the equivalent of a kind of hypothetical preverbal thought; and the play becomes its utterance, its articulation. In linguistic terms the sign of the dream is being linked in a straightforwad nominalistic manner with an object or reality to which it refers us, the reality of the natural fact of Polyeucte's death. We do not require the elaboration of five acts of drama to discover that Polyeucte is going to die: the transparency of the dream-sign tells us that he is dead from the very start. He goes through the play as a *memento mori*, a permanent presence of death itself.

What is important in the tragic theatre of Corneille, then, is the discovery of nature. This nature is apprehended in and through a postulated position of self-presence, as the dying character is placed in the position of the present, a present in which her or his consciousness is supposed to be entirely present to itself. This, I am arguing, is the position which Augustine called 'in death' or the present. In Corneille it is mediated as a present moment in which there is uttered an essence of nature, the truth, as it were, as seen, literally, through the dying character. Arising from this, the theatre of Corneille supposedly reveals the authority of the natural world 'as it is in itself'; in fact, however, the play sanctions a political perspective in which the interpretation of the state of nature, from the position of the self-present individual consciousness, is sanctioned as a fundamentally and essentially 'correct' one. There can be, for instance, no doubt in the audience's mind, any more than in Pauline's, about how to interpret the dream of Pauline: nature is supposed to be self-evident, revealed perfectly in fully transparent signs. There can be no doubt about the fact that Polyeucte is to die, either for Polyeucte or for us. There can be, in short, no doubt that the state of nature could be other than it appears to the self-present consciousness of the assured individual. Nature is clearly revealed here, and there is to be no scepticism concerning whether it might be different.

The major difficulty with this position, as argued here, is that it places the audience in the same position of self-assured consciousness as Polyeucte. If nature is present to us, then the only position in which this nature could reveal itself to our consciousness is the position which Augustine called 'in death'. But this accords fairly precisely with Corneille's prescription for the audience of his theatre. He wrote, in the *Discours du poème dramatique*, of tragedy and comedy and suggested that:

> Toutes les deux ont cela de commun, que cette action doit être complète et achevée, c'est-à-dire que, dans l'événement qui la termine, le spectateur doit être si bien instruit des sentiments de tous ceux qui y ont eu quelque part qu'il sorte l'esprit en repos, et ne soit plus en doute de rien.[17]

The spirit is to be at rest, and there is to be no further doubt about anything. But, as my earlier citation of Harvey and Hobbes has shown, this notion becomes problematic, for in life there is never such a resting point and stability of purpose or intension. For the writers who come later in the century, this will be of crucial importance.

Indeterminacy is made slightly more problematic in at least one play of Corneille; in *Horace* it threatens to turn a tragedy into a comedy. In the attempt to forestall outright war between Rome and Alba, there is proposed a ritualised fight between the three representative Alban brothers, of the family of Curiace, and the three Roman representatives, the Horace brothers. News of the struggle filters back to the father of the Horace family; and here, indeterminacy with regard to the interpretation of a sign, is crucial. Old Horace hears that two of his sons have been killed, and that the third one has fled. He rails against this third son (the central Horace in the play), saying that the flight is an unproblematical and clear sign of cowardice. But then more details are brought to light, and it becomes clear that this Horace has killed all three Curiace brothers, his flight having been a strategy allowing his successful ambush of them. He thus saves not only his name and reputation but also that of Rome, and more pertinently for our purposes here, he saves and maintains the name of his family and inherited blood. From the point of view of Old Horace, it is this sudden *volte-face*, this sudden revelation of the indeterminacy of signs, the realisation that 'nature' can be other than it appears to be, which turns the narrative of events, if not the whole play, from being a tragedy into a comedy. And certainly, were it not for the fact that the newly validated interpretation of events has dire consequences for the other characters present, especially Camille and Sabine, then Old Horace's sudden change of heart as regards his son would be extremely comic:

> *Le vieil Horace:* Que n'a-t-on vu périr en lui le nom d'Horace!
> ... O mon fils, ô ma joie, ô l'honneur de nos jours!
> O d'un État penchant l'inespéré secours!
> Vertu digne de Rome, et sang digne d'Horace!
> Appui de ton pays et gloire de ta race![18]

But what makes this tragic once more is that beneath the false interpretation there lies, not merely another interpretation which might in its turn be falsified, but rather an essentially correct one, referring us to the death of Camille's lover at the hands of her brother, the death of Sabine's brother at the hands of her husband, and the glorying in this of Old Horace, Horace himself, and indeed the whole city of Rome. An essential nature has once more been revealed, only here in an indirect way. But it is the fact that nature, meaning death and determinacy, has been revealed which turns the play towards tragedy.

Adulterate 'Nature' and Critical Interpretation

It is in Racine that we find the kind of radical doubt which McBride claimed, erroneously, to see in Corneille as a vital operational and organisational principle of the drama. Indeterminacy is crucial to Racinian tragedy. In Corneille the revelation of essential nature as death and self-presence was central to the fact of tragedy; in Racine, on the other hand, there is great doubt among characters and audience alike as to what constitutes 'essential nature', although there lingers a belief that such a nature actually does exist; simply, such a nature is slightly more alien to the human than it was supposed to be in Corneille, and remains difficult of access. In the comedies of Molière and the 'Restoration wits' in England, I shall argue that nature as an essential entity has been entirely lost, and all that remains is a series of deceitful and dubious linguistic counters which bear no direct relation to 'nature' in any way. Claude-Gilbert Dubois finds a historically progressive loss of nature in seventeenth-century writings. He argues that there occurred in that century a fairly steady alienation of the human from nature, and the world of nature is thus, as I have been arguing here, a kind of paradise lost for us:

> La manière d'appréhender le monde change elle aussi: le dualisme cartésien remplace progressivement la conception unitaire de la nature que ni le matérialisme ni le panthéisme cosmique n'arrivent à sauver. L'esprit se distingue de l'étendue, et la matière de la conscience. ... La nature devient inerte et silencieuse.[19]

This can be seen in the spectrum which I am indicating, from the hubristic self-present conscious certainty and belief in the accessibility of an authority in nature in Corneille's tragedy, through the indeterminacies of Racine's drama, and into the loss of nature in comedy, where an essential nature is lost and replaced by a self-consciously artificial linguistic construction of 'nature'. Two views with regard to nature as a source of essential authority are thus available in the later seventeenth century, the tragic and the comic views.

Racine's theatre, especially his tragic drama, occupies a kind of middle ground between these two views, a ground in which nature in its revelation as death exists still as an intractable essence, but an essence which cannot be understood or experienced as essence, because it is also inextricably mixed up with our interpretations of it.

In *Andromaque* the same kind of temporal compression which Corneille advocated occurs. Hermione tells Oreste that he must avenge her and kill Pyrrhus 'dans une heure'. Oreste, who has just arrived on the scene, replies to this in words which manage to contract the unity of the day into the evanescent moment of the present, a moment which is explicitly equated with death:

> *Oreste:* À peine suis-je encore arrivé dans l'Épire,
> Vous voulez par mes mains renverser un empire;
> Vous voulez qu'un roi meure; et pour son châtiment
> Vous ne donnez qu'un jour, qu'une heure, qu'un
> moment.[20]

Here, the 'time' of the play is reduced into the one present and literally revolutionary moment, the crisis which is the overthrow of an empire and the death or murder of a king.

Whereas in Corneille this moment became a determination and extreme clarification or revelation of nature or truth, in Racine the moment remains extremely indeterminate. The tragedies of Racine do not merely start according to the Horatian principle, *in medias res*, they are always 'in the middest', always on a point of indistinction between a past and a future, on a present moment which is never determinate. This moment in Racine is a moment in which the human consciousness is never understood as being fully present to itself; it is a moment which is characterised by extreme indecision and doubt, a fully 'critical' moment. Corneille's theatre provides answers to the knotty riddles which its plots have tied; Racine's theatre, by contrast, replaces one set of questions and doubts with another. Rather like the characterisation which I constructed of the Shakespearean stage when I suggested that it was in some ways gender-unspecific, the stage of Racine is always radically ambiguous. Racine's stage is in the position of the boundary between self-present certainty and the ultimate sources of authority which was earlier occupied by woman in the writing of the seventeenth century. Here, then, we never know precisely what it is that is being presented as nature on the stage, for it is always subject to ambiguous interpretation, and its own essence seems to be fading from view or relevance. Rapin, among others, complained about the increasing 'effeminisation' of the theatre; and this kind of uncertainty with regard to the identities of people and the objects of nature in the Racinian drama could have been the catalyst for such attacks. Corneille, on the other hand, had declared that tragedy, in order to be dignified, had to concern itself with more 'male' materials: 'Sa dignité demande quelque grand intérêt d'État ou quelque passion plus noble et plus mâle que l'amour'.[21] It was, however, not merely his material or content which was more 'male'; it was actually the manner in which that content was thought or experienced and mediated formally to the audience which gave such 'male' certainties. Racinian theatre, however, made room for the dubieties which a theorist such as Rapin had equated with weakness and woman, and which might better be equated with a pragmatically useful indeterminacy or critical scepticism.

In *Andromaque*, for instance, there are numerous doubts on the part of characters and audience alike: will Astyanax live or die; will Oreste live or die; will Andromaque marry Pyrrhus or not; would Hector have sanctioned such a marriage; such questions not only reverberate throughout the play, they also help actually to form the play. Similarly, *Phèdre* is a play characterised by huge uncertainties, beginning in the 'doute mortel' in which we discover Hippolyte, who wonders whether his father, Thésée, is alive or dead, and who is about to set off, like the audience, in the search for his father and for certainty. Most radically of all, perhaps, *Iphigénie en Aulide* is organised around an ambiguity concerning the very characters who are on stage before us: is Iphigénie or Ériphile the woman who is to be sacrificed in accordance with the oracular message as understood by Calchas and Agamemnon; is 'Iphigénie' or 'Ériphile' the answer to the riddle; and thus, is Iphigénie not confused with Ériphile?[22]

Racinian tragedy exists through indeterminacy and through or because of the constant deferral of speech: uttering is replaced by stuttering. These two phenomena, indeterminacy and speech-deferral, amount to much the same thing, in fact, but because they are two aspects of the same tragic phenomenon, that which Pascal identified in the *Pensées* as fear and doubt in the face of 'le silence éternel de ces espaces infinis [qui] m'effraie',[23] I propose to examine them separately through two different plays, *Iphigénie en Aulide* and *Phèdre*.

Iphigénie en Aulide opens at the moment of two crises or impasses. There is the spatial impasse of the journey of the Greeks, held in port for want of a favourable wind. As a corollary of this, there is a kind of temporal impasse or crisis, for the journey could be continued, it seems, if Iphigénie is sacrificed; she, or more precisely her death, is understood by Agamemnon to be the passage towards the future for the Greeks, their escape from their paralysis in port and in the moment of the play. The time, however, is already somewhat ambiguous. The play seems to open in the morning, but for Agamemnon there has been no sleep and he is still in the darkest night. Whether it is day or night, then, depends to some extent upon one's position or perspective with regard to these natural temporal 'facts'; to call it 'day' or 'night' is always an interpretation of the facts, facts which as essence remain alien to us. It is vital to this play that we remember that the central principle of the play is an act of interpretation: 'Iphigénie' has been understood by Agamemnon as the 'correct' interpretation or answer to the riddle of the oracle.

Iphigénie is on her way to Aulis, she thinks, to be married to Achille; Agamemnon, however, now thinks of her as on her way to be sacrificed. The resolution of these contrary viewpoints depends upon a further act of interpretation, the interpretation which the play will work out as its action. There are more confusions, however, and some confusions which focus on the question of singular identity. Who, for instance, is Iphigénie? Agamemnon raises this question, for he thinks of her in extremely intimate terms as the issue or flowing of his own blood. Accordingly, when thinking of the sacrifice of Iphigénie he begins to envisage the death of himself and of his whole familial heritage: 'Ma fille ... Ce nom seul, dont les droits sont si saints,/Sa jeunesse, mon sang'.[24] The moment of death here is understood by Agamemnon as a suicidal act on his own part; using his authority, as interpreter, to cause the death of Iphigénie leads him to the belief that he is sacrificing his own name, his own authority. He is thus in a critical situation; but no more, clearly, than Iphigénie or Ériphile or even the audience, primary interpreters of all the play's riddles. In this position the paralysis of sin seems to be the only avenue open for Agamemnon. He realises that something has absolutely to be done to appease the gods, and at the same time he realises his own refusal or reluctance to comply; and compliance in any case leads to the sin of suicide. In order, however, to try to avoid the sin, Agamemnon tries to defer the moment of death, of final resolution and certainty. Like Pauline in Corneille's *Polyeucte*, he struggles to evade the revelation of nature. Sin, of course, is understood theologically as 'that

which lacks existence', 'the thing which is not'. It is precisely
this sin which Agememnon falls into, as he tries to avoid the
death of Iphigénie and of himself. To defer the determinacy
of death, he writes 'the thing which is not', a fiction, a letter.

Calchas has some degree of authority, as a medium or
'diviner' of the will of the gods; but Agamemnon's very
specific use of authority here, in writing the letter which
strives to delay the arrival of Iphigénie and Clytemnestre, is
an attempt to betray or forestall the priestly authority of
Calchas. To establish his own *auctoritas*, once more a character has to betray an anterior *potestas*. The letter-writing,
however, opens the play to what might be regarded as its
central doubt: will Iphigénie die and will the letter arrive?
This question can be phrased in another way. Iphigénie, or
rather, 'Iphigénie' as the name of that character, is understood to be the letter or series of letters which responds to
the oracular riddle. Will 'Iphigénie', then, arrive; and how
close is the character Iphigénie to her name or sign, 'Iphigénie'?
There is, of course, someone else due to arrive in Aulis with
Iphigénie and Clytemnèstre, and that other person is called
Ériphile. Ériphile is coming to look for some kind of certainty
and identity, which makes her look almost exactly like
Iphigénie, who is coming to change her name and find her
identity as the wife of Achille. Ériphile comes to look for a
name, to look for a father. The play more and more begins to
confuse these two characters, and the riddle of the oracle is
solved precisely by driving a wedge between Iphigénie the
person and the sign of 'Iphigénie', the letters of her name.
Ériphile turns out to be the character who is to be sacrificed;
she comes to discover her identity, and her identity is, precisely,
'Iphigénie'. There is a *décalage* between nature and the language
which we use to describe it: Iphigénie is not precisely
'Iphigénie', as it were. As the play progresses, these signs
become more ambiguous, until finally, Ériphile can occupy the
position suggested by the letters 'Iphigénie'.

Such indeterminacies of identity as this are rife in Racine.
The ambiguity depends entirely upon there being a divorce
between nature and the signs or language by which we
understand it. In short, in this kind of theatre there is no
nature apart from its interpretations, made either by charac-

ters or audience. No essential nature can be found or revealed. It thus becomes uncertain who it is who dies, in fact. Is it Ériphile who dies, or Ériphile only insofar as she is 'Iphigénie'; is it thus Iphigénie who dies; and further, remembering the confusion of her blood with Agamemnon's, is it Agamemnon who dies; and so on. The identity of character is not the only locus of uncertainty and indeterminacy in Racine, however. Nature, though tantalisingly real, nonetheless cannot exist in a state unadulterated by interpretation: for the human, nature is as it is interpreted. As such, nature becomes radically indeterminate or relativised. This is so much the case that even hard physical objects in Racine begin to take on some surrealist fluidity; the altar, for instance, begins to mean and to be different things to different people.

This is at least one ambiguity in the play which is never resolved into a singular essentially true meaning. The word 'autel' appears on many occasions, but the word, and the object to which it supposedly refers, become diverse. In one case Iphigénie uses the word to mean one thing, while Agamemnon and his audience know it to mean something else. Firstly, the relations between these two characters (and thus their very identities) are stressed as being fluid. Agamemnon hints strongly at this when they meet upon Iphigénie's arrival:

> *Agamemnon:* Ma fille, je vous vois toujours des mêmes yeux;
> Mais les temps sont changés, aussi bien que les lieux.
>
> (lines 555–6)

And then a similar fluidity extends itself outwards to the 'natural' world of the real physical object of the altar. The altar is the place to which Iphigénie wants to come, to partake in witnessing the sacrifice prepared by Calchas; and at the same time it is the stone upon which Iphigénie is to be laid, to bear intimate witness, as martyr, to the sacrifice:

Iphigénie:	Calchas, dit-on, prépare un pompeux sacrifice?
Agamemnon:	Puissé-je auparavant infléchir leur injustice!
Iphigénie:	L'offrira-t-on bientôt?
Agamemnon:	Plus tôt que je ne veux.
Iphigénie:	Me sera-t-il permis de me joindre à vos voeux?
	Verra-t-on à l'autel votre heureuse famille?
Agamemnon:	Hélas!
Iphigénie:	Vous vous taisez!
Agamemnon:	Vous y serez, ma fille.

(lines 573–8)

And later, of course, the altar will become even more radically indeterminate, as it becomes both the scene of Iphigénie's marriage and also that of her imagined death or sacrifice. It is thus not simply invested with two different emotions depending upon how we look at it; it actually is on its way to becoming not simply one essential thing at all, but rather it becomes at least two distinct entities.

Clytemnèstre regards the handing over of Iphigénie in marriage not only as the culmination of her journey but as the culmination of her activity in giving birth to Iphigénie. As an integral part of this activity, she regards the marriage as urgent. Accordingly, she urges Agamemnon to hasten the marriage, to hasten Iphigénie's arrival on the altar:

Agamemnon:	Laissez, de vos femmes suivie,
	A cet hymen, sans vous, marcher Iphigénie.
Clytemnèsre:	Qui? moi! que, remettant ma fille en d'autres bras,
	Ce que j'ai commencé, je ne l'achève pas!

(lines 793–6)

In completing the act of giving birth and identity to Iphigénie, for which she has to hand her over to Achille and urge her on to the altar, Clytemnèstre serves to locate the temporal axis of the play at a moment which is one both of birth and death; giving birth to Iphigénie is completed when Clytemnèstre has laid her upon her death-stone. The play is set precisely at such a moment, of birth and death, morning and night, a moment of the present which contains *in nuce* the whole of life itself.[25] This collocation of birth and death is made clear because the altar is something else, according to Agamemnon, than the marriage-stone. Clytemnèstre con-

ceives of the altar as the locus of identity for Iphigénie
because it is the place where she finally completes giving
birth to her; Agamemnon thinks of it as the place where the
discovery of identity is made at the instant of death. As he
puts it, giving way to Clytemnèstre:

> *Agamemnon:* Madame, c'est assez: je consens qu'on le croie.
> Je reconnais l'erreur qui nous avait séduits,
> Et ressens votre joie autant que je le puis.
> Vous voulez que Calchas l'unisse à ma famille;
> Vous pouvez à l'autel envoyer votre fille:
> Je l'attends.
>
> (lines 778–83)

Here, the word 'autel' hovers uncertainly between 'marriage'
and 'death'; but more radically than this, the actual physical
object, the 'natural' fact of the altar as some given essence,
is called into doubt. What in fact is the altar? Nature itself
here is being questioned, as the altar has no real, natural,
unadorned, unadulterated or uninterpreted existence; it exists
and is experienced only in relation to its phenomenological
perceiver. There may indeed be *something* 'out there', some
real stone or material, but what it is in itself, its *quidditas*,
as it were, has by now forever disappeared to the human.
There is no longer a nature here which can be experienced
or comprehended from some supposedly transcendent point
of consciousness; or at least, that point of consciousness, if
it exists, is not present to the human subject but has become,
in the words of Goldmann (himself citing Pascal and a Jansenist
tradition), a *deus absconditus, le dieu caché*.[26] That is
to say, in less theological terms, that the point of such
transcendent consciousness, present to the human individual
according to the tragic theatre of Corneille, is always absent
to the human individual in the tragedy of Racine. Since such
a point of consciousness is abandoned in Racine, or since it
abandons us, the audience are left *in medias res*, as it were,
with no confidence in the idea of a fully self-present consciousness. Their authoritative judgements or statements are
now always subject to relativisation; aware that they have
no direct consciousness of nature, they are made to realise
that the experience of such 'nature' always finally eludes

them, is never wholly present to their consciousness, and that their judgement is based upon a pragmatic interpretation of 'nature', a nature which should now appear only 'under erasure'. The godlike position of self-present transcendent consciousness has here absconded; the 'truth' is always somewhere else, has always moved on from the consciousness of the individual interpreter.

The altar, then, in *Iphigénie en Aulide* becomes a kind of natural concrete pun, and it is here, perhaps, in the dialectical understanding of that pun, a pun which must never be resolved into singular meaning and whose univocal meaning is in fact denied it in the course of the play, that we find the source of the tragic emotions, as Racine understood them, of pity and terror.[27] The radical ambiguity or indeterminacy of the altar actually is its mode of existence. It may well exist, in the realm of nature, but cannot be purely comprehended; it is relativised, changed and adulterated in the very fact of its existing for us, in the fact of our perception of it.[28]

The evasion of the presence of nature within us, as here in Racine, still nonetheless leads to a tragic view of the human condition. Life in the present can never be a source of pleasure or happiness, for such happiness is always, by definition, deferred along with the deferral of death. Pascal had thought about this:

Nous ne nous tenons jamais au temps présent. Nous rappelons le passé; nous anticipons l'avenir comme trop lent à venir, comme pour hâter son cours, ou nous rappelons le passé pour l'arrêter comme trop prompt, si imprudents que nous errons dans des temps qui ne sont point nôtres, et ne pensons point au seul qui nous appartient, et si vains que nous songeons à ceux qui ne sont rien, et échappons sans réflexion le seul qui subsiste. C'est que le présent d'ordinaire nous blesse. Nous le cachons à notre vue parce qu'il nous afflige, et s'il nous est agréable nous regrettons de le voir échapper. Nous tâchons de le soutenir par l'avenir, et pensons à disposer les choses qui ne sont pas en notre puissance pour un temps où nous n'avons aucune assurance d'arriver.

Que chacun examine ses pensées. Il les trouvera toutes occupées au passé et à l'avenir. Nous ne pensons presque point au présent, et si nous y pensons ce n'est que pour en prendre la lumière pour disposer de l'avenir. Le présent n'est jamais notre fin.

Le passé et le présent sont nos moyens; le seul avenir est notre fin. Ainsi nous ne vivons jamais, mais nous espérons de vivre, et, nous disposant toujours à être heureux, il est inévitable que nous ne le soyons jamais.[29]

The present is to be avoided because it causes us pain; as Eliot was later to state it, 'humankind/Cannot bear very much reality'.[30] In the tragedy of Racine, two consequences follow from this evasion of the presence of nature. Firstly, there is a constant stuttering rather than uttering, as characters avoid making definitive statements or lead others to make such utterances for them. Agamemnon says that Clytemnèstre can send Iphigénie to the altar, but does not actually take it upon himself to send her; Andromaque decides to consult the dead Hector to find out what she should do about constantly deferring her answer to Pyrrhus's proclamations of love; and *Phèdre* is full of characters who refuse to speak for themselves, full of characters who have to be urged by others to say anything, and full of characters, like Phèdre herself, who are always putting themselves into the hands, and mouths, of others. Secondly, the identity of these characters is never finalised; constantly moving on into a future, as Pascal put it, they are never fully present to their own consciousnesses, and thus they never fully coincide with themselves: they are, in the terms of existentialism, entirely *pour-soi* and never reach the status of identifiable objects, *en-soi*; as such, their identity is conditioned by a notion of absence from the self, or exile. The characters of Racine's tragedy are all 'exiles' from the self and from identity. Thus they are never in fact capable of the kind of authority, identifiable or namable singular authority which goes with the utterances of those, such as the characters in Corneille, who know precisely who they are, but who are dead 'objects' as a result. The god of the self, if I may thus characterise the condition of self-present transcendent consciousness, has always absconded, exiled itself from the human individual. Truth may thus disappear, but relativised, pragmatic meanings can remain.

The fundamental question in *Phèdre*, according to Barthes, is 'Dire ou ne pas dire?'[31] This is certainly an important question in the play, as *Phèdre* hesitates about whether to utter her love for Hippolyte, Hippolyte debates whether to utter his love for Aricie, and whether to reveal to Thésée what has been going on while this paternal source of authority has been absent. Most of the characters desire to make some statement, an utterance which will reveal their nature. But the only way that 'nature' can be present to us, as I argued above, is if we are at the moment 'in death'. The desire for certainty among the characters in this play does, to some extent, equate with their desire for death, or at least for the satisfactory state of self-revelation, utterance. The play opens with Hippolyte searching for certain knowledge about his father, Thésée; doubts about whether Thésée is alive or dead reverberate through the play; Phèdre seeks her own death, and is suicidal from the moment she appears, and so on.

When Phèdre enters, she locates the time of the play once more at the moment 'in death', and she is spoken of in terms which constantly locate her in such a position; like Polyeucte, she is at least metaphorically dead as the play opens, and the play works to realise the metaphor.[32] Theramène links Phèdre's malaise to her supposed inability to speak in these opening remarks, but once she appears she is not at all silent. She speaks, however, only through a complicated series of manoeuvres, involving periphrasis, euphemism, *double entendre*, 'stuttering', and refusing herself the authority for the statements which she teases Oenone into making. Even in death, as it were, she falters and stammers, for the mere mention of the name of Hippolyte rouses her again. Phèdre is irresolute even about dying, and her entire performance is actually wholly her 'dying speech', one of the longest and most irresolute in the history of the theatre.

Once roused at the merest mention of the name of Hippolyte, Phèdre is advised to will herself to life and action by Oenone:

> Oenone: Mais ne différez point; chaque moment vous tue:
> Réparez promptement votre force abbatue,
> Tandis que de vos jours, prêts à se consumer,
> Le flambeau dure encore, et peut se rallumer.
> (lines 213–16)

But there is an error in such advice, because, to Phèdre, it is only through deferral, through the deferral of speech and action and commitment, and through the maintaining of silence, that she will remain alive. And that is part of her own dilemma; she will not be fully alive, not fully herself, while still in love with Hippolyte.

But is she so in love? The realisation that she is in love is made through a motion of deductive reasoning; Phèdre avoids stating that she is in love, at least early in the play. We do have a huge amount of circumstantial evidence, however, and of course she does not deny that she loves Hippolyte. She does, however, refuse to name her desired lover:

> Oenone: Aimez-vous?
> Phèdre: De l'amour j'ai toutes les fureurs.
> Oenone: Pour qui?
> Phèdre: Tu vas ouïr le comble des horreurs ...
>   J'aime ... À ce nom fatal, je tremble, je frisonne.
>   J'aime ...
> Oenone: Qui?
> Phèdre: Tu connaîs ce fils de l'Amazone,
>   Ce prince si longtemps par moi-même opprimé ...
> Oenone: Hippolyte! grands dieux!
> Phèdre: C'est toi qui l'as nommé!
>   (lines 259–64)

This act of nomination is taboo for Phèdre; and it is taboo because the act of sure nomination or identification such as this implies a sure identity for the nominator as well as for the nominee. She ventriloquises, euphemistically avoids mentioning the 'sacred name' herself, and thus 'stutters' over it in the attempt to delay her own settled identity as lover of Hippolyte, an identity which threatens her identity as wife to Thésée.

The name is important here. As in *Iphigénie en Aulide*, there is a dislocation between the name and what it supposedly signifies in essence. Phèdre thinks that the name 'Hippolyte' signifies one thing, a hater of women. Later she has to concede that this interpretation of the name can be relativised, as she comes to realise that 'Hippolyte' identifies himself as lover of Aricie. It is, in fact, at the moment when Phèdre comes to realise this alternative nomination, at the moment when the name of 'Hippolyte' is realised as according with the essence which Hippolyte claims for it, that this 'tragedy of nomination' begins to come to rest. When the name is identified with a supposed essence, that which loves Aricie and feels disgust for Phèdre, Hippolyte dies. Hippolyte had earlier stressed that Thésée could never invoke Neptune in vain: 'Neptune le protège, et ce dieu tutélaire/ Ne sera pas en vain imploré par mon père' (lines 621–2). In Act 4 Scene 2, Hippolyte reveals his love for Aricie, not for Phèdre, precisely at the moment when Thésée does in fact invoke (or 'name') Neptune to kill Hippolyte. Hippolyte is as good as dead already, then. And the revelation to Phèdre of the 'real' or alternative signification of the name 'Hippolyte' is made at the same moment as Thésée's repeated invocation:

> *Thésée:* Sa fureur contre vous se répand en injures;
> Votre bouche, dit-il, est pleine d'impostures;
> Il soutient qu'Aricie a son cœur, a sa foi,
> Qu'il l'aime.
> *Phèdre:*   Quoi, seigneur!
> *Thésée:*   Il l'a dit devant moi:
> Mais je sais rejeter un frivole artifice.
> Espérons de Neptune une prompte justice:
> Je vais moi-même encore au pied de ses autels
> Le presser d'accomplir ses serments immortels.
>   (lines 1185–92)

The act of self-revelation, an act of nominal identification of the self, made either by identifying oneself in a straightforward manner or indeed by 'naming' oneself indirectly through identifying or naming another historical character, is tantamount to death in this play. It is precisely at the moment when Phèdre herself reveals the dislocation between her name and what it signifies to Thésée, or more exactly, at the moment when she makes her name accord with her 'natural' self, that she will die at the close of the play.

The confusion of names and their referents is also important when Phèdre comes to stutter her love once more, this time to Hippolyte himself. In Act 2 Scene 5 she comments on how she loves Thésée, but confuses the name 'Thésée' with the person standing before her, Hippolyte. Here, Hippolyte is made to utter the pronouncement of love. Phèdre

stutters in order that others, notably Hippolyte, will make
the definitive utterance, thus absolving her of sin, guilt and
authority for the utterance. She thus contrives to restrain
herself from singular namable identity and manages to pro-
long her dying-scene. Phèdre speaks to Hippolyte of Thésée,
and they again wonder whether Thésée is alive or dead:

> Phèdre: On ne voit point deux fois le rivage des morts,
>   Seigneur. Puisque Thésée a vu les sombres bords,
>   En vain vous espérez qu'un dieu vous le renvoie;
>   Et l'avare Achéron ne lâche point sa proie.
>   Que dis-je? il n'est point mort, puisqu'il respire en vous;
>   Toujours devant mes yeux je crois voir mon époux:
>   Je le vois, je lui parle; et mon cœur ... Je m'égare,
>   Seigneur, ma folle ardeur malgré moi se déclare.
> Hippolyte: Je vois de votre amour l'effet prodigieux:
>   Tout mort qu'il est, Thésée est présent à vos yeux;
>   Toujours de son amour votre âme est embrasée.
>
>   (lines 623–33)

Here, then, Phèdre confuses the name of her husband with
the sight before her eyes, the physical presence of Hippolyte.
By this contrived euphemism, in which 'Thésée' euphemistically replaces Hippolyte, she can proclaim her love; but
she stutters even in this, and it is Hippolyte who articulates
her love.

The evasion of the presence of nature within the self, the
evasion of death which goes on in these linguistic contriv-
ances, involves the characters in a process of acting or dis-
simulation; or, to put it more crudely, it involves them in
the assumption of other voices and the ventriloquistic control
of other speakers. They constantly defer their own speech-
act or utterance by a process of stuttering, which causes
other voices to speak for them. The process is very close to
the Eliotic notion of 'impersonality', a procedure which itself
approximates towards 'impersonation'. T. S. Eliot writes
some of *The Waste Land*, but avoids his own identity, his
own personality, by contriving to make it appear as if Dante,
Marvell, Webster and others wrote most of it, and Ezra
Pound even manages to help here in editing some parts of
Eliot's own fragments.[33] The characters in Racine stutter like
T. S. Eliot because they must manage to make others assume

the authority for the pronouncements which they themselves wish to make, but which it would be death for them to make. Thus Oenone is made to reveal the name of Hippolyte; or Phèdre leaves herself entirely in the hands of Oenone: 'Eh bien! à tes conseils je me laisse entraîner' (line 363).

The presence of an audience, both on and off the stage, is of crucial importance to the stuttering of these characters. It is in the creation of some kind of dialogic mode of making definitive statements, the refusal of monologic authority, which allows the characters to defer death for a time. In Racine, such an audience is always implicit, and is usually necessary to the stuttering speaker. Thus we have Phèdre stammering a few phrases, and yet pleased that her audience has 'heard too much', which allows her to go on with her fragmented utterance:

> Phèdre: Ah, cruel! tu m'as trop entendue!
> Je t'en ai dit assez pour te tirer d'erreur.
> Eh bien! connaîs donc Phèdre en toute sa fureur:
> J'aime! Ne pense pas au moment qu je t'aime.
>   (lines 670–3)

Phèdre, although using her own name here, has still not identified herself fully as the lover of Hippolyte, but the weight of evidence for this interpretation is enormous, for Hippolyte as for us. Similarly, when Hippolyte stutters out his own love for Aricie, she interrupts in an effort to stop the utterance, but he protests that he has already gone too far, and the momentum of the utterance itself demands that it be made:

> Aricie: Quoi, seigneur!
> Hippolyte: Je me suis engagé trop avant.
> Je vois que la raison cède à la violence.
> Puisque j'ai commencé de rompre le silence,
> Madame, il faut poursuivre.
>   (lines 524–7)

In Racine, when the self is entirely present to itself, when there is no dislocation between the sign of the self, the name and what that name supposedly signifies as essence, then

authority can be taken and used to make a definitive utterance. But this utterance can only be thought of, in these
terms, as a revelation of the presence of nature within the
self, and thus, since the fact of nature is death, it becomes
death itself to make such a monologic authorial utterance.
When the self is in a condition of self-absence, as it were, in
a kind of exile like that of Thésée, then the utterance is
replaced with the fragmentary stuttering, and there is no
essential nature which ever comes to present itself in the self.
Racine's theatre heralds the death of the monologic author;
but it also replaces such an author with the principle of
dialogic authority, in which conventional conversational
gambits are offered in order to evade the direct identification
of self with singular name or identity. In the model of
stuttered conversation whose operation in *Phèdre* I have
outlined, there is an evasion of singular namable identity,
and thus a contrived evasion of the revelation of essential
nature through the self; but in Racine's tragedy such an
evasion is always transitory, and there comes a point at which
such a revelation of nature, such a collocation of name and
'essential self' occurs, bringing the death of the character.

Aricie's evasions before Thésée towards the close of *Phèdre*
finally turns the tables on Phèdre herself, and she is forced
to make her authoritative utterance:

> *Phèdre:*   Il faut rompre un injuste silence;
> Il faut à votre fils rendre son innocence:
> Il n'était point coupable.
> ...
> C'est moi qui, sur ce fils chaste et respectueux,
> Osai jeter un œil profane, incestueux.
> (lines 1617–24)

At this moment, then, she finally utters herself, reveals her
self to the others present. She assumes an authority which is
written, as it were, from the essential self within, an authority
which is truly Phèdre's; and she writes from the poison
which courses through her veins and brings her death. Even
though her authority is finally equated with death, the play
itself has offered an alternative model of authority, and one
which tried to circumvent the natural fact of death.

Phèdre might resolve the life of Phèdre into her natural death; but in one sense at least, it closes precisely as it opened, *in medias res*, critically in a state of indeterminacy. Thésée proposes that Aricie assume the position of his daughter, but no answer is given. The indeterminacy of the stutter as a mode of authority is one which can be characterised as a mode which is constantly *in medias res*: stuttered statements never finally resolve into singular identifiable utterances. Racine's tragedy operates precisely in this median, indeterminate, position. The self-present consciousness which was always finally discovered in the tragic theatre of Corneille has here, in Racine, absconded: exile from the self, a situation in which the name of the self never coincides with an essence of the self (until the instant of death), is the condition of human being for Racine. Such a position is rather close, in fact, to one of the thoughts of Pascal, in which he commented on the inability of the human to be content in a position of 'home', a condition of self-presence:

> Quand je m'y suis mis quelquefois à considérer les diverses agitations des hommes, et les périls, et les peines où ils s'exposent dans la Cour, dans la guerre d'où naissent tant de querelles, de passions, d'entreprises hardies et souvent mauvaises, etc., j'ai dit souvent que tout le malheur des hommes vient d'une seule chose, qui est de ne savoir pas demeurer en repos dans une chambre. ... on ne demeure chez soi avec plaisir.[34]

And Pascal, it might be noted, was another poet of the median and an advocate, at least in his practice in the *Pensées*, of a dialogic form between, for instance, the *honnête homme* and the apologist for Christianity.

Chapter 6

The Impossibility of Authenticity

Lear:	Dost thou know me, fellow:
Kent:	No, sir; but you have that in your countenance which I would fain call master.
Lear:	What's that?
Kent:	Authority.
Lear:	What services canst thou do?
Kent:	I can keep honest counsel, ride, run, mar a curious tale in telling it, and deliver a plain message bluntly.

(King Lear I. iv. 26–33)

Cornwall:	This is some fellow Who, having been prais'd for bluntness, doth affect A saucy roughness, and constrains the garb Quite from his nature. He cannot flatter, he, An honest mind and plain—he must speak truth.

(King Lear II. ii. 90–94)

Ériphile:	N'as-tu pas vu sa gloire, et le trouble d'Achille? J'en ai vu, j'en ai fui les signes trop certains.

(Iphigénie en Aulide, lines 1094–5)

Civil Authority: Gender, Genealogy, Nationalism

The vernacular languages in the later seventeenth and eighteenth centuries were becoming more self-conscious, as the
growth of vernacular literatures developed. An interest in
dictionaries, in England and France, is testimony to the
desire for the regulation, rationalisation and, indeed, identification and purification of national languages. But these
languages, to be 'purified', had to be related back to an

originary source, a 'pure' source in which the relation
between language and nature was supposed to be naturally
sanctioned and not arbitrary. The vernacular tongues claim
a kind of linguistic genealogy, similar to that which operates
in the family as I have described it in these pages, in which
they discover their pure identity through their more or less
clear direct lineage with the 'non-vernacular' languages of
Hebrew, Greek and Latin, not to mention 'purer', more
distant 'Oriental' forebears. Thus the vernaculars try to discover some source of an originary and thus incontrovertible
link between their constituent vocabularies and the world of
nature; among other things, the interest in etymology is an
interest in discovering identities, in discovering a grounding
for the language which the vernacular cultures use. To find
a personal history is, on one historical model, to find an
identity, a self; the analogy suggests that, similarly, to find
a root for a word is to discover the essential meaning, the
essence, of the word.[1]

In the period under discussion, the late seventeenth
century, tragedy was bound up with a kind of linguistic
nationalism. There was the belief, in English tragic theory
for instance, that the English person is comfortably 'at home',
as it were, in the English language. This language is the
mother-tongue and comes to one as intimately as mother's
milk or father's blood. Insofar as a person speaks English,
then, nature is immediately presented to her or him through
the words (whose link to nature has been fixed by
etymology), and the words themselves sit squarely and
necessarily in accord with nature. There is, as I showed in the
previous chapter, no dislocation between sign and referent in
what we might call 'high' tragedy. With such a belief in the
'naturalness' of a national language, there arises also the belief
that other languages are deviations from the norm of nature.
Interestingly, the civil disturbances which disrupted England
so much in the seventeenth century begin to turn outwards,
and civil war is replaced by national war. Again, the conflict
can be seen, among other things, as a conflict of authorities.

Some notion of exile, however, seems to be inherent to
comedy and the model of authority which that subtends. In
comedy there is the loss of a belief in a 'natural' tongue

because there is accepted in comedy a complete dislocation between vocabulary and nature. The human here is always exiled from nature, which remains forever alien and thus uncontrollable. There is no 'home' in language in comedy, and no certainties as regards the world of nature or truth. Truth is replaced by rhetoric; control of nature replaced by the control of other people's interpretations of 'nature'. In the present chapter I want to trace the death of the tragic view of life and its replacement with the comic at the period of the late seventeenth century; and I shall elaborate more fully the model of authority which comes to be available in writing.

Reuben A. Brower has argued that, provided we take him in a very specific tradition, 'Dryden marks the reaffirmation of "Europe" in English poetry and culture after an experiment in insularity and at a time of artificial essays in continental "Classicism."'[2] This is confused. Can 'Europe' be affirmed in a poetry which is simultaneously defining itself as distinctively 'English'? Moreover, how can this affirmation of Europe be squared with the many comments and essays of Dryden in which there is a constant attempt to differentiate the 'English' in terms of language, culture and theatre, from the 'French', the 'Spanish' and the 'Italian'? The mere fact that Dryden alludes to, imitates or parodies the 'conventions of other literatures' and that he drew on 'the large materials of philosophy and theology' and played on 'popular parallels between contemporary religious and political situations and those of ancient history, sacred and secular',[3] does not in any satisfactory way amount to any form of 'affirmation' of Europe; it simply means that Dryden is erudite and is aware of European traditions and literatures. His theoretical ideas were often constitutive of an attempt to create an 'England', a myth of England, through language.

In some of his more direct comments on this, in his criticism, we find a slighting of the French, especially of the French writers contemporaneous with himself. Thus he has Neander say in the Essay *Of Dramatic Poesy*:

> And these examples are enough to clear us from a servile imitation of the French.
> But to return whence I have boldly digressed, I dare boldly affirm

these two things of the English drama: first, that we have many plays of ours as regular as any of theirs; and which, besides, have more variety of plot and characters: and secondly, that in most of the irregular plays of Shakespeare or Fletcher (for Ben Jonson's are for the most part regular) there is a more masculine fancy and greater spirit in the writing, than there is in any of the French.[4]

And in the preface to his own version of the Antony and Cleopatra story, *All For Love*, he wrote that:

I should not have troubled myself thus far with French poets, but that I find our *Chedreux* critics wholly form their judgments by them. But for my part, I desire to be tried by the laws of my own country; for it seems unjust to me, that the French should prescribe here, till they have conquered. Our little sonneteers, who follow them, have too narrow souls to judge of poetry.[5]

Meanwhile, in France, Racine was claiming a similar kind of rectitude and autonomous *auctoritas* for the French, authorising, for instance, the sentiment of *Iphigénie en Aulide* by reference to its 'originary' classical counterpart. He wrote in the preface to this play:

J'ai reconnu avec plaisir, par l'effet qu'a produit sur notre théâtre tout ce que j'ai imité ou d'Homère ou d'Euripide, que le bon sens et la raison étaient les mêmes dans tous les siècles. Le goût de Paris s'est trouvé conforme à celui d'Athènes.[6]

Precisely in the same way as in his drama itself, there is a confusion or ambiguity of identity here: Paris is and is not Athens, and thus the archetypal city of good civilised writing; Racine is and is not Euripides.[7]

While Dryden was concerned to differentiate himself from the French, some of the French theorists and critics, such as Boileau and Rapin, were simultaneously trying to distance themselves from the Spanish and Italians. Thus Boileau, for example, attacks theatrical excess:

Évitons ces excès: laissons à l'Italie
De tous ces faux brillants l'éclatante folie.[8]

Or he defends the unities by using the Spaniards as his butt:

Que le lieu de la scène y soit fixe et marqué.
Un rimeur, sans péril, delà les Pyrénées,
Sur la scène en un jour renferme des années.
Là souvent le héros d'un spectacle grossier,
Enfant au premier acte, est barbon au dernier.
Mais nous, que la raison à ses règles engage,
Nous voulons qu'avec art l'action se ménage;
Qu'en un lieu, qu'en un jour, un seul fait accompli
Tienne jusqu'à la fin le théâtre rempli.[9]

There is a tacit claim here that the French vernacular is the natural source of rationality; in fact, each of the vernaculars were assuming themselves to be an embodiment of reason. This comes under closer scrutiny, in England at least, in the early eighteenth century.[10]

Similarly, Rapin argues that the Spanish and Italian writers have fallen from the heights of writing because they have, unlike the French, chosen to ignore or deviate from the rationality of Aristotelian 'regularity'.[11] But Rapin's admiration of the French theatre was not unqualified, and he in fact had many complaints about its degeneration, as he saw it. This degeneration arose, he thought, from an 'effeminisation' of society and its theatre. Pity and terror were central to Greek tragedy, but not so important in contemporary French drama because the French society had become more 'female'-centred:

C'est ce qui oblige nos poètes à privilégier si fort la galanterie sur le théâtre, et à tourner tous leurs sujets sur des tendresses outrées, pour plaire davantage aux femmes, qui se sont erigées en arbitres de ces divertissements, et qui ont usurpé le droit d'en décider.[12]

This complaint goes hand-in-hand with the rising prevalence of comedy over tragedy in the French theatre. The 'effeminisation' of society, as Rapin and others saw it, made it difficult for the society to sustain a kind of tragic theatre such as we have seen it in the avowedly masculinist Corneille, for example. Rapin himself commented on this particular effect:

Les Anciens ... ne mêloient la galanterie et l'amour, que dans la comédie. Car l'amour est d'un caractère qui dégénère toujours de cet air héroïque, dont la tragédie ne se défait jamais ... l'innocence du

thèâtre se conserveroit bien mieux selon l'idée de l'ancienne tragédie;
parce que la nouvelle est devenue trop éffeminée par la molesse des
dernier siècles.[13]

The concerns of nationalism were not an entirely new
phenomenon. The growing ease of communications with
other parts of the world served to relativise each of the
vernaculars; the language which had been considered 'natural', a kind of 'blood-right' or 'birth-right' was now seen
to be one language and cultural norm among many. Two
responses, at least, are possible in the face of this, and they
correspond to what I am characterising here as a tragic and
comic response to nature respectively.

Doubts about who and where we are, doubts about our
proximity to a state of nature, have to be entertained. But
we can respond to this in the manner of a Descartes, who
uses the extremes of doubt to found a new certainty: if I
doubt, at least I can therefore be sure that I exist; and the
rest of the world follows from this, in the *Méditations*. This
accords with the tragic approach of Corneille. In this the
response to doubts is one whereby we contrive to attain a
position of self-present authority. This is, by and large, a
position which pretends to ignore the social and historical
and geographical conditionings of the present self, a self
which becomes the container of nature and thus the source
of meaning for the world. To entertain doubts about the
authority of the self here would be to relativise that self, to
make it seem to be not fully present to itself, as it were. This
is a conservative view, hubristic, self-assured and unable to
question sceptically the rightness of self-present authority.
It is also, interestingly, in theatrical terms a kind of drama
which both Corneille and Rapin characterise as 'male'.

On the other hand, there is available the 'comic' response.
In this there is a realisation of all such doubts about identities
and essential natures, but there is also a refusal to worry
overmuch about these doubts. In this we are not so concerned
with establishing the present self as a container of nature and
as a source for the meaning of nature in the world. This
response leads to the realisation of the strict impossibility of
monologue; any statement made from the position in which

we find ourselves is immediately open to subsequent correction, commentary, response or re-formation. Hence, the only way to 'talk' or assume authority is through an even more radical kind of 'stutter' than that which I indicated in the theatre of Racine. In this response there is no credence in a continuing genealogy in which we have a language which accords with nature as some kind of inherent blood-right. As our blood, identity, becomes relativised, so, likewise, does our language. The language grows not through a link with an essential nature which can be rediscovered by academies and contained in dictionaries, but through usage.

The question of nationalism had been prominent earlier in the century. The writings of Milton betray his nationalism at some points. For instance, in 'At a Vacation Exercise', which was written half in Latin in fact, the English part begins with a paean to the English language as something 'inborn':

> Hail native Language, that by sinews weak
> Didst move my first endevoring tongue to speak,
> And mad'st imperfet words with childish trips,
> Half unpronounc't, slide through my infant lips,
> Driving dumb silence from the portal dorc,
> Where he had mutely sate two years before.[14]

The poem's arrangement establishes both the difference of English from Latin and also its intimate links with this originary, 'purer' language. It stresses, moreover, through its specific provenance, from within Milton, aged nineteen, the idea that the English language comes from within the 'present' body, or at least the self-present consciousness of Milton; the language comes from as intimate a source as the blood. In 'L'Allegro', further, there is a suggestion that this English language (despite the Italianate title) is in some kind of direct line of translation not from Rome but from heaven itself:

> But come thou Goddess fair and free,
> In Heav'n ycleapt *Euphrosyne*,
> And by men, heart-easing Mirth[15]

And in the prefatory address in *The Doctrine and Discipline of Divorce*, Milton urged great nationalistic fervour. Urging England to lead the world in the reformation of divorce law, he wrote:

> It would not be the first, or second time, since our ancient *Druides*, by whom this Island was the Cathedrall of Philosophy to *France*, left off their pagan rites, that England hath had this honour vouchsaft from Heav'n, to give out reformation to the World. Who was it but our English *Constantine* that baptiz'd the Roman Empire? Who but the *Northumbrian Willibrode*, and *Winifrede of Devon* with their followers, were the first Apostles of *Germany*? Who but *Alcuin* and *Wicklef* our Country men open'd the eyes of *Europe*, the one in arts, the other in Religion. Let not England, forget her precedence of teaching nations how to live.[16]

Nationalist feeling ran high, and appeared in concert with tracts such as this one just quoted, which stressed the dominance of 'male'-centred values. Contrary to Brower's thesis that this nationalism was countered by interlinguistic allusion, such nationalistic fervour continued to make itself felt in the writings of the latter part of the seventeenth century.

In the latter half of the seventeenth century, such nationalistic approaches to language were perhaps more of a reaction against the loss of social place and identity. The idea that 'who one is equals where one is' was coming into disrepute; the fact of the revolution had made it clear that no one was ascribed a 'natural' and hence necessary place and identity. The mobility of identity, the direct result of the mobility of nature (both in the cosmos and in the human blood), was becoming more acceptable as a norm. But the problem then arises that this model of human being, that of lacking stable identity, is fulfilled most clearly by the woman; 'male' or 'masculinist, 'patriotic' (if not, indeed, *patriarchal*) reactions, such as those of Rapin, set in. Nature, however, could no longer unproblematically be regarded as an eternally ordered regulation of the world, but rather the state of nature was seen to be more and more a result, a product, of our inter-relations with the world. This is to say that the tragic view of life and of nature was ceding place in some degree to the comic view. In the theatre itself, especially perhaps in England, tragedy gives way to comedy, and plays are organised around the confusion between nature and art.

The condition of exile has been linked to literary authority, most frequently perhaps in relation to writings of the Modernist period.[17] Some notion of exile, however, seems to have been the condition of poets during many periods. Medieval *troubadours* and *trouvères* had their work recited by travelling *jongleurs*; some seventeenth-century poetry was written by young poets during their great tours of Europe, and certainly a great deal of seventeenth-century verse was written from some position of exile or isolation from church and state (Crashaw is perhaps the most obvious example); Swift was an exile in both England and Ireland, feeling at home nowhere; Sterne based his writing of *A Sentimental Journey* and volumes seven and eight of *Tristram Shandy* upon the flight into exile, a flight from death, and so on. Some notion of exile seems also to have been important to Corneille's theorising about tragedy:

> Bien qu'il y aye de grands intérêts d'État dans un poème et que le soin qu'une personne royale doit avoir de sa gloire fasse taire sa passion, comme en *Don Sanche*, s'il ne s'y rencontre point de péril de vie, de pertes d'États ou de bannissement, je ne pense pas qu'il aye droit de prendre un nom plus relevé que celui de comédie.[18]

The peril of exile, banishment, is important as a constituent element of tragedy, argues Corneille here. As I pointed out earlier, however, such a peril of exile is always overcome; reinstatement is the founding principle of Cornelian resolutions. In *Horace*, for instance, there is a fear that the whole state of Rome will be lost in a sense; but it is returned to itself and is returned to its 'rightful' place by the close of the play.

Blanchot has argued that exile is the condition of poetry. He writes:

> Il est vrai: Saint-John Perse, en nommant l'un de ses poèmes *Exil*, a aussi nommé la condition poétique. Le poète est en exil, il est exilé de la cité, exilé des occupations réglées et des obligations limitées, de ce qui est résultat, réalité saisissable, pouvoir. ... Le poème est l'exil, et le poète qui lui appartient appartient à l'insatisfaction de l'exil, est toujours hors de lui-même, hors de son lieu natal, appartient à l'étranger, à ce qui est le dehors sans intimité et sans limite, cet écart

que Hölderlin nomme, dans sa folie, quand il y voit l'espace infini du rythme. ... Cet exil qu'est le poème fait du poète l'errant, le toujours égaré, celui qui est privé de la présence ferme et du séjour véritable.[19]

This looks fairly close to my own description or theorisation of the position of the comic author. The tragic poem is made from the reaction to the condition of exile, from a resultant reinstatement and rediscovery of eternal, 'natural' values. Blanchot's comment here, which is concerned most intimately with the writings of the twentieth century, is testimony to the fact that, *pace* D. H. Lawrence, the 'modern' age is one in which comedy dominates as a mode of organising literary experience and even, perhaps, consciousness itself.[20]

The French and English theatres looked to the ancient world for models for their language and for their drama; their 'home' was in Greece and Rome. It is instructive to consider, for example, the Theban plays of Sophocles in relation to the questions of exile and authority, and authority and the city. In the light of this, what becomes important to much of the theatre of the later seventeenth century in England and France is a notion of the city as a home which forms a steady and continuous backdrop against which the actions of the characters can be defined. The city, or in a wider sense, a stable home or *point de repère*, history or tradition, serves to give characters a point of reference which always allows them to orientate themselves safely and securely. The continuance and stability of the city guarantees the stability of the identity of its citizens. This is precisely the same, at a civic level, as the activities of a Dryden or a Boileau, generating an identity as English or French, citizens of stable 'homes'. The cities are also linked, more or less directly, to the notion of the stable continuity of identity guaranteed by the identifiable male-blood lineages and male history which the family, in its nuclear form, allows to be written.

In *Oedipus Rex* Creon comes from the oracle with the news that there is in Thebes someone who exists, like Phèdre in Racine, as a stain on nature, a concrete manifestation of sin, of the deviation from nature:

Creon:	There is an unclean thing,
	Born and nursed on our soil, polluting our soil,
	Which must be driven away, not left to destroy us.
Oedipus:	What unclean thing? And what purification is required?
Creon:	The banishment of a man, or the payment of blood for blood.
	For the shedding of blood is the cause of our city's peril.
Oedipus:	What blood does he mean? Did he say who it was that died?
Creon:	We had a king, sir, before you came to lead us. His name was Laius.[21]

Laius is swiftly made into an entire family history, so that what has been killed is in some sense an elaborate tradition, a whole historical lineage of male blood, the identity and name of the city itself and its historical stability:

Oedipus:	I mean to fight for him now, as I would fight
	For my own father, and to leave no way untried
	To bring to light the killer of Laius,
	The son of Labdacus, the son of Polydorus, the son of Cadmus, the son of Agenor.[22]

The flow of blood from Thebes has been aligned with the flow of blood of Laius's familial lineage, and thus has come to represent tradition and the authority of the past. Insofar as this tradition conditions the present experience of the characters, such authority carries the weight of *potestas*, a power which is to be obeyed in the present. In the present, however, Oedipus has established his own *auctoritas*, through the solving of a riddle and the murdering of a tradition: he thus marks a disruption in the regular flow of his family's blood. What is at stake, however, in these plays, is not simply the personal life and *auctoritas* of Oedipus but rather the very fact of the tradition, heritage and *potestas* of the city of Thebes. The city in this trilogy works at the same symbolic level of authority as the heritage of male familial blood in primogeniture in the plays of Shakespeare.

The city is important in the theatre of the later seventeenth century. At this moment the very concept of a native or natural identity has begun to come into doubt, as the bound-aries of England, or more radically, 'here', have become

visibly mobile. The Civil War, for instance, was precisely
about a redrawing of boundaries, and thus a relativising of
them. Boundaries are not 'naturally given', but fought over.[23]
Moreover, some writings have begun to fantasise, in one way
or another, the dissolution of the male-orientated nuclear
familial basis of a society.[24] In some of these cases of proto-
feminist writing there is a threat to the very notion of the
male blood line which is supposed to subtend the identifiable
and constant city, and which is also supposed to be upheld
by nature. If the location of nature was difficult of access
for Shakespeare, it was all the more evasive and elusive for
the writers of the Restoration period.

Corneille's *Horace*, written probably as early as 1637, but
not performed until 1640, was already the beginnings of an
exploration of the theme of national and natural identity.
Interestingly enough, the question in this play is focused
primarily upon female identity. Sabine, born in Alba, is
married to the Roman Horace. Alba and Rome are now at
war; Sabine, therefore, is in a state of crisis, indeterminate
about where her affections, and her identity, are to be found:

> Sabine: Je suis Romaine, hélas! puisque Horace est Romain;
> J'en ai reçu le titre en recevant sa main;
> Mais ce noeud me tiendrait en esclave enchaînée,
> S'il m'empêchait de voir en quels lieux je suis née.[25]

In historicising the present conflict, she places Rome in the
position of the child who murders its parents, Alba, in order
to establish its own transhistorical individual identity; in
order, in short, to establish itself as the presentation or
manifestation of an essential nature:

> Sabine: Je sais que ton État, encore en sa naissance,
> Ne saurait, sans la guerre, affermir sa puissance,
> Je sais qu'il doit s'accroître, et que tes grands destins
> Ne le borneront pas chez les peuples latins,
> Que les Dieux t'ont promis l'empire de la terre
> (lines 39–43)

She urges Rome to conquer many different lands, but then
goes on:

Sabine: Mais respecte une ville à qui tu dois Romule.
         Ingrate, souviens-toi que du sang des rois
         Tu tiens ton nom, tes murs, et tes premières lois.
         Albe est ton origine: arrête et considère
         Que tu portes le fer dans le sein de ta mère.

                                              (lines 52–6)

Sabine here indicates the intimate relationship which exists between Rome and Alba, a relationship of maternity and paternity. Rome, she claims, derives its identity, even its very name, from its parental forebear, Alba. The boundaries between Rome and Alba disappear in this speech; and as the boundaries fall, so too national and individuated identity collapses. Camille is in a similar situation to Sabine. Although a Roman and a sister of Horace, she is in love with the Alban, Curiace. There is a slight discrepancy between their comparable situations, however, in the fact that Camille is not yet married. But this is a vital discrepancy; for the play questions, through this factor, the solidity of the boundary which distinguishes Camille's identity as daughter of Old Horace from her identity as wife to Curiace. Thus the geographical boundary between Roman identity and Alban identity is probed even more fundamentally. At what moment does Camille stop being a Roman and start to be an Alban; in her betrothal to Curiace, even in her love for him, is there not some suspicion of her identity already being in a state of transition? Natural and national identity are questioned by the fundamental exposition of the situation in the play. Sabine, now a 'Roman', can also be an 'Alban'; Camille, born in 'Rome', can in some ways be an 'Alban'. This is to say, of course, that in this play, at least, indeterminate identity can be seen as potentially treacherous to the integrated nation. In metaphysically redrawing the boundary around Rome to include part of Alba, Sabine is betraying Rome, bringing Alba inside Rome, in the 'wooden horse' of her mind. These two women are seen by the other 'nationalists' in the play, those whose (male) identity is stable and assured, as being precisely such traitorous threats.

Sabine and Camille manifest one of the first 'modern' positions in the literary and cultural debate over the relative values of the ancients and the moderns. The Roman self subscribes to the values of a certain tradition, that of Rome as a kind of familial blood, as a permanence of identity against which it derives its defined identity as 'Roman'. The permanence of the city, the fact that the city of Rome contains within itself all its past heritage, grants Horace the authority to act in entire accordance with the city's values, which demand, for instance, the murder of an Alban who happens to be the lover of his sister and brother of his wife. Rome is in Horace's blood, as it were, and gives him, he thinks, an incontrovertible natural authority, the authority of the past, of the ancient tradition. Camille and Sabine, on the other hand, hovering between two nations and two identities and thus in a state of exile already, both want the world to be recentred upon themselves and their own personal and individual experience.

As against this wavering lack of self-definition in these female 'exiles', Corneille provides the inevitable triumph of the ancients, the triumph of the city and of its male blood and self-identity. Tulle excuses Horace for his murder of Camille and reminds us that the nation of Rome was built precisely upon an act of fratricide. This makes Horace not simply a Roman but a present manifestation of Romulus himself: the history of Rome is present in the character of Horace, and its very name is articulated through his action of killing Camille:

> *Tulle:* De pareils serviteurs sont les forces des rois,
> Et de pareils aussi sont au-dessus des lois.
> Qu'elles se taisent donc, que Rome dissimule
> Ce que dès sa naissance elle vit en Romule:
> Elle peut bien souffrir en son libérateur
> Ce qu'elle a bien souffert en son premier auteur.
> (lines 1753–8)

Horace thus carries within himself the identity of Rome as a city. In saving himself, he has saved the city, saved the past, and guaranteed the permanence of the names of both family and city.

The city of Venice is perhaps one of the central 'characters' in Otway's *Venice Preserv'd*, a play which is about the preservation of the city and of its values and authorities. But the city is itself in a state of extreme indeterminacy, under threat from the revolutionaries who wish to change its meaning and authority. The revolutionaries consider Venice to be in a state of degeneration. The 'natural' or 'just' order of its citizens, they claim, is in a condition of disorder, usurped by the cowardly senators. They characterise the city as a female whore:

> *Pierre:*   How lovely the Adriatic whore,
> Dressed in her flames, will shine! devouring flames!
> Such as shall burn her to the watery bottom
> And hiss in her foundation.[26]

The vision which Jaffeir offers of the city in revolution is one in which there is a strange prosopopoeia. The father of Belvidera is one of the senators. When Jaffeir tells her that he is to kill her father, she is in a crisis situation similar to that of Desdemona and Cordelia in Shakespeare, having to choose between love for a father and for a lover or husband, allegiances which both, fundamentally, support the same masculinist ethos and ideology of male priority and authority. Jaffeir's conception of his action turns the city into a bleeding human, and the action itself is seen as the destruction or murder of the burden of the ancients:

> *Jaffeir:*   Nay, the throats of the whole Senate
> Shall bleed, my Belvidera: he amongst us
> That spares his father, brother, or his friend,
> Is damned: how rich and beauteous will the face
> Of Ruin look, when these wide streets run blood.
>   (III. ii)

The arteries of the city itself here, confused with the blood of the senators or Jaffeir's forebears, are the object of Jaffeir's revolt. But insofar as the blood of the senators is the blood of her father, it is also in some measure the blood of Belvidera herself. Venice, further, is identified as female. But it is precisely the flowing of female blood which is forestalled. Venice, the city and all its values, is preserved; in death, the blood of Belvidera does not in fact flow. Such a preservation of the city is tantamount here to the failure to establish a present 'modern' *auctoritas* in the face of the triumphant *potestas* of the permanence of the city itself, along with the (male) blood of its real authorities, the senators.

These plays, in some respects, represent a final attempt to reinstate the tragic view of life as I have characterised it in this book. This tragic view is one which attempts to discover the presence of nature; but the very notion of an 'essential' nature and an unchanging eternal presence of that nature is now treated with scepticism. The structure of the city is tenuous, always under threat of disruption from 'moderns', always trying to consolidate the power of its heritage or 'ancients'.[27]

This view, that these plays represent the end of tragedy in some sense, is one shared by R. J. Kaufmann, although he arrives at his conclusions by a very different route from the one taken here. Kaufmann writes of the 'cycle' of Dryden's plays, from *The Indian Emperor* (1665) through *Tyrannic Love* (1669), *The Conquest of Granada* (1669–70) and *Aurung-Zebe* (1675) to *All for Love* (1678), and argues that:

> This intense episode of heroic plays can be described historically as the death agony of the tragic drama in England, and as the last phase of Renaissance experimentation with high individualism. Thus these plays provide an obituary, somewhat hysterical perhaps, of tragic heroism as it had been understood.[28]

My own argument is not that tragedy 'died' at this moment but that it simply became contentious to write it. Steiner's argument about the death of tragedy thus also corroborates, but overstates, my own argument. Steiner concludes *The Death of Tragedy* with an interpretation of a parabolic tale, in which he writes that:

> The bearing of this parable on our theme, I take it, is this: God grew weary of the savagery of man. Perhaps He was no longer able to control it and could no longer recognize His image in the mirror of creation. He has left the world to its own inhuman devices and dwells now in some other corner of the universe so remote that His messengers cannot even reach us. I would suppose that He turned away during the seventeenth century, a time which has been the constant dividing line in our argument. In the nineteenth century, Laplace announced that God was a hypothesis of which the rational mind had no further

need; God took the great astronomer at his word. But tragedy is that form of art which requires the intolerable burden of God's presence. It is now dead because His shadow no longer falls upon us as it fell on Agamemnon or Macbeth or Athalie.[29]

The burden of the presence of God may not finally be necessary to tragedy; but at least some burden of the past, the tradition, the weight of an essential nature does seem to be crucial. Nature as some kind of blood-right, a blood-right which is externalised in the permanence of the city or the family, is central to the conflict between tragedy and comedy in the seventeenth century. When the presence of nature is understood as being tenuous, then such tragedy as we have in the neoclassical French theatre, or in England's Restoration theatre, becomes impossible. The state of nature, most clearly in an age of the artificial ritual of the civic arrangement of human life, is now an area of contention. Nature as an eternal presence has finally been acknowledged as lost. Paradise was lost, perhaps for the first time, in the seventeenth century when Milton wrote the loss of paradise. As such, all that remains possible is the artificial construction of a mythic or deceitful 'nature', a state which will be called nature by various characters even at the very instant when they know that it is their own artifice. This is the situation of comedy with its purely linguistic indeterminacies in this period of the later seventeenth century.

Play's the Thing: The Demise of Epistemology and the Triumph of Hedonism

When Harvey published his findings concerning the circulation of the blood in 1628, he began a major controversy in medical circles, a controversy which gave added impetus to the movement towards empirical observation and away from the theoretical principles of medical authorities. Jean Riolan the younger and Gui Patin, Dean of the Faculty of Medicine at Paris, refused for some time to believe Harvey's discoveries. The kind of medicine which they practised, out of the theorems of Hippocrates and Galen, required the body to be conceived of as a static container of four elemental humours: blood, phlegm, choler and melancholy. As such, they believed that nature itself was present in the human body in these four elements, and that all illness arose from some imbalance among them. Thus they believed that the blood, for instance, had to be stagnant, or at least non-circulating; when they diagnosed an illness which was a result of a prevalence of blood, they would simply drain some of it off. They thought of themselves as working directly upon nature itself, as being in direct contact with nature, which simply required adjustment now and again; they were regulators, even 'legislators', of a nature which never changes in its elemental make-up.[30]

Molière, an ill man in a country whose medics lingered under the beliefs of Patin, with his pathological love of bleeding patients,[31] was extremely sceptical of the whole institution of medicine. His work shows his belief that nature was not quite so easy of access as Patin, Riolan or even Harvey himself would lead us to think. *Le Malade Imaginaire* was Molière's last play, written at a time when he had a vested interest in exposing fallacious medicine. In this text there is a very specific link between writing and death, and one which goes beyond mere theory. Molière, an ill man, played the part of the imaginary invalid, a character who is not as ill as he would have us believe, although he does require to be cured of something. In a kind of Wildean paradox, in which art prefigures nature, Molière's fourth performance of the play, on 17 February 1673, brought on his death. He took ill on stage and died shortly after the performance ended. A man acting illness becomes 'really' ill. This fact is of importance in the theoretical understanding of comedy in the later part of the seventeenth century.

Amidst these Wildean paradoxes, Béralde expresses the view that more people die from the intervention of doctors upon nature than would die if nature were left to its own devices:

> *Béralde:* Votre monsieur Purgon, par exemple, n'y sait point de finesse; c'est un homme tout médecin, depuis la tête jusqu'aux pieds; un homme qui croit à ses règles plus qu'à

toutes les démonstrations des mathématiques, et qui croirait du crime à les vouloir examiner; qui ne voit rien d'obscur dans la médecine, rien de douteux, rien de difficile; et qui, avec une impétuosité de prévention, une raideur de confiance, une brutalité de sens commun et de raison, donne au travers des purgations et des saignées, et ne balance aucune chose. Il ne luit faut point vouloir mal de tout ce qu'il pourra vous faire: c'est de la meilleure foi du monde qu'il vous expédiera; et il ne fera, en vous tuant, que ce qu'il a fait à sa femme et à ses enfants, et ce qu'en un besoin il ferait à lui-même.

Argan: C'est que vous avez, mon frère, une dent de lait contre lui. Mais enfin, venons au fait. Que faire donc quand on est malade?

Béralde: Rien, mon frère.

Argan: Rien?

Béralde: Rien. Il ne faut que demeurer en repos. La nature d'elle-même, quand nous la laissons faire, se tire doucement du désordre où elle est tombée. C'est notre inquiétude, c'est notre impatience qui gâte tout; et presque tous les hommes meurent de leurs remèdes, et non pas de leurs maladies.[32]

Perhaps much the same thing could be said of King Lear at the beginning of the century as well. Already, however, there is in this interchange the seeds of a belief that any human contact with nature is interference, intervention; and moreover, nature is by definition that which alien to the human, beyond human knowledge and perception.

Dryden subtitled *All for Love* with the phrase, *The World Well Lost*; it was, however, only in comedy that the world was finally lost to humanity. The comedies of this period are full of characters who have clearly lost their grip on an alien nature. The clearest example is once again from Molière, in *Tartuffe*. Most of Orgon's household can see that Tartuffe is an impostor, and by no means a natural manifestation of an essential piety; Orgon and Mme Pernelle, however, are fully taken in by him. Orgon is so enamoured of Tartuffe that he decides to marry off his daughter Mariane to him. The problem is, of course, that Mariane is in love with the handsome Valère, and despises Tartuffe. Orgon demands that Mariane love Tartuffe: 'Mais je veux que cela soit une vérité'.[33] Dorine, the servant, complains vociferously, and her interruptions begin to make Orgon's speech degenerate into a comic faltering or stuttering:

Orgon: [*A part.*] Fort bien. Pour châtier son insolence extrême,
Il faut que je lui donne un revers de ma main.
[*Il se met en posture de donner un soufflet à Dorine; et, à chaque mot qu'il dit à sa fille, il se tourne pour regarder Dorine, qui se tient droite sans parler.*]
Ma fille, vous devez approuver mon dessein ...
Croire que le mari ... que j'ai su vous élire ...
[*À Dorine.*] Que ne parles-tu?
Dorine: Je n'ai rien à me dire.
Orgon: Encore un petit mot.
Dorine: Il ne me plaît pas, moi.
Orgon: Certes, je t'y guettais.
Dorine: Quelque sotte, ma foi! ...
Orgon: Enfin, ma fille, il faut payer d'obéissance,
Et montrer pour mon choix entière déférence.
Dorine: [*en s'enfuyant.*] Je me moquerais fort de prendre un tel époux.
Orgon: [*après avoir manqué de donner un soufflet à Dorine.*] Vous avez là, ma fille, une peste avec vous ...

(lines 570–80)

In this we have an explicit failure on the part of Orgon to come to touch reality; his failure to strike Dorine is a manifestation or enactment of his inability to maintain any genuine contact with nature in the play, or with the natural essence of Tartuffe. As he tries to slap Dorine, he realises that she has already moved on, moved away; he fails, in the play as a whole, to connect with reality, for it has always moved on into its next guise, its next imposture.

The revelation of the presence of nature in the human was coterminous with the enactment of death, I argued earlier. This, perhaps, is why the contact with nature is not allowed in these comedies. Even *Le Malade Imaginaire*, insofar as it concerns an 'imaginary' invalid, is an attempt to forestall the presence of death. In *Tartuffe*, the avoidance of death as a real event is again made more explicit. The fact of death becomes reduced to the status of a purely verbal or linguistic event. Mariane is devastated at the news that she is to marry Tartuffe. Dorine, after provoking her to speak up for herself, asks Mariane what she expects from such a marriage to the hypocritical impostor:

Dorine: Sur cette autre union quelle est donc votre attente?
Mariane: De me donner la mort, si l'on me violente.
Dorine: Fort bien. C'est un recours où je ne songeais pas.

Vous n'avez qu'à mourir pour sortir d'embarras.
Le remède sans doute est merveilleux. J'enrage
Lorsque j'entends tenir ces sortes de langage.

(lines 613–18)

The threatened death here, then, is converted by Dorine into an empty or purely rhetorical linguistic gambit, a word which bears no direct relation to the deed which it supposedly indicates. The presence of nature, in the form of a real death, is again evaded, or literally translated into an imaginary event, a rhetorical fiction; in Sausurrean terms, pure 'signifier'.[34]

By and large, in Restoration comedy the pursuit of nature has been replaced by the pursuit of pleasure. The biological 'fact' of blood, from which Shakespeare started in his pursuit of nature, has, after Harvey, been shown to lead into a never-ending pursuit of 'blood-identity'. The blood, always on the move, was now never in fact 'identical' with the body, whose empirically visible movement it helped to propel; the body itself was no longer stable enough to be identified with, or according to, its blood. It is no great step from realising this[35] to deciding that there is no point in pursuing essential nature at all, or even in worrying about it. The existentialist pleasure, a delight in acting for its own sake, replaces this now discredited notion of an essential nature. The pleasure itself is intimately tied up with play in language (in every sense, from the pun to the Barthesian 'plaisir du texte'), with 'the play' in the notion of theatre (acting and dissembling or fictionalising), and with fashion, with the pleasure of living 'in the moment'.

The pleasure of the moment, rather than the nature of the world, occupies the central position in the stage for these plays. Congreve calls a play not 'The Nature of the World' but *The Way of the World*, indicating even in that title his interest in the transitory, the fashionable and the manners of the world at the present relativised moment. The play itself corroborates such an understanding of its title. For instance, at one point, some of the characters await the arrival of Mrs Millamant, and then question her as to why she was so late in her arrival on the scene:

Mrs Millamant: Ay, that's true—O but then I had—Mincing, what

	had I? Why was I so long?
Mincing:	O mem, your laship stayed to peruse a pecquet of letters.
Mrs Millamant:	O ay, letters—I had letters—I am persecuted with letters—I hate letters—nobody knows how to write letters; and yet one has 'em, one does not know why—they serve one to pin up one's hair.
Witwoud:	Is that the way? Pray, madam, do you pin up your hair with all your letters? I find I must keep copies.
Mrs Millamant:	Only with those in verse, Mr Witwoud. I never pin up my hair with prose. I think I tried once, Mincing.
Mincing:	O mem, I shall never forget it.
Mrs Millamant:	Ay, poor Mincing tift and taft all the morning.
Mincing:	'Till I had the cremp in my fingers, I'll vow, mem. And all to no purpose. But when your laship pins it up with poetry, it sits so pleasant the next day as anything, and is so pure and so crips.[36]

In this brief and seemingly inconsequential interlude, Congreve links the play of language, in verse, with the play of fashion, in hairstyle, and with the play of acting, in Mrs Millamant's adoption of her social role. These three modes of artifice dominate Restoration comedy.

Many of these comedies are 'plays about plays', insofar as acting is their dominant theme, concern, and organisational principle. But more pertinently, they are plays about *play* itself. There is here at least one link between the comedy of the Restoration period and an Aristotelian notion of tragedy, or of acting, as described in the *Poetics*. In the *Poetics*, Aristotle had argued that 'The instinct for imitation, then, is natural to us'; such imitation is in itself a source of epistemological pleasure:

> The creation of poetry generally is due to two causes, both rooted in human nature. The instinct for imitation is inherent in man from his earliest days; he differs from other animals in that he is the most imitative of creatures, and he learns his earliest lessons by imitation. Also inborn in us is the instinct to enjoy works of imitation. ... The reason for this is that learning is a very great pleasure.[37]

Aristotle bases this upon his own empirical observations, that people do seem to enjoy the representation of something whose presence they could not bear; for in the representation, which acknowledges itself to be a mere imitation, something can be learnt about the object presented. But the idea of imitation and its pleasurability will bear more analysis. The fact of imitation leads to (at least) two corollary considerations: deindividuation and inauthenticity. In being reproduced or imitated, an object loses its specificity and individuality, and becomes no longer a purely autonomous and self-directing subject. To impersonate another person, as Shakespearean twins demonstrate, is to question the very individuality of the person thus duplicated. As a result, the question of the authenticity of the 'original' is raised. When one person stops imitating or impersonating another, she or he does not return to an authentic selfhood, but returns instead to an impersonation of the 'originary' self. This is to say, in fact, that the impersonator has no self; like a Sartrean waiter, she or he can only play the role of the self, now simply one role among many. The Aristotelian fact of imitation serves to offer the theoretical possibility (a possibility adopted in Restoration comedy) that there is no essential or natural self; rather, there is only a series of Goffmanesque 'presentations of the self in everyday life'.[38] Through these results of imitation, deindividuation and inauthenticity, there arises a realisation that the question of an originary source becomes simply unanswerable: an essential nature gives way entirely to the play and pleasure of art, of artifice and artificiality, which might be called duplicity. If, as Benjamin suggests, 'The presence of the original is the prerequisite to the concept of authenticity',[39] then, in the Restoration duplicitous character, imitating and acting out various roles, and where the very notion of the original is lost, what we have is precisely the impossibility of authenticity in Restoration comic theatre. Benjamin goes on:

> The authenticity of a thing is the essence of all that is transmissible from its beginning, ranging from its substantive duration to its testimony to the history which it has experienced. Since the historical testimony rests on the authenticity, the former, too, is jeopardized by reproduction when substantive duration ceases to matter. And what is really jeopardized when the historical testimony is affected is the authority of the object.[40]

In the terms of my own argument here, this translates neatly into the loss of the authority of nature itself, in the process of imitation in Restoration self-conscious 'play' and pleasurable imitation.

There are many scenes in the comedy of the late seventeenth century in which the characters on stage adopt roles, or are 'directed' by other characters. In *Tartuffe*, once more, Mariane and Valère eventually confront each other with the news that Mariane is to wed Tartuffe. Mariane says she is at a los˜ what to do; and this indeterminacy gives Valère his own cue. He urges her to marry Tartuffe, since her indeterminacy reveals no repellance towards him, and her hesitancy about proclaiming love for Valère indicates her lack of such an affection. This in turn gives Mariane another cue, and she now believes that since Valère has not tried to talk her out of marrying Tartuffe, and has in fact encouraged her to marry him, then Valère cannot love her. Dorine, who is on stage at this point, withdraws to let them act out their little scene; as she does this, she becomes, voyeur-like, a kind of 'director' of these two characters who refuse to reveal their 'real' selves and who act the part of rejected lover.

Two things primarily require to be said about this scene. Firstly, there is some avowed refusal of autonomous authority on the part of both characters. But this is done in order to pursue greater degrees of authority over each other. There is nothing to be gained from a direct proclamation of love, for, with the marriage between them now uncertain, such a proclamation would simply hand the power of choice, of rejection or acceptance, and thus the power of authority, over to the silent partner. There is much, however, to be gained from rhetorically persuading the partner to speak first, and thus retaining such authority, the power of autonomous choice, for the self. It is for this reason that Valère 'stutters' his departure, or merely imitates the role of the departing, rejected lover. In going, he thinks he will force an avowal of love and a demand for his return from Mariane; when this is not forthcoming, he is forced to return himself, pretending that he has heard her speak, or adding a final word to his 'farewell', or whatever. Dorine intervenes and tries, with great difficulty, to force them together. She has here precisely the same difficulty with regard to grasping 'nature' that

Orgon had when he tried to strike her earlier: whenever she thinks she is in contact with nature, whenever she thinks she has a grip on each character, the other character slips away from her.

The second thing to be said, however, concerns just this resultant bringing together of Mariane and Valère by directorial force. Are they, in fact, in their rightful positions; are they in love with each other at all? It must be stressed that all through the scene, they have precisely refused to protest that they love each other, and, on the contrary, they have in fact acted severe dislike of each other. The normal interpretation of this scene rests upon the assumption that they are really in love, and that Dorine, and we, know this better than they themselves, blinded by pride or whatever. Instead of this, however, there is an interpretation pressing itself upon us which suggests that it is now extremely uncertain as to whether they are 'naturally' in love with each other at all. The authority of nature or 'reality' has been lost in their very acting out of their parts; and this is replaced with the authority of a directorial rhetoric, here that of Dorine (although their acted parts are also heavily rhetorical). Their hesitations at the start of the scene and their stuttered departures from each other are open to a radically different interpretation. They are, perhaps, not rhetorical manoeuvres to persuade the partner to make the first declaration of love; rather, they are manoeuvres which contrive to place the partner in the position of the authority which states definitively that they must indeed separate. Although Dorine does indeed bring them together, the whole scene has demonstrated the arbitrariness of this; their 'love' for each other is clearly not a 'natural' phenomenon dictated by the necessities of authority of nature at all. The 'rhetoric of the signified' (Benjamin's 'authority of the object') is here replaced by the rhetoric of the signifier, as it were. Natural authority and necessity is replaced by rhetorical and politic manoeuvrings in the quest of power, the power and authority invested in choice. The being of the characters of Mariane and Valère is no longer a given at all; their rhetorical manoeuvrings are the pleasurable counters in a game of *self-construction*. Their identities, if indeed they have any such, are artificial, attained through play, through theatre, through the pursuit of pleasure. Such pleasure is, moreover, related to power.

Perhaps the most consistent piece of such acting is in Wycherley's *The Country Wife*. Horner allows it to be thought that he is impotent; like Antony in Dryden's *All for Love*, he has been 'unmanned'. In fact, at a period when it had become conventional for women, rather than boys, to act the parts of women on stage, here, in Horner, we have a harkening back to the Shakespearean stage, almost, as Horner becomes, in the eyes of Jasper Fidget and others, to all intents and purposes a man lacking a man's part, but playing a woman's. The authoritarian structures of such a convention are now laid bare, however. By using the pretence that he is a eunuch, and by pretending to hate women, Horner gains more intimate access to the position of women, and thus demonstrates a greater sexual potency or power. As 'woman', he can unashamedly work himself into the 'parts' of women, and into their private parts as well. Another way of approaching this particular disguise or role-play is to examine it on the grounds of gender ambiguity. If Horner is a 'man', but devoid of testicles, then in what sense is he still a 'man' at all. The biological boundary between genders comes into question here.

It has been argued (possibly erroneously) that the French Salon, especially at its inception by Catherine de Vivonne at the Hôtel Pisani and its quasi-institutionalisation at the Hôtel de Rambouillet, contributed to the refinement and delicacy of French manners in the late seventeenth century.[41] Rapin was to speak deprecatingly of the power and social influence thus gained by women in the effeminisation of society. An increased attention to woman was also being paid in England, in the predominantly male milieu of the coffee-houses. This is not to say that in England women began to become liberated in any real terms from their social shackles; but the question of gender-specifics was being more openly addressed (by men), perhaps as a result of fear at the tacit authority of woman, perhaps as a genuine attempt at discovering wherein lie gender-specifics. Steele, for instance, argued for women to be more active, exercising their bodies as men did. This very attention to the female as a carnal body, and not as either idealised spirit, angel or as equally idealised genitalia, was in some ways an advance:

> I am apt to believe there are some parents imagine their daughters will be accomplished enough, if nothing interrupts their growth, or their shape. According to this method of education, I could name you twenty families, where all the girls hear of, in this life, is, that it is time to rise and come to dinner, as if they were so insignificant as to be wholly provided for when they are fed and clothed.
>
> It is with great indignation that I see such crowds of the female world lost to human society.[42]

In this kind of thinking, there is perhaps at work a desire to defuse the threat of woman to male society; the demand for exercise on the part of women is a desire to make them hygienically conformative with healthy manhood. Similarly, among the fops of the coffee-house society at least, there is an approach of the male towards an idealised ornamental femininity. In fashions, and in the presentation of the self as an ornamental image of the self (through the mirror), there is a growing aestheticisation of the male body as well as of the female; and this contributes to their growing indistinction. If the self is conceived and constructed through the mirror, then it exists as a kind of primal work of art, framed and hanging as a portrait on the wall or on the washstand. In this conception of male and female there is no great gender differentiations, at least in principle, for both sexes are composed entirely of pigment and paint.

Rochester attended to the body of woman in a more intimate and specific way in his writings; but he seemed to conceive of woman as a mere manifestation of genitalia (rather similar to his conception of men, in fact):

> But whilst her busy hand would glide that part
> Which should convey my soul up to her heart,
> In liquid raptures I dissolve all o'er,
> Melt into sperm, and spend at every pore.
> A touch from any part of her had done't:
> Her hand, her foot, her very look's a cunt.[43]

This, apart from being a specific reduction of the materiality

of woman to its symbolic realisation as mere genitalia, serves
also a function in a wider strategy in Rochester's writing
of the human body. More and more, the body is almost
dematerialised in fact, as it is made to appear almost indistinct
from its environment. In *Sodom*, for instance, we hear of
women who use any material object that comes to hand as
a dildo. One such woman has a passion for dogs, and once
tried to have intercourse with a horse, but the horse proved
to be too faithful to its mare. Apart from being a titillating
example of bestiality, this also serves quite seriously to erode
the boundary between the human and the non-human
environment. If all human bodies, both male and female, are
seen in such a way, as empty vessels awaiting interaction
with an environment, then the question arises as to where
the human body stops and where the environment begins.
The soldiers in Bolloximian's army, in *Sodom*, are vessels
just as much as the women, for their whole sexual activity
seems to consist of buggery. These people, then, are rather
like the empty signs of the name, such as 'Iphigénie', which
I indicated in Racine; they are mere signifiers, if you will,
who attain their signification through an act of coition with
an environment which can be as inhuman as you please. Not
only gender-specifics but also human specificity, according to
this, is nothing more or less than a sociological construction.
Sexuality is not given; humanity is not even given. Rather,
such classifications are constructed through our existential
activities, through our social 'actings'.

What this amounts to saying, and what both Hobbes and
Rochester suggest, though in different ways, is that there is
in fact no such thing as a given nature; there is no 'nature'
apart from its rhetorical, and historically enacted, construction. Such constructions are made in the pursuit of power
or pleasure. All that is left, now that an 'originary' nature is
discredited, is a series of pragmatic interpretations. These
interpretations, however, are in no way derivative, for there
is no original with respect to which they can be regarded as
secondary.

The very word 'original', of course, undergoes some semantic change at this time. Whereas it meant 'with reference
to an anterior origin', and thus 'old-fashioned', it now begins

to echo with its more contemporary meanings of 'new', 'novel', 'a departure from the norms of the past'. In Congreve's *Way of the World*, there is an interchange which neatly balances both these meanings. Mirabell begins a description of Sir Wilfull Witwoud, and Fainall interrupts, as Witwoud himself enters:

> *Fainall:*   If you have a mind to finish his picture, you have an opportunity to do it at full length. Behold the original.[44]

Fainall, foppishly or bizarrely dressed, enters; he is both the 'original' from which Mirabell's description derives its existence, and also an 'original' in the sense of an odd-ball, weird and bizarre, a Boileauesque 'bizarre portrait'. The word here hovers between its meanings as 'model' (itself an ambiguous word) and 'bizarre'. But the important point here is that Witwoud's actual appearance on stage is no more authoritative a presence than Mirabell's description; for Witwoud himself is merely 'modelling' himself, acting a part, performing an interpretation, as it were, of himself.

With this conflict of interpretations as a vital principle of the comic theatre, it is not surprising that innuendo, *double-entendre*, ambiguity and pun all generate the condition of much of the comedy. The pun is a more radical development of the stutter. When one stutters in speech, a determinate final meaning for the pending utterance is deferred; one is in a state of uncertainty about the meaning of the message for it is not completed. The pun, while giving a complete word, nonetheless does not allow for any rest in a final and determinate single meaning. It keeps us, therefore, entirely in the realm of the linguistic, more precisely the written, and refuses to make the translation between language and singular nature which is so important to tragedy. In the tragedies of indeterminacy which I have discussed, the indeterminacy finally does manage to refer us to nature, a nature which either becomes clearly defined, as in Corneille, or remains surrealistically shimmering, as in Racine. In the comedy of indeterminacy, however, the indeterminacy exists entirely at the level of the language itself; for the pun to work, the final translation of the word into some referent must always be resisted and deferred. When we do make such a translation, the pun is no longer a pun at all, for one meaning out of two possibles has been accepted and the other rejected; the pun-word thus becomes determined into singularity of meaning, as with any other nominalistic vocabulary.

Perhaps the most famous such *double-entendre* in Restoration comedy occurs in Wycherley's *Country Wife*, where there is extensive play on the word 'china'. Horner and Lady Fidget disappear into a locked room in order to examine Horner's 'china'. As they reappear, Lady Fidget says:

Lady Fidget:	And I have been toiling and moiling for the prettiest piece of china, my dear.
Horner:	Nay, she has been too hard for me, do what I could.
Mrs Squeamish:	Oh, Lord, I'll have some china too. Good Mr Horner, don't think to give other people china, and me none; come in with me too.
Horner:	Upon my honour, I have none left now.
Mrs Squeamish:	Nay, nay, I have known you deny your china before now, but you shan't put me off so. Come.
Horner:	This lady had the last there.
Lady Fidget:	Yes indeed, madam, to my certain knowledge, he has no more left.
Mrs Squeamish:	O, but it may be he may have some you could not find.
Lady Fidget:	What, d'ye think if he had any left, I would not have had it too? for we women of quality never think we have china enough.
Horner:	Do not take it ill, I cannot make china for you all. [45]

It is important to note that, despite the great temptation to translate the word 'china' into the referent 'semen' here, Lady Fidget has indeed appeared carrying a piece of china. The word refers us, but indeterminately, to both the piece of china and also to Horner's sexual capacities. In order for the play to work at this point, both meanings must be retained. There is no originary referent in nature to which we are directly referred here.[46] Horner, or rather the body of Horner, is of course a kind of concretised carnal pun in itself, with its indeterminate gender. The body itself becomes an indeterminate sign in many of these plays of acting and disguising, and as such it becomes ripe for play, for the playing and pleasure which closely resembles the linguistic pun.

Play in Plain Style

Molière's *Le Misanthrope* is a play which satirises the very notion of a 'plain style', and is thereby testimony to what I am calling here the impossibility of authenticity. In *Le Misanthrope*, it becomes clear that 'plain speaking' or 'plain dealing' is in fact impossible and self-contradictory. Alceste demands some kind of 'tragic' relation to nature; like Cléante in *Tartuffe*, he has a belief in some essential nature which is to be found, appropriately enough, in the source of the blood, in the heart, which then becomes understood as the locus of sincerity:

> *Alceste:*   Je veux que l'on soit homme, et qu'en toute rencontre
> Le fond de notre cœur dans nos discours se montre,
> Que ce soit lui qui parle, et que nos sentiments
> Ne se masquent jamais sous de vains compliments.[47]

Like a latter-day Sidney, who wants to follow the muse's advice to 'look in thy heart, and write', or a Herbert who believes that with God in his heart any writings are guaranteed authenticity and truth if only they come sincerely from the heart, Alceste here suggests that the way to truth is clear and easy: all he need do is to reveal his heart in his speech. In many interpretations and productions of the play, of course, the part of Alceste has been mediated as precisely such a 'tragic' character; but such a view of Alceste misses the essential point that this kind of 'tragic' view of life is, according to the tenets of this play, inherently incongruous, necessarily a pose (and hence self-contradictory, not genuine at all). Philinte tries to persuade Alceste of the social inviability of 'plain speaking', in terms of decorum. But the play demonstrates a much more fundamental inviability of plain dealing, and shows it to be, in fact and in theory, socially impossible.

Alceste rails against the poetry of Oreste, claiming that poetry should be 'significant' in a very specific way: it should constitute a referential revelation of an essential nature instead of being simply a play of words, a play of signifiers in the manner of the sixteenth-century *rhétoriqueurs*, such as Octovien de Saint-Gelays or Jean Molinet.[48] The whole dichotomy between the tragic and comic views of life is summed up in terms of the conflict between referentiality and 'pure' poetry, when Alceste comments on Oreste's sonnet:

> *Alceste:*   Ce style figuré, dont on fait vanité
> Sort du bon caractère et de la vérité,
> Ce n'est que jeu de mots, qu'affectation pure,
> Et ce n'est point ainsi que parle la nature.
> (lines 385–8)

More and more clearly, Alceste begins to adopt the *role* of plain speaker; the desire for plain speaking becomes the merest pretence of plain speaking. But he also begins to discover himself as a rhetorical poet of sorts; he is in the Shandean position whereby the more plainly he speaks, the more his statements seem to be at odds with his sentiments.

He confronts Celimène, whom he supposedly loves, and tells her that unless she make a plain statement of love for him, they must separate. It is here that the play offers one precise locus in its demonstration of the theoretical impossibility of authenticity in speaking. A plain statement of Celimène's love for Alceste would, in ideal terms, demand that she never in fact speak again, that she never allow the possibility that the present statement of love be controverted or even modified at any other moment. Plain speaking demands that a local, present statement operate as a transcendent utterance, standing as a revelation of an eternally unchanging essential nature. Alceste's request for sincerity goes hand-in-hand with his desire for individuation and singularity; and the individuation he demands is one in which an individual becomes an allegorical manifestation of her or his essential self, forever fixed and abstract. He complains, for instance, to Celimène that she receives too many suitors for his liking:

Celimène: Mais de tout l'univers vous devenez jaloux.
Alceste: C'est que tout l'univers est bien reçu de vous.
Celimène: C'est ce qui doit rasseoir votre âme effarouchée,
              Puisque ma complaisance est sur tous épanchée:
              Et vous auriez plus lieu de vous en offenser,
              Si vous me la voyiez sur un seul ramasser.
Alceste: Mais moi, que vous blâmez de trop de jalousie,
              Qu'ai-je de plus qu'eux tous, madame, je vous prie?
Celimène: Le bonheur de savoir que vous êtes aimé.
Alceste: Et quel lieu de le croire, à mon cœur enflammé?
Celimène: Je pense qu'ayant pris le soin de vous le dire,
              Un aveu de la sorte a de quoi vous suffire.
Alceste: Mais qui m'assurera que, dans le même instant,
              Vous n'en disiez peut-être aux autres tout autant?

                                        (lines 495–508)

The problem here is that, even when she has made her
'sincere' or 'plain' statement of love, Alceste realises that it
is a statement which is always subject to subsequent deformation or contravention. At another time and place she
may still feel the same, but it is not certain; another set of
circumstances might allow her to say the same thing to
another person, or might allow her to change her mind,
change her heart, as it were. Alceste's demand here is seen
as a logical absurdity or impossibility, for spoken discourse
is attached to its historical location in some way, and what
he demands is a kind of transcendent or transhistorical word
which will be a binding utterance for all time and in every
situation. Even when she makes a 'plain' statement, Celimène
is open to the charge of not speaking plainly enough, of not
telling the eternal truth and revealing the essential nature of
her heart.

Celimène sees the difficulties enjoined here, in making
statements which are not plain enough for Alceste, though
she could not make them any plainer, even if she wanted to
(and her statement of love is, in fact, ambiguous; she does
encourage her other suitors). She indicates the paradox within
which Alceste finds himself when he claims that his love is
without parallel or precedent, and she retorts:

Celimène: En effet, la méthode en est toute nouvelle,
              Car vous aimez les gens pour leur faire querelle;

Ce n'est qu'en mots fâcheux qu'éclate votre ardeur,
Et l'on n'a vu jamais un amour si grondeur.
                                            (lines 525–8)

The more he professes his love, the more Alceste's words
and actions become incongruous with such love; the more
he loves, the more he says he dislikes, in fact. His plain style
leads him into straightforward falsehood. This is further
elaborated by Éliante, who points out that feigning is integral
to poetry, to love and therefore to loving social communication. Alceste continues to use the words of a scold in
'plainly' speaking his love. Communication, or direct communication between two essential individuated selves such as
Alceste would have it here, is shown to be no longer possible.
Alceste's real problem turns out to be precisely related to
this. Having lost contact, in comedy, with an essential nature,
the self is now, in a sense, always out of step with itself and
with its own nature. The nature of the self can never be
present to the consciousness of the self, but instead has
always moved on whenever the consciousness tries to focus
itself upon the self. Self-consciousness, which is a result of
such a loss of integrated contact with the essential nature,
brings about a radical split in the self. The individual, conscious of her or himself *as* individual, is always caught in
the paradox of being unable to locate precisely the distinct
individuality which constitutes the self. Celimène says of
Alceste:

Celimène: L'honneur de contredire a pour lui tant de charmes,
              Qu'il prend contre lui-même assez souvent les armes;
              Et ses vrais sentiments sont combattus par lui,
              Aussitôt qu'il les voit dans la bouche d'autrui.
                                            (lines 677–80)

The problem, then, is one of self-distinction and individuation. As soon as possible corroboration of one's 'plain
statement' is achieved, that is, as soon as it is accepted as
'true' by someone who agrees with it, then it is tantamount
to having that other person repeat the plain statement. But
the plain statement which comes from the heart is a marker
of the essential nature of the self; if someone else repeats,

agrees with, or 'imitates' that statement, the very rehearsal of it leads to the deindividuation of the former self. The essential nature of the individual and distinct self or heart becomes, according to this, the essential nature of someone else, as soon as direct communication takes place, but this contradicts the fundamental principle of distinctive and subjective authenticity. 'Plain speaking' is an oxymoronic contradiction in terms. The only real possible 'plain speech' is silence, a refusal of speech entirely; and Alceste's exile at the end of the play is entirely in accord with this: it is an imposed exile from society, from any need to communicate whatever: a 'comic death-scene' of sorts.

Towards the close of the play, when Celimène finds herself in the position of having to choose between two suitors, Oreste and Alceste, her choice is a choice between two equally rhetorical styles, two 'representations' or 'interpretations' of the selves of the characters involved; it is not at all a choice between two essences or realities. She can choose the 'poetic and metaphorical' or 'figurative' style of Oreste on the one hand, or she may opt for the 'plain style' of Alceste on the other. The plain style is still a style and has its own kinds of figuration. Neither style has any greater degree of authenticity or natural authority than the other; both are merely competing discursive practices, competing for rival interpretations or constructions of 'reality'. In fact, in the Molièresque world of comedy, there is no real choice, since the plain style has been shown itself to be simply a specific kind of poetical style, involving Alceste in subterfuges and in protestations of hatred when he 'feels' love and so on. The plain style, as embodied in Alceste, necessitates a refusal of social linguistic intercourse, refuses, in fact, the possibility of communication, and hence the self-imposed exile at the end is quite logical, and even necessary. Alceste has been in some state of exile, misunderstood by the other characters in the play, for the whole duration of the comedy. The plain style itself can lead to the greatest incomprehensions.

Celimène comments on the validity of inconstancy (what we might be tempted to call inauthenticity, or at least double dealing), and on the validity of a purely relative activity of judgement to Arsinoé:

Celimène: Madame, on peut, je crois, louer et blâmer tout;
Et chacun a raison, suivant l'âge ou le goût.
Il est une saison pour la galanterie,
Il est une aussi propre a la pruderie.

(lines 975–8)

This echoes Ecclesiastes 3, when the preacher remarks that 'To every thing there is a season, and a time to every purpose under the heaven'.[49] In the Molière play the time is determined by the fashion of the age or of the hour. All things change (like Racinian altars) dependent upon their time, place and milieu; and here this location is understood to be dependent upon the position from which they are interpreted, and the whimsical fashion of such a position.

The passage I quoted earlier, from Congreve's *The Way of the World*, in which poetry is literally tied up with fashion, used as curlers for hair, is also relevant at this point. For what determines the authority of writings or of rhetorical styles in these comedies, what decides between one 'interpretative construction' of reality and another (between one fiction and another) is, quite simply, fashion. Whichever poem ties up Mrs Millamant's hair in the fashion which is most 'up to the minute' becomes valorised as the authoritative statement, and thus dictates, entirely pragmatically, fashion, taste and belief. This pragmatic mode of authority can be seen as a purely expedient mode of satisfying purely subjective whim. In Vanbrugh's *Provoked Wife*, for instance, there arises a conflict of interpretations of the concept of 'good'. The meaning of the word, and even the word itself, slips into its opposite, 'evil', purely in accordance with the whims of the present thoughts of Lady Brute:

Belinda: Ay, but you know we must return good for evil.
Lady Brute: That may be a mistake in the translation.[50]

Without some kind of secure source or origin of authority, without, as Benjamin would have it, the 'authority of the object' or the authenticity of an essential nature, such rhetorical manipulation as this becomes possible.[51] Questions of different authorities now become more radically involved with the conflict of critical interpretations and hermeneutics.

The quarrels of the 'ancients' and 'moderns', in writings

such as Perrault's *Parallèles des Anciens et des Modernes* (1688), Temple's *Essay upon the Ancient and Modern Learning* (1690) and Wotton's *Reflections upon Ancient and Modern Learning* (1694), has to do precisely with the conflict between critical interpretations. Once God and nature as a source of authentication of authorities disappear, then what is left is either tradition (a kind of intertextual authority) or the authority of the present 'individual talent' struggling both with and also against such a tradition. Some attempts to rediscover authenticity were made in the production of dictionaries; but again, these were always interpretative texts themselves. When Swift came to join in the ancient and modern controversy, all he could do, finally, was write a battle between texts, a *Battle of the Books*.

The stage was set, then, for the struggle of authority which was much later to be posed as a fundamental philosophical question by Humpty-Dumpty, in another text where the reflexive mirror plays a huge role, Lewis Carroll's *Through the Looking-Glass*:

> 'When *I* use a word', Humpty Dumpty said in rather a scornful tone, 'it means just what I choose it to mean—neither more nor less.'
> 'The question is', said Alice, 'whether you *can* make words mean different things.'
> 'The question is', said Humpty Dumpty, 'which is to be master—that's all.'[52]

PART III
Novel Authorities

Chapter 7

Enthusiastic Carnal Knowledge

Cette unité logique de moi-même, ce n'est pas quelque chose. C'est une forme; je n'existe que par le contenu. Mais où est ma vraie nature? Pour la nature des choses, encore qu'elle se rappelle durement à nous et nous tient serré, encore faut-il la chercher. Tout ce qui se montre est faux. ... Le Moi psychologique n'est donc pas la personne; et il n'y a aucune vertu, même intellectuelle, dans cette unité qui reçoit tout. Aussi personne ne vit selon la psychologie, excepté les fous, qui seuls se croient absolument eux-mêmes.

(Alain, 'Que suis-je?', *Études*)

Jusqu'au début du XIXe siècle ... les fous restent des monstres—c'est-à-dire des êtres ou des choses qui valent d'être montrés.

(Foucault, *Folie et déraison*)

Media Studies

At the threshold of the eighteenth century the understanding of authority has undergone a significant transition. An authoritative act is coming to be thought of as an act of interventionist mediation or pragmatic interpretation of an origin or nature which has been lost. At least two modes of authority, ancient and modern, are now available and in conflict with each other. The 'ancient' demands conformity in a writer to the authority of tradition or precedent; the 'modern' demands spontaneity or innovation. In both cases, indeterminacy is important: the eighteenth-century author is always *in medias res*. The two positions can be aligned closely with the opposition Rorty makes between metaphysicians and intellectuals in philosophy.[1] The metaphysician starts from doubt and scepticism, but only in order to resolve such doubt and replace it with certitude. In this respect the metaphysician is in the position of the archetypal Cornelian hero, Descartes, in whom doubt is a method of guaranteeing a hubristic self-assurance. A self-centredness, prioritising the subjective individual, is integral to the Rortean metaphysician, then. Intellectuals, on the other hand, are characterised by Rorty as sceptics whose doubt never allows them to rest in a final 'final vocabulary', never to reach the position where there are no more questions to be asked. Intellectuals work to generate more questions rather than absolute and guaranteed answers. This more closely resembles the pragmatic mask-changing of comedy. The intellectual, then, rather like the 'modern' authority, not only starts in but also remains in a position of indeterminacy, endlessness.

In contradistinction to Descartes, Pascal can be considered as a kind of representative of the Rortean intellectual position. For Pascal, the human body was caught very much in the midst of nature, but in indeterminate form: 'Car enfin qu'est-ce que l'homme dans la nature? Un néant à l'égard de l'infini, un tout à l'égard du néant, un milieu entre rien et tout, infiniment éloigné de comprendre les extrêmes'.[2] According to this intellectual mode of thought, the human consciousness can never be located as an authenticating point of reference for understanding the world; that consciousness is always in an indeterminate position, always *in medias res*, always relative. The implication of this, which is worked out fully in Swift's *Gulliver's Travels*, is that the present space which is the locus of the human body becomes unavailable as an objective entity: there is no fixed, stable or absolute such space. Further, it is no easier to locate the present temporal moment as any kind of 'originating' or authenticating force in terms of authority. The question of 'originality' itself, not to mention that of sincerity, becomes central. The debate focuses on the status of the human body or consciousness itself: can the human consciousness be whole, unified, 'present' to itself?

Evil Optimism: The Denial of the Historical Body

In 1757 Johnson reviewed Soame Jenyns's *A Free Inquiry into the Nature and Origin of Evil*, piercing the complacent Optimism which had permeated not only Jenyns's work but also some of the poetry of the earlier eighteenth century. The Optimistic thought of Jenyns, or of Pope (in the 'Essay on Man'), depended on ideas of nature which were untenable in 1757 by thinkers such as Johnson. The philosophical position of Optimism depends on a notion of nature as a spatial plenum and history as a consequential continuum; but the eighteenth century began to think about these things differently and, most importantly, to regard the very presence of the human body and consciousness itself as a radical interruption in the state of nature from which it was, consequently, in exile. The human became thought of as discontinuous with nature, and the human body was identified as that locus of experience marked by a series of interruptions into the plenum of nature or the world.

Leibnizian Optimism, fairly accurately summed up in the trite phrase 'all is for the best in the best of all possible worlds', is tenable only in a philosophy which remains 'in the boudoir', like that of Descartes or Sade, and which refuses to countenance empirical or historical realities. Taken to its logical limits, the Leibnizian position leads to the arguments of Mandeville, who could suggest that local vice was an absolute necessity to universal virtue, and thus that the evil in the world was not only to be condoned but also encouraged, at a local level. In Willey's reading, Mandeville's position is taken to be an audacious one:

> Many had urged that God and Nature knew how to evoke good from ill, to turn private vice to public advantage, but the orthodox view (as stated by Butler) was—Woe unto him through whom the scandal cometh! We must not put too great a strain upon the moral refineries of Providence; and the world would be an even better place without any vice at all, than it is with vice being constantly turned, by divine alchemy, into good. Mandeville alone had the audacity to declare that the refinery *needed* the raw material: that the public benefits existed not in spite of, but because of, the private vices.[3]

Not everyone pushed Leibniz to such extremes. More typical is the response of Voltaire, who could accept the position with some reservations in the 1720s, but who made an abrupt turn-about on the morning of Sunday 1 November 1755, when the Lisbon earthquake shook everyone's determined Optimistic ignorance of local disasters. This was a movement of the earth which easily rivalled in importance the movement instigated by the new Copernican astronomy 200 years previously.

The Optimism of the Pope who wrote that 'all must full or not coherent be'[4] in the world, elaborating the notion of the plenitudinous 'chain of being', was already under philosophical attack in England in the late seventeenth century. When Locke produced his *Essay Concerning Human Understanding* in 1689–90, the belief in a whole and unified scale of natural being became less tenable, for Locke conceived here of the possibility of the vacuous, empty and discordant or incoherent space:

> But not to go so far as beyond the utmost bounds of body in the universe, nor appeal to God's omnipotency to find a vacuum, the motion of bodies that are in our view and neighbourhood seems to me plainly to evince it. For I desire anyone so to divide a solid body, of any dimension he pleases, as to make it possible for the solid parts to move up and down freely every way within the bounds of the superficies, if there be not left in it a void space as big as the least part into which he has divided the said solid body. And let this void space be as little as it will, it destroys the hypothesis of plenitude.[5]

Newton's thought, in the *Opticks* of 1704 tended in this same direction:

> Between the parts of opake and colour'd Bodies are many Spaces, either empty, or replenish'd with Mediums of other Densities; as Water between the tingling Corpuscles wherewith any Liquor is impregnated, Air between the aqueous Globules that constitute Clouds or Mists; and for the most part Spaces void of both Air and Water, but yet perhaps not wholly void of all Substance, between the parts of hard Bodies.[6]

Voltaire understood Newton in this respect, and commented wittily on the discrepancy of thought between England and France at this time. In the fourteenth of his *Lettres Phi-*

losophiques, he wrote: 'Un Français qui arrive à Londres trouve les choses bien changées en Philosophie comme dans tout le reste. Il a laissé le monde plein; il le trouve vide.'[7] The impetus of such thought is orientated towards an accept-ance of radical spatial discontinuity. As with Donne's 'flea', Pascal's 'cheese-mite', Swift's Gulliver, the determinant stan-dards of measurement and objectivity become relativised: there is a universe within the flea, or within the Blakean 'Bird that cuts the airy way' as well as outside the 'senses five' of the human.[8]

Pope's defence of Optimism, in the 'Essay on Man' is itself riddled with problematic lacunae; even while arguing for a plenitudinous and coherent world, he posits a gap, a dis-continuity, between human and beast:

> How Instinct varies in the grov'ling swine,
> Compar'd, half-reas'ning elephant, with thine:
> 'Twixt that, and Reason, what a nice barrier;
> For ever sep'rate, yet for ever near![9]

A more strict reading of the Essay would perhaps show that the argument suggests a striving towards an unattainable Optimism rather than a complacent defence of it, for Pope too is aware of these and similar discontinuities.

Some writers, however, such as Jenyns, want to retain the belief in the plenum in support of Optimism. For con-servative thought, such Optimism is desirable in that it sanc-tions belief in pre-established or naturally authorised essential and hierarchical social order. But Johnson's review of Jenyns stringently opposes such notions, primarily by questioning the plenitudinous state of nature:

> It does not appear even to the imagination, that of three orders of being, the first and the third receive any advantage from the imperfection of the second, or that indeed they may not equally exist, though the second had never been, or should cease to be

and Johnson continues:

> The scale of existence from infinity to nothing, cannot possibly have being. The highest being not infinite must be, as has often been observed, at an infinite distance below infinity. ... Between the lowest

positive existence and nothing, wherever we suppose positive existence
to cease, is another chasm infinitely deep; where there is room again
for endless orders of subordinate nature, continued for ever and for
ever and yet infinitely superior to non-existence.[10]

Johnson goes on to attack the position on moral grounds.
Here, it is important to recall the enormous popularity of
Milton's *Paradise Lost*, attested to by Addison's *Spectator*
essays, for the eighteenth century. Johnson's review of
Jenyns relates to this poem, and satirises the position of
Optimism as a Satanic one. He writes: 'Having thus dis-
patched the consideration of particular evils, he comes at last
to a general reason for which *evil* may be said to be *our
good*.'[11] This should recall to mind not only a whole body
of self-deceivers in rhetoric from Shakespeare's Duke Senior
through to Vanbrugh's Lady Brute, all adept at translating
evil into good; it also alludes directly to Milton's Satan, who
in Book IV of *Paradise Lost* utters precisely the words 'Evil,
be thou my Good'. Optimism, accordingly, becomes for
Johnson an evil philosophy, and Optimists become agents
of deception, a deception whose efficacy depends upon a
denial or ignorance of historical experience and the historical
body. Optimists bring to accident or local evil a 'mind not
to be chang'd by Place or Time',[12] like Milton's Satan, like
Descartes, or like 'metaphysical' subscribers to the notion of
self-presence.

The possibility of a different tradition exists, at least by
implication, and by fact from the empiricism stemming from
Bacon; and it is in this, more 'intellectual' tradition that
Newton should be placed. Where Optimism implies passive
quietism and complacent acceptance of the 'state of nature',
a scientist such as Newton works by making a series of
experimental 'interventions' of her or his own consciousness
into the 'natural' environment outside that consciousness,
and even outside that material and physical or historical
body. Here, philosophy becomes active, and the thinker tries
to place or locate her or his body within some plot or scheme
or plan of nature. Such a problematic informs not only
science but also, later, Romantic poetry, where the poet's
body or consciousness becomes an intervention, a rupture
or medium in and through which authority authenticates and

validates itself. The human becomes, then, what Heidegger was later to call a 'clearing', coming into Being discontinuously and representing a radical interruption into the space of the world.

Literary History: Tradition, Modernity, the Body

The problem of spatial discontinuity affects the understanding of time and history as well, and this articulated itself in the form of the debate between ancients and moderns, between tradition and individual talents. 'Originality' was the issue, but the word undergoes a change of meaning. Where it used to mean 'with reference to an origin', it begins to be understood as 'novel'; in both cases it is invoked in the name of authenticity or authority. The atavistic search for a tradition among the 'ancients' (theorised, in different forms, by Bate and more generally by Bloom) is, once more, a nostalgic quest for a pure source of natural authority or truth. But how 'ancient' were the models to be: Pope translates Homer but edits Shakespeare and imitates a whole series of much more recent writers, for instance. The difference between ancients and moderns is not a simple one of chronology. For the 'ancients', authority lay in the corpus of tradition, an external source for their present writings; for the 'moderns', it lay instead in the subject herself or himself, in the present body and its immediate 'experience'.

Both modes have their problems. The ancients had to invent, more or less arbitrarily, a tradition which they claimed to be absolute (like Eliot, Leavis and Bloom in our own century); the moderns had to be adept at 'writing to the minute', and thus faced what Ryle, in our own time, has called 'the systematic elusiveness of "I"'. For the ancients, true authenticating and authorising nature lay, like a palimpset under the writings of the past; for the moderns, it lay under the consciousness of the present body writing.[13]

The problem of 'writing to the minute' informs Swift's *Tale of a Tub*, where the author claims total authority, the authority which comes from being the (as yet) latest unquestioned medium upon nature as it is immediately experienced: 'But I here think fit to lay hold on that great and honourable privilege of being the last writer. I claim an absolute authority in right, as the freshest modern, which gives me a despotic power over all authors before me.'[14] This occurs in Section V; does it thereby invalidate the previous four sections? Is this tale a Fishian self-consuming artifact, like Robbe-Grillet's *Les gommes* proceeding under self-erasure? The notion of truth in this kind of writing cedes place to mere certainty, the certainty of the immediate moment: 'I profess to your highness, in the integrity of my heart, that what I am going to say is literally true this minute I am writing: what revolutions may happen before it shall be ready for your perusal, I can by no means warrant.'[15] This modern, open to temporal discontinuity, can never generate self-identity or self-presence; unlike Proust, say, he cannot construct an identity between two disparate, discontinuous temporal moments. It is for this reason that the author must remain anonymous; anonymity thus becomes an operational principle in the determination of authority in this modernist writing: the author has no namable, individual, authority or 'title'.

Where Shakespeare started from the fact of blood in his search for authority, Swift started from that of the breath; but he conflates that breath with air, wind and spirit, as in the *Tale*, where he utterly materialises the human body:

> For whether you please to call the *forma informans* of man, by the name of *spiritus, animus, afflatus,* or *anima*; what are all these but several appellations for wind, which is the ruling element in every compound, and into which they all resolve upon their corruption? Farther, what is life itself, but as it is commonly called, the breath of the nostrils?[16]

Prefiguring Beckett's *Foirades*, Swift's body is materialised as a machine for producing belches and farts; here lies the fundamental source of authority for this 'modern'. The mediating body, for Swift, manufactures incoherent words or noises on bad breath. The Aeolists 'affirm the gift of BELCHING to be the noblest act of a rational creature',[17] and their modernist 'texts' comprise the gripings and physical bodily distortions caused by wind, with its attendant noises.

The belief in an internal, 'modernist' source of authority, according to this, will discover that the only thing within the human body is breath; but such breath is ambiguous. It may be, as a founding principle of the 'spiritual' life, sacred; it may equally be nothing more than wind, stressing the material bestiality of the human body and its liability to corruption. Here, then, is the counter to Optimism. It accepts the indeterminacy of the 'breath' which constitutes human life, the historical and material body, but is disturbed by it. It also accepts both spatial and historical discontinuity, thus losing its bearings on an originary source of authority; authority is replaced by enthusiastic mediation. While accepting the need for intellection and rationality, it points out that history in the form of the corrupting, discontinuous and vacuous human body and breath, cannot be ignored.

The metaphysical rationalism of Descartes, divorced from historical or empirical sense-data, is alluded to satirically at the opening of Swift's Tale. The modern writer: 'had endeavoured to strip himself of as many real prejudices as he could; I say real ones, because, under the notion of prejudices, he knew to what dangerous heights some men have proceeded'.[18] After Locke, the Cartesian ignorance of history is not so tenable. That satire on metaphysics remains right through all Swift's attack on religious 'enthusiasts', as in *The Mechanical Operation of the Spirit*:

> The Practitioners of this famous Art, proceed in general upon the following Fundamental; That, *the Corruption of the Senses is the Generation of the Spirit*: Because the *Senses* in Men are so many Avenues to the Fort of *Reason*, which in this Operation is wholly block'd up. All Endeavours must be therefore used, either to divert, bind up, stupefy, fluster and amuse the *Senses*, or else to justle them out of their Stations; and while they are either absent, or otherwise employ'd or engaged in a Civil War against each other, the Spirit enters and performs its Part.[19]

What Swift and his age seems to fear, in the suppression of consciousness such as Descartes or the 'modern' practised it, was not the unconscious itself so much as the threat of 'madness'; the fear that the spirit might be not a rational god at all but rather a *malin génie*, that Satanic breath which can transform, rhetorically, evil into good. This fear is the anxiety caused by the threat of the loss of self-possession, that 'title to property' or title, here to self-presence or an identifiable proper name. Yet this 'madness' itself can no longer be ignored for the 'intellectual' or modern writer. At some level, the 'madness' of the bestial human body has to be explored, together with the indeterminacy of the discontinuous human consciousness, the anonymity of the human space or 'clearing'. The opposition is set now around the question of the authorial *will* or intention: to what extent is this determined and 'sanitised' by the writer, and to what extent can it remain indeterminate, a matter for 'insane' interpretation?

Chapter 8

Betraying the Text

the Church by the public reading of the book of God preacheth only
as a witness. Now the principal thing required in a witness is fidelity.
(Hooker, *Ecclesiastical Polity*, vol. V)

Her story altered, at first, in the retelling, but finally it settled down,
and after that nobody, neither teller nor listener, would tolerate any
deviation from the hallowed, sacred text. This was when Bilquís knew
that she had become a member of the family; in the sanctification of
her tale lay initiation, kinship, blood. 'The recounting of histories,'
Raza told his wife, 'is for us a rite of blood.'
(Salman Rushdie, *Shame*)

Camera Obscura: The Human's Room

In the eighteenth century the human body began to become
understood as a medium or vehicle of air, the breath itself
being the mark of life; and later, metaphorically, the human
was also the bearer of light in some sense. Some writers
would want to claim that the spirit or air being mediated
through them was in fact the inspirational *Ruach* or, more
romantically, Hegelian historical *Geist*. But if the poet is
merely a medium through whom poetry comes to light or
announces itself, then in what ways could the poet be credited
as an 'authority'? The Romantics themselves were keen to
confuse the bare mediation of pure nature with their own
sympathetic mediation of it;[1] and some degree of attention
to authorial will or 'intention' seemed to be demanded.

The question of validity or authenticity of this intention

brought into play the dominant metaphor of light. Some writers would want to claim their own 'inner light', a light which would reveal the state of nature in clearest and most distinct form; others might claim that all such light is as a fading coal or a pathetic reflection of an exterior light, the world as it revealed itself to sight. Both Locke and Newton advanced models of the human as a sort of camera obscura, a dark *room* or space in the domestic house or 'dwelling' that is the body. But there are vital differences in their conceptions of this 'camera-human', and these differences focus the questions of intention and authority.

Locke posited the notion of the human as a tabula rasa, upon which the pre-existent world impressed itself:

> Let us then suppose the mind to be, as we say, white paper, void of all characters, without any ideas; how comes it to be furnished? Whence comes it by that vast store which the busy and boundless fancy of man has painted on it with an almost endless variety? Whence has it all the materials of reason and knowledge? To this I answer, in one word, from *experience*.[2]

Reflection follows upon such experience for Locke; but this impressive experience as such has priority. Here is a notion of a naïve photography, a belief in the 'innocent' disinterested eye of the camera which simply, as if *im*mediately, represents the real. Dewey's attempts to reconcile nature and experience in the twentieth century revitalise this Lockean position, but with important pragmatic qualifications. The temporal sequentiality of reflection following upon experience is removed in the Deweian formulations, and there is no sensation without reflection. Reflection, in neo-Romantic fashion, is partly constitutive of and responsible for the experience. This is an attempt on Dewey's part to reinstate the importance of real historical contingency; for Dewey was as aware as most other philosophers from Plato to Althusser of the ideology which is to be found in 'experience', an experience understood as prereflective or untheorised. The position underlying Dewey resembles the Newtonian version of the camera.

Newton's description offers an analogy with human consciousness: 'Whenever the Rays which come from all the

Points of any Object meet again in so many points after they have been made to converge by Reflection or Refraction, there they will make a Picture of the Object upon any white Body on which they fall.'[3] Newton was extremely aware of the pragmatic artifice of his experiments: even in this brief citation, light is 'made' to converge by the manipulation of the prism. Light behaves here, the scientist knows, due to the conditions of the experiment. Newton, through his introduction and manipulation of a prism into a small (discontinuous) opening in a wall, makes a series of radical interventions into the otherwise seemingly plenitudinous world of nature. His experiment is a 'criticism' of nature, an intervention into it which concentrates on one abstracted aspect, light; and this 'betrayal' of nature's 'wholeness' makes the light 'betray' or reveal itself in its full colours. Here we have genuine photography, light-writing; Newton's prism is the equivalent of the writer's intervening or informational consciousness; and, like the writer's pen, its movements are determined not entirely by nature itself but to some extent by the pragmatic and ideological concerns of the writer herself or himself. Nature here, and this is the important point, is not available in unmediated form.

In these understandings of the human body as a medium, *in medias res*, we have a philosophical repetition of the discrepancy I outlined in neoclassical French theatre. There, some writers adhered to the belief that language could 'innocently' represent nature, immediately. That tragic, though Optimistic position, gave way to the comic stance in which there was no longer any accessible essential nature but merely mediations or interpretations of a 'nature' which is lost or missing, and such interpretations would themselves be immediately subject to interpretation or mediation, usually by other characters. Such interpretations are always a 'betrayal' of nature, for the interpretative act is a labour of transformation effected by the human mediating consciousness. Further, the mediations are instrumental in the revelation not of nature as such but of the relativities of all such interpretations of nature, of all discourses. The interpretations or mediations—that is, the discourse of this 'comic' language as such—are always rhetorical, and, as de Man puts it, 'Rhetoric radically subverts logic and opens up vertiginous possibilities of referential aberration'.[4] The position is comic in a sense close to Lyotard's conception of 'l'humour':

> L'humour dit: il n'y a pas de point de bonne vue, ni les choses du monde ni les discours ne forment un tableau, ou s'ils le forment, c'est par décision arbitraire du regardeur, prince ou savant. Exhibons cet arbitraire non pour le tourner en dérision, mais pour le saisir infiltré d'une logique, d'un espace, d'un temps qui ne sont pas ceux du tableau représentatif, logique des singularités, espace des voisinages (des infinis), temps des moments. L'humour n'invoque pas une vérité plus universelle que celle des maîtres, il ne lutte même pas au nom de la majorité, en incriminant les maîtres d'être minoritaires, il veut plutôt faire reconnaître ceci: qu'*il n'y a que des minorités*.[5]

This comedy is non-totalising and radically critical or heretical: betrayal and misreading are its modes. The activity of mediation, interpretation, even reading itself, becomes, in such a case, a dialectic between a posited intentionality on the part of a writer and a constructed intentionality on the part of the critic, herself or himself a writer too.

Criticism Is Fundamental to Modernity

Criticism, in England, began to be institutionalised between the period in which Dryden wrote his prefaces and theoretical essays and that in which Johnson wrote his *Lives of the Poets* and *Preface to Shakespeare*. Clearly, there was critical and theoretical writing before this, as in Sidney's *Apology* or Jonson's *Timber*; but criticism as such begins to get under way when an indigenous culture and literature become isolated as its object. During the period of the primary acculturation of criticism, writers, such as Pope and Swift, seemed to fear critical activity; Pope especially feared (mis) interpretation. Writers were considered by Pope as Dunces precisely to the degree to which they lacked a preverbal shadowy 'intention' which was to be realised perfectly by the words of their poems. Dunces, like Philemon, stumbled into sense and meaning, betrayed by demons: 'Some Daemon stole my pen (forgive th'offence)/And once betray'd me into

common sense'.[6] This marks Pope's own fear of being 'possessed' by voices other than his own (including, necessarily,
that of readers and critics or even 'unconscious demons').
More basically, this is an anxiety over the possible loss of
control over his own words, meanings or verbal 'issue'; such
controlled meaning serves to stabilise his own identity. The
linguistic and intentional indeterminacy of Dulness, whose
'random thoughts now meaning chance to find';[7] finding
meanings as a father might adopt a son, was an arbitrariness
which Pope saw as a threat to his own self-stability and
identifiable name or even identifiable style. It indicates a
distrust of readers who might 'find' meanings of which Pope
himself remained unconscious; but this is no less than a fear
of being read critically at all. 'Readings' of Pope, according
to this, are meant to be uncritical rehearsals, on the part
of a now unconscious reader, of Pope's own words and
intentions.

As was the case with Molière's Alceste, however, such a
monologic plain style is a logical abstraction and impossibility: Pope, like Alceste, is always in a dialogue with himself,
if with no one else. Yet Pope tries to deny such dialogue. His
linguistic utterance is supposed to operate as an enactment
or articulation of an essential nature, as a manifestation or
revelation of a truth which pre-exists its articulation. This
nature, truth or originary source, in the poetry, is the authenticating thought, intention or 'voice' of the poet himself. If
the critic is to read this poetry at all, she or he must precisely
occupy the 'intentional space' of Pope as he wrote or (supposedly) spoke. There can be no 'finding', much less constructing, a critical sense or meaning by this reader; interpretation is the purest repetition, rehearsing the authorial
intention, personality and identity of Pope and re-estab-
lishing, at least for the duration of the reading, Pope's own
historical conjuncture. If 'valid' reading is thus carried out,
Pope's identity is assured; there is an identity or at least
complicity between the reader reading the poem and Pope's
self-understanding through its writing. The stability of
Pope's identity, here, is a kind of mental stability, a hygienic
sanity: Pope fears unconscious meanings because they may
contaminate the purity and singularity of his identity as

'sane writer', an identity maintained constantly against the identification of the Dunces who surround and differ from him, with their unconscious dreaming poetry and their sleeping unsure 'intentions'.

Swift shared a similar concern, but responded differently. Pondering criticism in the *Tale*, Swift's author writes:

> The author is informed, that the bookseller has prevailed on several gentlemen to write some explanatory notes; for the goodness of which he is not to answer, having never seen any of them, nor intends it, till they appear in print; when it is not unlikely he may have the pleasure to find twenty meanings which had never entered into his imagination.[8]

Swift was alive to the possibility of a multiplicity of interpretation which becomes constitutive of the 'intention' in a poem. He drew attention to this, in a passage whose irony perhaps bemoans the instabilities of language and sense, but which nonetheless indicates that a multiplicity of readings are sanctioned by the words of a text, independently of a supposedly prelinguistic authorial intention or psychology:

> I do here humbly pose for an experiment, that every prince in Christendom will take seven of the deepest scholars in his dominions, and shut them up close for seven years in seven chambers, with a command to write seven ample commentaries on this comprehensive discourse. I shall venture to affirm, that whatever difference may be found in their several conjectures, they will be all, without the least distortion, manifestly deducible from the text.[9]

A criticism which understands this solely as a jibe at Swift's author for producing a confused text is missing the point and assuming *a priori* that all 'valid' texts are unified and univocal. Swift, here and elsewhere, produces texts which question this assumption of monologicity. Intention is more complex than some present-day critics of Pope and Swift suggest. Swift goes so far as to offer a criticism of the Popean notions from the 'Essay on Criticism', which argued for a monological intentionalist orthodoxy. The return of the critic to the supposed pristine intention of the writer leads to a phenomenological situation in which it is thought possible that a critic can map her or his intentional space upon that of a precedent writer. But Swift addresses this issue in a way which carves an image of Pope as 'modern' writer:

> whatever reader desires to have a through comprehension of an author's thoughts, cannot take a better method, than by putting himself into the circumstances and postures of life, that the writer was in upon every important passage as it flowed from his pen, for this will introduce a parity and strict correspondence of ideas between the reader and the author. Now, to assist the diligent reader in so delicate an affair, as far as brevity will permit, I have recollected, that the shrewdest pieces of this treatise were conceived in bed in a garret; at other times (for a reason best known to myself) I thought fit to sharpen my invention with hunger; and in general, the whole work was begun, continued, and ended, under a long course of physic, and a great want of money.[10]

Swift was clearly uncomfortable with simplistic notions of a critical return 'home' to an originary informing intention through 'sympathetic' reading; if anything, what is suggested here is more like a 'symptomatic' reading. It is perhaps all the more alarming, given Swift's satire here, to see such a position reiterated, in various ways, in contemporary criticism. Hirsch, for instance, argues that:

> The interpreter's primary task is to reproduce in himself the author's 'logic', his attitudes, his cultural givens, in short, his world. Even though the process of verification is highly complex and difficult, the ultimate verificative principle is very simple—the imaginative reconstruction of the speaking subject.[11]

The subject Hirsch attends to is that subject which is supposedly the author's unified self and vocalised intentionality.

Paul de Man, surprisingly, comes rather close in some ways to intentionalist orthodoxy such as this. One example of this is when he discusses his own reading of a brief passage from Proust. In the reading of a scene concerned with the 'dark coolness' of Marcel's room in *Swann's Way*, de Man deconstructs the supposed superiority of metaphor over metonymy. But he goes on to write:

> The deconstruction is not something that we have added to the text but it constituted the text in the first place. A literary text simultaneously asserts and denies the authority of its own rhetorical mode, and by reading the text as we did we were only trying to come closer to being as rigorous a reader as the author had to be in order to write the sentence in the first place.[12]

The final part of this proposition looks extremely like Hirsch's quite serious proposal, and Swift's pre-emptive modest proposal which satirises the entire quasi-phenomenological notion. But de Man's argument is not so simple, for the whole practice of reading here has been instrumental in showing that the supposed 'primary' text is itself always already a deconstruction, and one which, literally, 'prevents' reading: 'Poetic writing is the most advanced and refined mode of deconstruction'. With de Man here, reference to any anterior source of origin, be it the world itself or an authorial consciousness, is modified if not entirely forestalled. There is no 'sympathy' here, for there is nothing prelinguistic to be sympathetic to; rather, there is a Lyotardian *apathy*: 'Seuls n'y perdront pas la tête et le cœur ceux qui sont guéris du pathos théorique, les apathiques'. [13]

The rigours of this 'apathy' allow de Man to make confident statements about the 'truth' of the text; though this truth is perhaps 'une affaire de style', in Lyotard's words. Not entirely different from this is the position of eighteenth-century 'apathetics'. Swift lamented the instability of the language which was supposed to be the medium for truthful propositions; if the language was degenerate, then how could truthful statements be made in an unadulterated form? This metaphor of 'adulteration' is chosen with express purpose. Many Augustans had recourse to classical languages because they were thought of as a primary 'fathering' source for English, which stood in a familial relation of descent from them. But English was a deviation, and as such its 'purity' or consanguinity with its classical forebears was not self-evident. In short, English was a bastard tongue. The use of classical language and precedent as a source is an attempt to secure stability and continuity of identity by transcending history; and this bears a close analogical resemblance to the workings of the nuclear family, as I have outlined that organisation here. The contemporary thrust towards the generation or discovery of etymologies is an attempt to think of history as a continuum and to stabilise the relation between 'parent'-tongue and potentially threatening bastard-tongues. The discovery of a classical root for a given word establishes the authority of the present idiolect through an atavistic appeal to the weight of tradition and to a 'familial' lineage in words which assures them of their purity and transcendent 'identity' of meaning.

If 'intention' can be successfully translated into stable self-evident words (words whose meaning is, as it were, present to their own orthography), then the writer is not only sure of being 'understood' in a specific way (and thus is assured a place in the community of 'sane' people, according to Foucault),[14] but is also, more importantly, safe from interpretation and from criticism. This 'community' of sane people includes only representations (all, supposedly, identical) of the writer. It is as if both 'speaker' and 'hearer' articulated the words simultaneously: a phenomenological correspondence demonstrating the incipient totalitarianism of such a (vocal) authority model.

The attempt to stabilise language in this way would serve, if successful, the corollary purpose of assuring writers of their own self-evident authority and of their own knowable and self-present identity. Authority, and the authorial ownership and control of meaning would become indubitable, for the meaning of the words would be self-evident, spoken as if by the consciousness which 'originally' articulated them. It is not surprising, then, given the concern for stability, that the first really effective copyright act dates from 1709; nor is it surprising that Pope, for instance, exercised this control of meaning to the full. Interpretation and criticism are precluded in a state of affairs where meaning is stable, 'pure' and self-evident; and as such, these critical practices are legislated against, as 'plagiaristic'. The whole theory depends upon the assumption of a self-present intentionality which is prior to linguistic articulation. This is, of course, a reiteration of the concern for authority which affected writers during the entire previous century; only, the question of familial lineage has moved into the analogous territory of linguistic etymology. A writer such as Pope is clearly reactionary as he tries to forestall the modern 'comic', 'pessimistic', 'apathetic' understanding of how language and authority work; for authority is coming to be known as a phenomenon dependent upon the betrayal of a tradition and of a history, and as a mode which works to destroy individuated identity. It is precisely against this that Pope struggles. Swift's attitude is more ambivalent, with the effect that the texts become anonymous (whether we eventually ascribe them to the historical individual, Swift, or not). He was well aware that what he 'meant' by a word in 1697 might not at all match the present reception and understanding of the 'same' word in 1710. He knew, similarly, that what he meant by a word might differ by the time he finished its transcription. In short, he understood that 'he' did not mean; rather, 'language' or texts meant. Language was in a state of entropic decay or degeneration, understood as self-bastardising; Swift both lamented, and made productive use of, this situation.

The entry into public, historical life in the seventeenth-century organisation of domesticity threatened patriarchal authority. Similarly, publication in the eighteenth century presents the paternal author with a threat of betrayal, as interpretation threatens to betray the identifiable authorial will. But publication constitutes an even more fundamental threat: the merest fact of an author's words being *read*, according to this theoretical assumption, is already a plagiaristic imitation of the poet. Thus the individuality of the poet, supposedly marked by guaranteed 'authoritative' identity, is already mitigated as the authorial intention is repeated or rehearsed in the mouth or mind of another, the reader. Just as this destroys the logic of Alceste's 'plain speaking' in Molière, so also it posits a threat to the logic of a 'sympathetic' phenomenological theory of communication. If the intention is to be the poet's, specifically, and identified strictly with her or him, then the poetry must be, in a profound sense, unreadable. Publication on those terms requires the most rigorous copyright control: theoretically, it requires that even the poet may not repeat or rehearse the work, for the intention, by definition, is not iterable. Intentional information is always, by definition, a *hamartia*, always 'missing the mark', even when the reader or interpreter of a text is the consciousness which writes it. If such (mis)reading betrays the writer, always (comically) missing the mark in an interpretative deformation of authorial intention, then the writer is threatened always, on publication, by incomprehension on the part of her or his audience. She or he is threatened with linguistic isolation, which is precisely how Swift, for one, understood the constitution of madness. Madness was the condition of being linguistically out-of-step with an audience or environment; madness, in short, was a corollary of having univocal authorial intention and retaining a belief in the viability of its linguistic control and currency.

Swift's Gulliver ponders a similar issue:

> In my first voyages, while I was young, I was instructed by the oldest mariners, and learned to speak as they did. But I have since found that the sea-yahoos are apt, like the land ones, to become new-fangled in their words; which the latter change every year, insomuch as I remember upon each return to mine own country, their old dialect was so altered that I could hardly understand the new. And I observe, when any yahoo comes from London out of curiosity to visit me at mine own house, we are neither of us able to deliver our conceptions in a manner intelligible to the other.[15]

Language, far from being something which is 'natural' to us, or even something which has a fundamental essential link to 'nature', remains artificial, a ritual with which we must engage if we are to speak at all. There is no natural or authenticating source of authority here. It is a matter, for Gulliver, of adapting conventions which will allow him to master language rather than being himself ruled by it. This is tantamount to suggesting that if we want to speak or understand at all, we must always be in a position where we betray language or 'read against' it; we modify its codifications and intervene in order both to write and to contribute to the ongoing creation of the language system as such. In differing ways, both Humpty Dumpty and Heidegger remarked on the same thing: 'Language speaks. Man speaks only insofar as he artfully complies with language', or 'Man acts as though he were the shaper and master of language, while in fact language remains the master of man'.[16]

Pinter's *Betrayal* offers a demonstration of the point that not only interpretation but even articulation itself, the 'originary' writing, is possible only as an act of betrayal of 'nature'. The characters constantly betray each other in extramarital affairs, and the play consists largely of varied repeated versions or narratives of supposed 'facts'. Such a multiplicity generates a state of indeterminacy, especially in disentangling the 'facts' from the rhetoric which mediates them. One such narrative concerns some event when Jerry perhaps threw up Charlotte when she was a child in someone's kitchen. The story is alluded to on three separate occasions, and is indeterminate even on the first telling. As it gets told, the tale gets betrayed and changed: the 'source' or origin of the tale, its basis in fact, becomes less and less accessible. For the present argument, that source can be understood as an authorial intention; but Pinter shows that such intention is never entirely present to consciousness; and, in its transcription, it is deformed. Moreover, even as it is told, the story changes, as Emma, for instance, commenting on Jerry's version, radically changes his text, betrays it:

> *Jerry:*   Yes, everyone was there that day, standing around, your husband, my wife, all the kids, I remember.
> *Emma:*   What day?
> *Jerry:*   When I threw her up. It was in your kitchen.
> *Emma:*   It was in your kitchen.[17]

It should not escape notice that Emma's commentary is the most faithful rehearsal of Jerry's text. She repeats his words verbatim, but even in that bleakest of plagiarisms, there is a betrayal as she changes the scene of the story. Thanks to the deictic, 'your', this betrayal is effected through the greatest possible fidelity to the original text upon which she comments. Even the most faithful reading of a text, like this, is already its betrayal and an interpretative modification of the text. But the basic point to be made is that even the 'original' text itself is a critical betrayal, a 'missing the mark' or deformation, through narrative, of a history lost to consciousness.

Betraying the Name of the Father

Swift's *Tale* prefigures some contemporary attitudes to interpretation and textual criticism, and an exploration of some of the critical strategies exemplified there will clarify some of the distinctions in modern critical authority. When Peter's father, the author of the will, dies, then Peter is born in Barthesian manner as its creative reader. He is exceptionally creative, and ingenious in the production of meaning from his text. Firstly, for pragmatic reasons of style, the sons need an authorisation in the will for the wearing of shoulder-knots. There is no such explicit authorisation in the will for this; or so it seems. Peter firstly turns to seek out the constituent phonemes of the words 'shoulder-knots', and when that fails he has recourse to searching out the letters. He almost finds them, when he finally makes do with a punning letter 'c' for the 'k' of 'knots'; and thus he finds the words in the text, and an authorisation is rapidly made. The critical practice here may look wild; but the twentieth century has seen some exact counterparts to this methodology.

Starobinski published extracts from Saussure's notebooks, where Saussure had pondered the presence of *les mots sous les mots*. In his extensive examinations of Saturnian verse, Saussure claimed to be able to isolate a basic hypogram for each text. This entailed the uncovering of a secret or taboo name within the text, a name which was disseminated and disguised among the phonemes of each line or segment. One type, for example, is indicated by the line:

Taurasia Cisauna Samnio cepit.
Ceci est un vers *anagrammatique*, contenant complètement le nom de *Scipio* (dans les syllabes *ci + pi + io*, en outre dans le *S* de *Samnio cepit* qui est initial d'un groupe ou presque tout le mot *Scipio* revient[18]

Saussure had to go to some lengths, like Peter, to make the texts subtend the names; but, as even the sceptical Starobinski indicates, the names do turn up with a remarkable degree of accuracy and frequency. In a letter of 14 July 1906, which Starobinski reproduces, Saussure is counting the vowels in many lines of Latin verse to prove their hypogrammatic structure. There is not a world of difference between that and Swift's writer in the *Tale* advising critics that:

> first, I have couched a very profound mystery in the number of O's multiplied by seven, and divided by nine ... whoever will be at the pains to calculate the whole number of each letter in this treatise, and sum up the difference exactly between the several numbers, ... the discoveries in the product will plentifully reward his labour.[19]

My alignment of Swift and Saussure (as mediated by Starobinski) is meant neither to disparage Saussure nor to ignore the fact that Swift may have considered the method 'mad'. Rather, it is meant to indicate Swift's awareness, perhaps reluctant, that there may be ghostly intentions, *revenants*, informing writing as they return to haunt the text. Swift is open to two possibilities which dominate much modern theory: he is open to the possibility of an unconscious articulating itself through writing; and he is open to the possibility of dialogue, the dialogic relation with a reader being the condition of writing. The texts may be informed by voices other than Swift's, voices whose tympanum may be in Swift's unconscious, or in the consciousness or unconscious of his reader, or even in the language system itself. It is for this reason that the *Tale* is an anonymous text: there may be subdued identities, if not actual names, returning as ghostly presences in the writing. Swift, like Derrida, knows the difficulties inherent in the strategy of the appropriative signature, especially when used as a marker for intention in respect of a written text.

Saussure's manoeuvres have not been so very uncommon in the twentieth century. Tzara, for instance, was excited by the discovery of François Villon's name, acrostically revealed, in that poet's 'will', *Le Testament*;[20] and for Tzara, what was of interest was the level of automaticity involved here. Was the proper name the origin, an emanatory source for the text; or did it appear, somehow dictated beyond the conscious control or authority of the poet? To what extent are these hypogrammatic names the founding containers of meaning for the texts?

Two attitudes develop here in twentieth-century theory. On the one hand, the text is seen as an elaborate euphemism for a name which haunts it and appears through it; the text, more or less covertly uttering the name or *mot-thème*, utters it as an authorising source of meaning for the text as a whole. This view would regard the discovery of the *mot-thème* as being of crucial importance in delimiting the meaning of the text. On the other hand, while the text remains a euphemism for the name, what becomes important is the relation established between the identity of the name which haunts the text and its supposed present historical speaker, the reader who 'conceives' (make a conceit of) the name. On this view, the discovery of the *mot-thème* is the discovery of unconscious factors which determine the conditions and possibilities of the meaning of the text, or better, the meaning of the event of reading. These factors might include not only the individual psychopathology of the writer but also more transindividual factors which contribute to the specificity of the text: such factors might, then, be social and historical, as the 'voice of a society', the *Geist*, or ideology articulate themselves through poetry.

The two attitudes can be exemplified in the practice of Riffaterre and Hartman, respectively. Riffaterre concerns himself with the reduction of a given text to its fundamental *mot-thème*, which he understands as a basic generative matrix which the poem itself articulates only covertly and implicitly. Thus, Baudelaire's 'Spleen (1)', according to Riffaterre, is an elaboration from the fundamental matrix 'no refuge from misery'. Everything in the poem, he argues, can finally be referred back to this grounding matrix for its explication. Here the discovery of the name or *mot-thème* which suffuses the text becomes also the discovery and guarantee of the text's authoritative meaning.[21]

Hartman's approach is entirely different. In *Saving the Text* he cites Hegel's 'It is by naming that we think', and he thinks his way through Derrida's *Glas* by laying bare some fundamental 'spectral names'. Through gradual manipulations and permutations, the clipped words 'je m'éc', that 'moignon d'écriture' from the opening page of *Glas* (in the Genet column), become IC, read as the initials of Christ, which in turn become ICH ('I', 'je'), an abbreviation of ICHTOS (the fish symbol for Christ). Hartman proceeds in this way until he reinstates the signature of Derrida himself. Derrida closes *Glas* with a very shadowy kind of signature: the text ends with the words 'le débris de', which is not even a very good pun on his name. But Hartman produces Derrida's name in the text as a ghostly presence, under the cryptic four-part name, 'Dionysos Erigone Eriopétale Réséda', which appears, isolated, in the Genet column. This, says Hartman, puts the name of Genet's counterpart, 'Georg Wilhelm Friedrich Hegel', 'in the shade', making that name 'ghost', like a 'shade', the Genet column. He goes on:

> This plush vocative with its internal doublings seems to restitute what was torn into little pieces at the beginning. Someone is named, certainly. But is it Dionysus alone? There is a word under the words, a disseminated sound. If we look at the cryptic fourfold as a Saussurean hypogram, then that other name is Derrida.
> So that the one time Derrida names himself is within a feminine constellation and in conjunction with Dionysus.[22]

This is clearly different from Riffaterre's method. In Hartman's exploration of spectral, shady names, what is important is the discovery of some kind of Christian name behind, or in front of, Derrida's own, as a kind of authorising principle for the textual encounter of Derrida with Hegel and Genet; but this Christian name is also understood as female in some sense. So, as this now womanly, now Christian author, the male Jew Jacques Derrida is named, s/he is named only through a further identification or encounter with Hartman himself, as the authority which isolates, speaks and brings to revelation the name in question. Here, identity of person or of meaning and name is not singular, and not gender-specified as male and univocal. Authority has been disseminated in both the text and the interpretation (now inseparable) which Hartman constructs.

Hartman remarks that 'It would be a vulgar though affective simplification to say that Derrida is exhibiting in *Glas* the difficulty of bringing a truly womanly speech to light';[23] but some kind of female voice is being elaborated here. If Derrida is identified through Hartman's nominalisation as Christ and woman, then we have a recognition of Derrida as a Shakespearean Jessica from *The Merchant of Venice*, betraying a patriarchal authority as he refuses the possibility of referring to himself as source of meaning in *Glas*: he is, as it were, not the father of this issue, and his 'own' proper name is not the '*mot-thème*' to which the text can be referred for its explication. Further, as a kind of womanly speaker, s/he betrays the notion of patriarchal tradition and historical continuity of identity; this is precisely the position which I outlined for a womanly mode of authority in seventeenth-century poetry. Hartman, then, has 'adulterously' stolen or appropriated Derrida from Dionysus. The text of *Glas* cannot easily be signed, for singular identity is disseminated in its reading/writing. The text is written from a position of self-exile, a position which accepts the impossibility of being fully present to oneself; it comes from a literal no-*man*'s-land. Even *Glas* itself is disseminated between the two works, one on Hegel, one on Genet. These two works not only reflect upon each other and adulterate each other, but also betray each other's authoritative priority. Betrayal is the fundamental principle of *Glas*; and that betrayal can focus on the revelation or 'betrayal' through the text and Hartman's interpretation, of the spectral names which not only haunt the writing but also undermine its singular meaning and authority. For Riffaterre, the discovery of such a name or *mot-thème* would be the finding of an authorising and authenticating source of meaning, a matrix, for the text. For Hartman, the name is there to be betrayed, in every sense. Its revelation is, literally, its betrayal. The text is not Derrida's, nor is it Hartman's (though *Saving the Text* may be 'his'); the comparable comment is de Man's on the reading of Proust: 'The reading is not "our" reading', argues de Man, 'since it uses only the linguistic elements provided by the text itself; the distinction between author and reader is one of the false distinctions that the reading makes evident'.[24] If this is the case, then this perhaps womanly authority is one which renders criticism less tainted by individualistic idiolects which would strive to appropriate (and 'name') the text as their own. The approach which saves the text, paradoxically, is the one which betrays it; *Glas* is written with the forked and self-betraying tongue of the pun and dialogue. *Glas*, the passing-bell, announces the death of the author and of the reader as identifiable, namable, individuals appropriating or encapsulating the source of a singular authorial univocal meaning.

Hartman owes some of this thought on nomination to Burke, who reconsiders the Freudian psychopathology of everyday life and asks about the possibility, alongside the bad puns which betray our unconscious, of 'good' puns:

> the 'bad' pun (arising from a conflict of impulses where one states an attitude despite himself) is the kind most amenable to study. But should we not look for 'benignities' that correspond to such 'malignities'? Should there not also be 'good' puns? As there are cases where we, in roundabout ways, pronounce the unutterable 'four-letter-words', might there not be corresponding cases where we, in roundabout ways, pronounce the unutterable 'Tetragrammaton'?[25]

Might there not be good ghosts to correspond to the *malin génie* who punningly speaks through our writings?

This kind of punning dialogism appears as a textual phenomenon before the ages of Bakhtin and Derrida. Swiftian 'irony' looks, in many ways, precisely the same, and produces the similar result of a refusal to categorise rigidly or authoritatively; there is never a final vocabulary, in Rortean terms, in this irony. The fictionalisation of the Transubstantiation in the *Tale* elucidates the point. Peter invites Martin and Jack to partake of some excellent mutton, and then offers them stale bread. In objecting, Martin and Jack are making an appeal to a verifying or authorising essential nature; they know that 'bread' is not 'mutton', and make not only linguistic but also corresponding essential distinctions between them. Such an appeal to nature, however, is useless here, for Peter lives entirely in the realm of the punning signifier, where bread and mutton can surrealistically interfuse. Apart from the religious component of this allegory, there is an important point to be made about the construction of the *Tale*. The narrative is constructed between these two varying and opposed approaches to language and its authoritative base: on the one hand, nature authorises words; on the other the pragmatic use of words, language itself, authorises meaning. In fact, the whole of the *Tale* is an extended pun or dialogue; like *Glas*, its two narratives betray and reflect upon each other in varying degrees of ironical relation. Their ironic counterpointing is only the first kind of interpretation which is integral to the reading of the *Tale*. The entire text begs for interpretation, for the mediation of its allegories; but this, of course, places the reader in precisely the position of 'interpreter' satirised and attacked within the text: this betrayal is its fundamental irony. Not only must we interpret, we must also interpret our interpretations in potentially never-ending dialectical series.

Dyson, in an analysis made in fairly conventional terms of Swiftian irony, indicates that the mode of authority which this subtends is based on betrayal:

> The technique is, of course, one of betrayal. A state of tension, not to say war, exists between Swift and his readers. The very tone in which he writes is turned into a weapon. It is the tone of polite conversation, friendly, and apparently dealing in commonplaces. Naturally our assent is captured, since the polite style, the guarantee of gentlemanly equality, is the last one in which we expect to be attacked or betrayed. But the propositions to which we find ourselves agreeing are in varying degrees monstrous, warped or absurd.[26]

It is significant, of course, in the light of the theory advanced in the present study, that it is the 'gentlemanly' which is attacked here, with its male titles to names, identity, property and singular authority.

Criticism: Heresy. Poetry: Feminism

Cleanth Brooks warned his fellow New Critics of the dangers of the 'heresy of paraphrase'; to paraphrase a poem would threaten the specificity and purity of the text with contamination by the reader's own subjectivism. The voice or consciousness of the reader in the activity of criticism is potentially 'heretical', a swerving away from the text as it truly is; and criticism as such, then, is seen to be based on the same eccentricities and indeterminacies as the pun in rhetoric. Brooks provides an appendix of all the poems discussed in his *Well Wrought Urn*; and, according to the logic of the essay on the heresy of paraphrase, this appendix should be the most careful criticism of the poems. The texts, in their supposedly innocent reproduction are allowed to speak for themselves, as it were. However, this has to be weighed against two facts. Firstly, their reproduction in such a critical context transforms them and their purpose, if not their authorial informing intentions (and, indeed, any repetition of them would transform them); secondly, Brooks's procedure in his study depends precisely upon paraphrasing, severely heretically, many of the texts under his consideration.[27]

The 'good poem', Brooks argues, sets up a 'resistance ... against all attempts to paraphrase it'; and, as the reader tries to find a proposition which says what the poem 'says', she or he will have some problems:

> As his proposition approaches adequacy, he will find, not only that it has increased greatly in length, but that it has begun to fill itself up with reservations and qualifications—and most significant of all—the formulator will find that he has himself begun to fall back upon metaphors of his own in his attempt to indicate what the poem 'says'. In sum, his proposition, as it approaches adequacy, ceases to be a proposition.[28]

In short, the proposition, increasingly metaphorical, becomes another poem. But, in practice, such heretical paraphrase seems the only possibility for criticism at all; all reading is such heresy, such an alternative to the 'authorised version' or a betrayal of the Scriptural text itself. These heresies are, further, deviations or turnings (figurings) which are eccentric with respect to the 'primary' text itself: 'The truth of the matter is that all such formulations lead away from the centre of the poem—not towards it'.[29] Unable, logically, to repeat the poem 'innocently', all critics become eccentric heretics; as Brooks suggests, this makes of criticism itself a poetic intervention. Or, in the words of Bloom, 'The meaning of a poem can only be another poem'.[30]

Bloom's refinements of the New Critical position, which Lentricchia sees as Bloom's own anxiety of influence,[31] remain caught up in a quest for origins and for the source of meaning or pathos in poetry. The theory is based on a tenet of intensional integrity, or the identifiability of authorial will, in a text. All the ephebe poet can do is to revise, heretically misread, the strong precursor. As I argued with reference to Shakespeare, all that can happen here in a male-centred neo-Freudian family romance is that the son or ephebe simply reinstates the will of the father at the very moment when he thinks he has appropriated it. Perhaps Bloom's real anxiety is misplaced, not so much an anxiety of influence as an anxiety about the challenge to this male lineage or literary history and tradition which comes from the 'womanly' text. The ephebe or critic (both mis-readers) can never, in the logic of this theory, establish an independent authority at all; the poetry or writing will be a (failed) representation of a 'fatherly' name and intention. The lineage which Bloom traces leads backwards, implying an authorial script in some theistic source, authorised by the unnamed patristic or patri-archal 'father'-poet. This Bloomian position, in its agony of thinking through the name of the father, approximates in its tragic pathos to the neoclassical tragic ideology of the verifiability and authority of an essential truth of nature, and to a univocality of meaning which is to be found and guaranteed there.

Similar in impetus is the theory of E. D. Hirsch, Jnr. For Hirsch, the correct critical manoeuvre for understanding the 'meaning' of a text involves suppression of the knowledge of the text's 'significance'. To find meaning, we find and ident-ify an authorial source, which leads, in fact, to the sup-pression of our own historical consciousness and vocal speech; it is thus that the poet speaks to us, speaking in our own voice as we (innocently) recite the poem. But we cannot, of course, occupy the same intentional space as the poet; nor can she or he come to inhabit our intentional space and moment. Further, it is difficult, not to say unwise, to sup-press one's own critical consciousness as a method of enabling the discovery of the meaning of another active consciousness and its informing intentionality. If we 're-present' a past intention in our present rehearsal of a text, we come closer to the kinds of phenomenological reader-response criticism from which Hirsch in fact distances himself. He sees the positions of Fish, Holland, Bleich, even Gadamer, as basi-cally positions which assume too much in the way of response or responsibility: such 'response' is appropriate only to the

realm of Hirschian 'significance', and irrelevant to the authorised meaning of a poem.

Just as Swift had prefigured and satirised the Hirschian
position, so too he had foreseen some of the extravagances
of reader-response criticism. Bleich, for instance, is a model
of the modern Enthusiast, in whom an interest in reading
the text is rapidly displaced onto a self-interest, an interest
in hearing one's own subjectivist rantings. It is useful to
eradicate critical consciousness in the Bleichian position:
'Recording a response requires the relaxation of cultivated
analytical habits'.[32] There remains a belief in an authenticating source of meaning, as in Hirsch and Bloom; but
Bleich displaces this centre and origin of meaning in the
subjective self of the reader. The responses to the text
demanded by Bleich are not in fact responses to a text at all,
so much as responses made by critics in the interests of the
generation or production of an interesting and imaginative
self-image. The method of interrupting reading, in order to
freely associate, not only encourages the construction of
narrativised images of the self but also make that selfhood
the origin or source of meaning for both text and world; the
subsequent continuation of reading is done in the light of,
or through the ideology of, this individualist fiction. The
equivalent of the pathetic search for an essential nature in
the world outside is displaced here onto an equally pathetic
(though even more ideologically blind) search for an essential
selfhood or personality or personal identity. As the subject
relaxes her or his critical consciousness, supposedly, the truth
or inner light reveals itself. This, too, matches the hubris of
Cornelian tragic characters, in their self-centred location of
authoritative meaning. Bleich is in a position similar to Jack
in Swift's *Tale*, and it is Jack's madness which leads him to
believe in a nature which is entirely present to his own
consciousness and which therefore authorises his Enthusiastic
and paranoiac rantings.

In opposition to such theoretical stances, we can range the
theories of critics such as Said and de Man. Such a critic
practises a mode of 'ec-centric' criticism, one which while
saving the text, forever spirals away from any notion of the
priority of authorial intentional meaning as the source of

truth in a text. De Man, for instance, is frequently at pains to indicate that the supposedly 'original' poetic text is itself always already a critical text, an act of reading and of self-reading rather than an act of 'pure' writing. In his suggestion that readers should strive to occupy the position of the writer as she or he wrote, it is because the act of writing is always its own primal act of self-criticism, contaminated by its own deconstruction. His criticism, then, is not concerned to return us to an authenticating authorial origin for a text, for such an origin is already 'double' or duplicitous, 'blind' to the insights which the critic will use to reveal the truth of the text, not of its author. In this mode of criticism, working by betraying the text, there is no pathetic tragic belief in the absolute verifying power of an essential nature; there is only a 'comic' series of *double-entendres* from which social or historical meaning can be constructed. The text is always fundamentally punning; and criticism operates by activating such puns, revealing the duplicity of texts, and making us self-conscious with regard to our own pragmatic critical or historical duplicities. In contradistinction to the monologic authority proposed by Hirsch, and, in different forms, Bloom or Bleich, criticism which 'betrays the text' not only saves that text for rereading but also posits a mode of dialogic authority, a mode which disseminates *potestas* towards a wide range of *auctoritas*, and which generates more writing, itself potentially productive of more historical voices and critical consciousness.

Insofar as this kind of interpretation is betrayal, these theories can be aligned with that mode of authority which I characterised in its seventeenth-century manifestations as specifically 'female'. Clearly, this is not to say that post-structuralist practice, and deconstruction, is feminist by any necessity; but in its questioning of a state of essential pre-linguistic nature which supposedly determines human identity, place and historical possibilities, it can be a strong ally of feminist criticism, which would also want to question such 'natural' necessities as the place assigned to women by a non-historical and supposedly authoritative 'nature'. In the interpretations of the paternal will in Swift's *Tale*, which I have taken as an analogue for interpretation of proprietorial authorial intention in any text, the betrayal of the text is related to 'degeneration'. Just as the degenerate or bastard in Shakespeare was what characterised the possibility of some kind of non-identifiable 'female', dialogical or conversational authority, so likewise in Swift and his 'modernist' or 'post-modernist' counterparts, interpretative betrayal might be aligned with just such a preference for dialogue.

Betraying the text proposes a mode of criticism which explicitly demands a revision of the prevalent understanding of literary history. Bloomian literary history, which is fundamentally conventional in some senses, is a story of fathers and sons, and an endless repetition of precisely the same stories and fictions or agonies. The mode of literary history which has constituted the present study has been concerned with critical interventions and disruptions into this seemingly homogeneous web of literary exercises. The 'new literary history' must concentrate upon such discontinuities, such 'degenerations' and 'betrayals' of the familial domestic under-standing of literary history which dominates not only Bloom-ian but also most conventional criticism. Instead of a generic theory of literary history, as proposed by Fowler, what is called for is a 'degeneric' mode, one which will examine not only the echoes which align writers but, more crucially, the areas of differentiation which wedge them apart historically. It is perhaps only through such a promiscuous mingling of heterogeneous writings that criticism could ever begin the task of 'thinking forward through the mothers'. Further, if criticism is simply a different degree of deconstruction from the poetic text, then the critical text must itself enter into consideration of its own historical production and its own historical relation to the text which it purports to criticise: it is through such a dialectical self-criticism and text-criticism that history itself moves. It will not therefore be a tran-scendent evocation of the truth concerning an authorial inten-tion, but rather a historical act or engagement which is itself productive of knowledge, a basis for historical therapy.

Chapter 9

Experiments in Writing

were not the letters that pass between
these ladies of a treasonable nature?
(Richardson, Clarissa)

So he vanish'd from my sight,
And I pluck'd a hollow reed,
And I made a rural pen,
And I stain'd the water clear
(Blake, 'Introduction' to
Songs of Innocence)

Adultery in the Novel

He goes back under the covers while she pads around on bare feet getting dressed. Funny how she puts on her bra before her underpants. Her putting on her underpants makes him conscious of her legs as separate things: thick pink liquid twists diminishing downward into her ankles. They take pink light from the reflection of each other as she moves. Her accepting his watching her flatters him, shelters him. They have become domestic.

(Updike, Rabbit, Run)

In medieval times and after, the education of girls was often intensive and produced effective managers of households. ... When they began to enter schools in some numbers during the seventeenth century, girls entered not the main-line Latin schools but the newer vernacular schools. ... Women writers were no doubt influenced by works that they had read emanating from the Latin-based, academic, rhetorical tradition, but they themselves normally expressed themselves in a different, far less oratorical voice, which had a great deal to do with the rise of the novel.

(Ong, Orality and Literacy)

265

One of the clearest results of the battle between ancients and moderns was the production of two new forms of writing: criticism as such, and the novel. Four factors shaped the condition of the novel: modernity, experimentalism, criticism and illegitimacy. It was a 'modern' form *par excellence*, with authors who disavowed their own authority, as if they were mere vessels through whom history articulated itself. In its relation to the contemporary, it was empirical or experimental to the degree that it was rooted in recent historical 'experience'. It was also, however, a commentary on such experience, and thus became an exercise in the new genre of criticism; its closeness to the experiments in living which opened the present study should be obvious, for many of these first novels were utopian or quixotic travelogues. Finally, insofar as it was modern, critical, experimental, the novel was also radically 'de-generic', always deviating from conventions, even its own. This might explain why the first 'anti-novels' were written even before the genre itself got fully under way.

This is not the usual theoretical conception of the novel. Perhaps the dominant conception of the novel genre has been that which has concentrated on the dialectic of character and society, self and other; and, more specifically, the recurrent organisation of the novel has been centred by theory on the establishment of familial relations or of a 'house' for its central character. Heath makes the most astute remarks here:

> In this 'individual and society' organization, the family has occupied a decisive position, proposed as a kind of mediation between the two: assuming the production of the new individuals needed for the reproduction of the social work-force, it is the first arena of socialization, preceding and then running alongside the systems of formal education, and, equally, it is the given arena of sexual relations, of the social ordering of the sexual. The great subject of the novelistic was thus crucially the family. ... That so many nineteenth-century novels end in marriage, the union with the perfect mate, is not, of course, by chance or simply some formal convention: the marriage-union ending represents the resolution of 'the individual and society', a firm social unit offered as the privileged mode of the individual, the haven of his or her personal happiness, personal life.[1]

If anything, however, the novel seems in fact to be concerned not so much with the establishment of families as with attending to the artificiality of this social organisation. The married family is rarely mediated as a 'natural' solution to the problem of the 'individual and society'; that problem, in fact, often arises precisely because of discordant familial relations. Many novels are also concerned with the destruction of the family. Engels drew attention to two forms of marital relation, in his study on *The Origin of the Family*, and commented that:

> The best mirror of these two methods of marrying is the novel—the French novel for the Catholic manner, the German for the Protestant. In both, the hero 'gets it': in the German, the young man gets the girl; in the French, the husband gets the horns.[2]

Some ('French', 'Catholic') novels, at least, might be concerned with adultery; and Tanner has indicated that this affects other modes of fiction.

Those novels which do propose the family as socially normative use that family as guarantor of stable identity for a character: these fictions are about the discovery of a character's 'real' identity, the discovery of a fathering, naming source or origin. The problem of the adulterous relation threatens, on the other hand, to undermine this; and often, the adultery is the province of the female character. This is perhaps apt, for it is she who most radically lacks an autonomous identity in the socio-cultural ideology of proprietorial marriage, and she, also, who lacks the authority that goes with such identity. It is in the light of this that we can reconsider authority in the novel.

Dialogue and Duplicity in the Novel

One fundamental aspect of twentieth-century modernism is its collocation of criticism with poetry or fictional narrative. Modernist writing is self-consciously intertextual, a response to other writings. *The Waste Land*, for instance, is largely a tissue of anterior writings, becoming an allusive criticism (almost a 'critical edition') of them. It is written in response to these texts, and to the letters of criticism which Pound wrote concerning both this tradition and the poem's own gestation. With Eliot as catalyst, the ghostly voices of the tradition are to be mediated, producing this textual 'com-Pound', a text which includes its own criticisms in Pound's editing. This is the dialectical relation between tradition and the individual talent:

> The existing monuments form an ideal order among themselves, which is modified by the introduction of the new (the really new) work of art among them. The existing order is complete before the new work arrives; for order to persist after the supervention of novelty, the *whole* existing order must be, if ever so slightly, altered; and so the relations, proportions, values of each work of art toward the whole are readjusted; and this is conformity between the old and the new. Whoever has approved this idea of order, of the form of European, of English literature, will not find it preposterous that the past should be altered by the present as much as the present is directed by the past.[3]

This 'influence' moves in both directions. The new work exists as a criticism of the past; but it is also already an aspect of that past tradition, has already been inserted into it; and thus it exists in critical juxtaposition to the other works of the tradition, which now comment critically upon the new work too, in terms at least of its conformity to tradition. The Eliotic poem, then, contains its own criticism internally. *The Waste Land* is not simply a response to the writing which constitutes the tradition prior to *The Waste Land*: it is a critical response to the tradition which includes *The Waste Land*. The tradition does not exist as such without *The Waste Land* in the first place, for it is generated by the writing of the poem. That is to say, *The Waste Land*, as poetic exercise in writing, is a response to its own reading, a criticism of itself, *before* it has actually been written. In modernist terms, a poem is a response to its own reading, an activity which is temporally coterminous with and logically anterior to its own composition or writing.

This is of relevance to the eighteenth-century modern form of the novel. Richardson's Lovelace is an extremely literary figure, a Donnean 'great frequenter of plays' who construes his own actions in terms of play. His letters are often fictionalised dramatic dialogue; and they provoke a response in his own critical readings of the drama, a mode of response which is clear in his correspondents too.[4] Richardson's own 'critical edition' of these letters or correspondence is already, then, a kind of Eliotic criticism of another writing; but this other writing is not itself 'originary', for it is already a criticism. For example, Lovelace has begun a process of intercepting and editing the writings of Clarissa and Anna: 'Hast thou a mind to see what it was I *permitted* Miss Howe to write to her lovely friend? Why then, read it here, as extracted from hers of Wednesday last, with a few additions of my own.'[5] In such a letter, there are a number of authorities at work. Firstly, there is that of Anna (but the letter is a response to a previous letter and has thus already been informed by the authority of that previous text); secondly, there is that of Anna's correspondent whose reading-interpretation of the letter construes authoritatively its own meanings; thirdly, there is that of Lovelace, editing and altering the sense of the letter; fourthly, there is that of Lovelace's reader, who is not only Clarissa but also Belford, Richardson and us. There is, then, a tradition of authorities into which Richardson inserts his writing; *Clarissa*, like *The Waste Land*, is a modernist exercise in self-reading.

A novel such as this radically requires a reader, not for its completion, but for its articulation in the first place: it is an act of reading rather than an originary act of writing. It is fundamentally 'experimental' in that it is based upon the empirical act of critical reading, 'based on experience, not on authority', in the words of the OED. It has to be experienced, or read, in order to be written at all; and it exists, therefore, primarily as a mode of dialogue with itself. This makes a slightly different sense of Jameson's notion that 'texts come before us as the always-already-read', saturated with cultural beliefs and previous interpretations. In the sense elaborated here, this would be the case not only for the 'reader' of a text but also for the writer who now transcribes a text which she or he has always already read. Such an 'experimental' text is thus always a critical response to an experimental reading of itself.

In the serial publication of high realism in the nineteenth century, the pace of production of a fictional text allowed time for this exercise in criticism to contaminate more clearly the writing. Writers such as Dickens or Thackeray received feedback from their public and modified their texts accordingly, writing with criticism firmly in mind. This led to 'experiments' in a sense, and to some textual inconsistencies, making some of these 'realist' novels look like their postmodern successors. These, then, are cases where real historical dialogue informs the authority of the novel.

Conditioned in this way, the novel becomes that which, in a sense, is never finally written; it has no 'final vocabulary' and always demands revision and rewriting or rereading. The novel is that which exists to be reread, and this stuttering condition of the novel aligns it to the comic pattern of authority outlined in Restoration and neoclassical theatre in this study. The novel demands to be written, seeking a poet rather than a reader to articulate it. Melville, in *Moby Dick*, comments on the radical incompletion of the novel, on its condition as a (heretical) beginning:

> I now leave my cetological System standing thus unfinished, even as the great Cathedral of Cologne was left, with the crane still standing upon the top of the uncompleted tower. For small erections may be finished by their first architects; grand one, true ones, ever leave the copestone to posterity. God keep me from ever completing anything. This whole book is but a draught—nay, but the draught of a draught.[6]

The perfect modernist manifestation of this same phenomenon occurs in Woolf's *The Waves*, where Bernard is not able to finish his story to Neville; and this is repeated precisely in the post-modern criticism of Hartman, who is 'not good at concluding' and whose criticism is itself endless, demanding its own revision or, sometimes, deconstruction.[7]

The precursor for this modernist trait is the figure of Lovelace, who at the moment of the rape, cannot complete his story. He writes what is possibly the briefest letter in the novel, saying 'I can go no farther' (III. 196), leaving a crucial aposiopesis in the text, a space which looks for interpretative closure. The point of the incompletions like these is to generate more writing, and to avoid being the last word; in short, the point is to expose the fundamentally dialogic condition of this modernist writing. The writing thus becomes not only dialogical but also, insofar as it suggests closure, duplicitous, for that closure is always forestalled. Reading does not provide closure; rather, in this modernist phase it is constitutive of the writing itself, of the text itself, and thus provides only the necessity of further rereading. Authority as such is never finalised but always disseminated.

Critical Novel: Degeneric Authority

The novel is critical in that it organises itself around a series of critical instants, moments of crisis. This critical modernity was the factor in its contemporaneity, its relation to the supposedly extremely recent past or 'modern times'. Richardson's project of 'writing to the minute' is a logical extrapolation of this tendency. The aim is to make the text approximate as closely to experience as possible, to repeat the 'narratively' sanctioned historical 'facts' of reality. This is supposed to make the text pure from the contamination of critical or subjective informing consciousness and to grant a measure of authority to the 'facts' of history themselves. Fielding's parodic *Shamela* rapidly exposed the ludicrous impossibility of the notion of 'writing to the minute':

> Mrs *Jervis* and I are just in Bed, and the Door unlocked; if my Master should come—Odsbobs! I hear him just coming in at the Door. ... he is in Bed between us, we both shamming a Sleep, he steals his Hand into my Bosom, which I, as if in my Sleep, press close to me with mine, and then pretend to awake.[8]

Writing to the minute may seem preposterous, but it was the same kind of aversion to critical information which impelled the modernist interest in automatic writings and the dictates of the unconscious. Criticism, however, is present even in these cases; *Shamela* cannot help but be a critique of the Richardsonian precepts.

Lennard J. Davis, contesting the Scholes and Kellogg thesis that the novel grew out of the synthetic romance, offers an alternative precursor of the novel in the last will and testament which constituted the criminal ballad. Such a mode of writing is clearly critical, made on the point of death

itself; and, interestingly, criticism and crime are etym-
ologically linked, through the shared Indo-European root -
skeri. These ballads and news-sheets, argues Davis, in their
recording of executions, form the novel's link to the recent
past. More pertinently, the ballads told stories that their
authors obviously could not finish, like Woolf's Bernard.
How does a first-personal narrative relate the death of the
narrator? In one example cited by Davis, the answer is to
make a sudden mutation from first to third-personal
narration, incidentally making a text which looks like a
Donleavy 'experiment'. For the ballad to be authenticated
and punctual, it had to be claimed as first-personal and thus
authoritative. This is what Richardson claims for his own
letters, of course; he must assert that his character actually
wrote them. But this serves to indicate that the novel, like
the ending of the criminal ballad, is actually a 'betrayal of
the text', a criticism of a criticism: in the case of the ballad,
a criticism of a confessional exercise in self-criticism or self-
justification; in that of the novel, Richardson's critical edition
of letters themselves already critically edited. Davis explains
this contradictory position; 'In maintaining that the authors
were actual criminals, writers of these ballads reveal the
inherent contradiction of the news/novels discourse—that
affirmation of veracity is tantamount to denial.'⁹ The very
fact of claiming a true, authenticating individual source for
the writing constitutes part of the lie of the fiction itself.
This is close to my own argument that the closer one comes
to authentic monological rehearsal or reproduction or representation of a text, the more one critically betrays it. This
is only a bad thing if one regards the betrayed text as having
been pure and unadulterated before the act of reading. But
I have shown that such 'original' writing is in fact always
already adulterated by criticism, always fundamentally dialogical, always already read and always a critical act in itself.

This dialogic form of the novel becomes more dialectical
in the light of Lukács's theorisation of the form as ironic, an
irony which allows no final resolution into clear and unified
compartments of self and other:

> The self-recognition and, with it, self-abolition of subjectivity was
> called irony by the first theoreticians of the novel, the aesthetic phil-
> osophers of early Romanticism. As a formal constituent of the novel

form this signifies an interior diversion of the normatively creative
subject into a subjectivity as interiority, which opposes power com-
plexes that are alien to it and which strives to imprint the contents of
its longing upon the alien world, and a subjectivity which sees through
the abstract and, therefore, limited nature of the mutually alien worlds
of subject and object ... and, by thus seeing through them, allows the
duality of the world to subsist. At the same time the creative subjectivity
glimpses a unified world in the mutual relativity of elements essentially
alien to one another, and gives form to this world. Yet this glimpsed
unified world is nevertheless purely formal; the antagonistic nature of
the inner and outer worlds is not abolished but only recognised as
necessary; the subject which recognises it as such is just as empirical—
just as much part of the outside world, confined in its own interiority—
as the characters which have become its objects.[10]

The supposed unification, through irony, leads instead to a
further empirical position for subjectivity; it leads, in short,
to a generation of a further thetical position, an irresolute
'dialexis', which requires further historical realisation. Thus
this position generates further vocal expression or the writing
of another novel or criticism, another critical novel or novel
criticism.

The novel, thus, becomes always a criticism of or commentary upon the writing or reading of the novel itself. But
criticism plays, often, a more obvious role in the novel than
is suggested by this theorisation of its dialogic principles.
McKillop, for instance, indicates that Fielding 'was certainly
more interested in criticism than any other novelist of the
age';[11] and *Shamela*, clearly, is a critical 'betrayal' of *Pamela*,
just as its title is a grotesque parodic misrepresentation or
repetition of its precursor text. The historical digressions at
the start of *Joseph Andrews*, or the introductory chapters to
each book of *Tom Jones*, also provide many examples of
Fielding's criticism entering the novel. But these 'digressions'
are Shandean, in the sense that critical digressiveness is the
very foundation of the novel form. Not only does it digress
from its precursor texts and generic conventions, it also
continually digresses from itself. In this respect, *Tristram
Shandy* might less dramatically, but more substantially, be
hailed as the 'most typical' novel, as Shklovsky called it.[12]

Shandy is not so different from Fielding's fiction. *Joseph
Andrews*, for instance, proceeds from crisis to crisis, generating constant forks in the direction the narrative might

take, and thus stressing the novel's divagative, extravagant
and quixotic form. Lady Booby's critical doubts about the
dismissal of Joseph leads to prevarications in which she
imagines scenes which digress from the kernel-story. Her
'crisis' is echoed by that of Leonora, in the tale within the
tale, when she has to choose between Bellarmine and
Horatio. More radically, the story of Leonora, as an interpellation in the main story and as a digression from that, is
in its turn interrupted by the 'main story', which itself now
becomes a digression. There arises a crisis at the level of
narrative itself: which is the tale and which the digression?
In fact, in the novel, there is no main or kernel tale; there
are only satellites, digressions, *divertissements*. The model
for this, clearly, is Swift's *Tale of a Tub*, a grotesque criticism
of Hobbes's *Leviathan*, in which the two tales, of religion
and learning, cross themselves in a deconstructive turning
which forestalls the recuperation of a single authorised meaning or tale.

Fielding comments on his chapter titles, advising us to use
them as critical indices, 'bills of fare'; if we do not like the
menu, he suggests that we skip the chapter. Taking this
seriously makes his work like post-modern experimental 'cut-
up' or 'shuffle' novels in the manner of Burroughs or
B. S. Johnson. The reader becomes explicitly a critical editor,
like Richardson who passes over his own editorial condition
in silence. Fielding further compares his novel to the writings
of Montaigne with respect to titles: 'And in these Inscriptions
I have been as faithful as possible, not imitating the celebrated
Montagne, who promises you one thing and gives you
another'.[13] Three points arise from this. Firstly, this is criticism, in a novel, of Montaigne's *Essais*. Secondly, Fielding
asserts his own deviation from an anterior model of biographical writing. Thirdly, insofar as his chapters are Brook-
sian paraphrases of the Inscriptions, they are precisely heretical digressions from the sacred headings of his 'menu'. The
critical modern novel is nothing less than a constant critical
divergence from itself, as even *Joseph Andrews* turns to give
us the story of Parson Adams, for instance. The novel is a
Dysonian 'betrayal' of the reader, who takes her or his
revenge by misreading the novel, adulterating it in dialogical

criticism, digressing from its narrative to tell another tale and give their own version or turning of the story.

Digression and extravagance are among the most recurrent features of the novel. Melville offers a history of whaling; Balzac gives a history of printing in *Illusions perdues*; Nabokov offers criticism as digression in *Pale Fire*; Beckett often comments on his own writings in the midst of the texts; Barth comments in *Letters* on all his previous writings, and so on. Post-modern 'experimental' writing makes explicit the self-readings which constitute the basically dialogical form of the novel since its inception. In its digressiveness and lack of central authority, the novel turns out to be about the continually deferred birth of authority as such.

In this dialogic state, the novel is construed as inherently duplicitous and criminal, or tautologically, 'fiction'. Richardson hands the novel over to his correspondents to write, but their letters are never a direct revelation of truth. Frequently circuitous and euphemistic, the letters are open to multiple readings, even at the hands of their writers. The action of the novel depends upon their interpretation; that is, it depends upon critical reading rather than upon writing; but characters, letters, deceive rather than reveal.

In the case of Defoe, the writing of a novel is handed over to a Robinson Crusoe or a Moll Flanders, outcast and criminal, respectively. Moll's story is always duplicitous, and it remains in doubt whether she has reformed or not. Defoe, in his supposed journalistic plain style and a Puritan mistrust of dialogue, is an active mediator of the ghostly voice of Moll Flanders (whose 'real' identity, of course, is never established), shaping her voice into the configurations of his own:

> It is true that the original of this story is put into new words, and the style of the famous lady we here speak of is a little altered; particularly she is made to tell her own tale in modester words than she told it at first, the copy which came first to hand having been written in language more like one still in Newgate than one grown penitent and humble, as she afterwards pretends to be.[14]

In other words, *Moll Flanders* turns out not to be *Moll Flanders* after all, but Defoe's critical edition of an anterior 'copy' or text; it is his altered bastardisation of the tale which we have here. Duplicity is written into the very fabric of the novel and is constitutive of its writing and authority. The relation of the novel to crime and illegitimacy, and of both to criticism, is apparent in such duplicity. Illegitimacy, in the form of an adulterated contamination of a supposedly pure text is a precondition of the very fact of the novel. The novel is degeneric, and for this reason always fundamentally experimental. 'Realism' is, as it were, simply one specific form of experimentalism; the novel has usually avoided that 'realist' pretence of a monological authority, and retains the dialogical dissemination of authority which is axiomatic to its 'form' or degeneracy.

Adultery in Criticism

In the light of the foregoing, it seems apposite to suggest, *contra* Heath, that adultery is the primary concern of the novelistic. The novel is not concerned so much with the generation of familial identity for its characters; rather, it toys with experimental constructions of alternative, 'heretical' identities, novel masks for its characters and interpreters, who strive to establish authority or authentic self-identity through the elaboration of the narrative. Critics work in the form of narrative just as much as novelistic characters and writers; but, especially in the case of the novel, it is only through deviation, heretical digression from a hypothetical central or kernel narrative that critical authority is attained.

Before adopting an attitude of remorse, the male members of Clarissa's family view the rape and subsequent death of Clarissa as the culmination of her quasi-'adulterous' separation of herself from her patriarchal lineage. She has 'heretically' or critically separated herself from the family will, intention or identity (the intention that she marry Solmes; the will intended for her by her grandfather) and in the eyes of the male characters has established a rival identity as the property and co-respondent of Lovelace.

Clarissa is organised around the critical moment of the

rape and the critical aposiopesis which constitutes Lovelace's description of it:

> Tuesday Morn., June 13
>
> And now, Belford, I can go no farther. The affair is over. Clarissa lives. And I am
>
> Your humble servant,
> R. LOVELACE.
>
> (III. 196)

This 'evasion' of a direct narration of the rape turns the central novelistic concern with female identity back towards another concern which now poses as logically prior, the question of *male* identity and property. This pouring of female blood might be the core of the novel; but as in Shakespeare, though in a contrary direction, there is a swerve away towards the opposing gender. The novel opens with the proleptic parallel of the rape of Clarissa, as Lovelace spills the blood of the male primogenitive child of the Harlowes, when he attacks James. This ghostly prefiguring of the rape transforms Lovelace's sexual act into an assault upon the entire family and upon the continuity of its name or identity. The novel makes this male blood more clearly central when questions of paternal control or authority come to the fore. Early on, it is established that Clarissa is due to inherit from her grandfather; but this authorial 'will' is superseded by a more recent, more 'present' authority, that of Clarissa's father and her uncle Antony: 'And my uncle Antony, in his rougher manner, added that surely I would not give them reason to apprehend that I thought my grandfather's favour to me had made me independent of them all. If I did, he would tell me, the will *could* be set aside, and *should*' (I. 30). Clarissa, then, threatened with this disinheritance at the hands of her male forebears, finds her own authority at risk. She is in a dilemma: if she writes to Lovelace, she loses inheritance, Harlovian identity and whatever authority that subtends; if she does not write, then, *per definitio*, she loses at least that measure of authority which is 'writerly'. After this, her every letter is seen as more or less overt duplicity, more or less overt betrayal of patriarchal intentional authority. Her very activity as a writer establishes

her as a 'degenerate bastard' with respect to her male forebears; every letter, even those written against Lovelace and
exonerating herself, compounds the 'felony' or 'adultery'.
Every critical letter is read as another act of betrayal of a
dominant paternal will and authority.

The assault upon James Harlowe, which frames the rape
of Clarissa and in some ways conditions the response of male
characters in the book to that rape, is an attack upon the
principle of a continuous (and, finally transcendent) history
as established through citied, male, civilisation. The family
interpret Lovelace's wounding of James as a kind of Romantic radical questioning of the very stability of civilised life
itself, understood in male terms. Meanwhile, and paradoxically, Lovelace is himself looking for such stability,
through the offices, and body, of a female. Like Belford,
who seems to have killed his father (IV. 169), Lovelace is a
kind of rebel-son, and he requires a woman of a certain class
to construct his own identifiable authority, trading in 'the
good old path of my ancestors' (II. 337).

What is at stake in the novel is the question of a continuous
historical lineage, the question of a transcendent perenniality
of masculinist will and intention or authority, together with
the threat of betrayal posed by the interpellation of adulterating intentions in critical writings. It is as if the very act
of writing, which male characters in Clarissa's family try to
inhibit, as a stain upon 'virginal' white paper, were itself the
act of betrayal of nature or truth (understood to be 'contained' in its patriarchal mediators); and such writing poses
a threat to the civic family and a mode of authority based
upon 'male-rights' and 'titles'. The novel is organised around
a critical point in that historical process of identity-con-
struction, a process which generates authority; and that critical point is the scene of the rape, Clarissa's vagina or body.

Eagleton has commented on this, taking issue with critics,
such as Judith Wilt, who question the 'reality' of the rape
as historical or narrative event:

> The 'real' of *Clarissa*—the point around which this elaborate two
> thousand page text pivots—is the rape; yet the rape goes wholly unrep-
> resented, as the hole at the centre of the novel towards which this huge
> mass of writing is sucked only to sheer off again.[15]

There is a complication in this. Certainly, this aposiopesis in the most crucial moment of the text demands interpretative completion. When faced with emptiness, Clarissa can write, thanks to the presence of Anna, her correspondent (I. 472); and similarly, Richardson's text requires a readerly corespondent for its articulation. Further, the weight of evidence implies, irresistably, the interpretation or articulation of the aposiopesis which posits the rape as the 'real' of *Clarissa*. This suggests, incidentally, the presence of a reality or nature, prior to its linguistic codification, to which the text refers, and to which the critic then refers as an authorisation for her or his propositions or narrative. However, even while a critic such as Eagleton tries to construct the critical narrative of *The Rape of Clarissa* from a womanly voice, this critical procedure betrays his position as incipiently masculinist. For the appeal to a verifying originary source for authority is not only the position adopted by all the male readers in and of *Clarissa*; it is also, in its appeal to a singular 'essential' or natural 'truth', easily aligned with the patriarchal modes of critical interpretation which I have attacked in the present study. Despite the admirable impetus of a study such as Eagleton's, there remains the residual belief in a singularity of truth as a meaningful, self-evident and self-present source of authority behind the critic's propositions. This position implies a faith in a world 'behind' the text which can be recuperated 'innocently' and authoritatively from a position of self-present transcendent consciousness; the counter-position for which I am arguing here subtends a greater pressure to construct a world, in Ricoeur's phrase, 'in front of' the text. This is not to deny, of course, the pressure to read, or 'counter-read' *Clarissa* in the way Eagleton does; it merely points out one way in which the text itself, in its reading or interpretation, 'betrays' the (male) reader. This kind of novel writing is not only critical and heretical, it is also, like the criticism which it engenders, adulteration: criticism can only be 'illegitimate' and especially so when it is criticism of the degeneric novel.

In discussing Brooks on the heresy of paraphrase, I noted the proximity to Bloom's argument that the meaning of a poem can only be another poem. This is perhaps especially the case in narrative fiction. The heretical paraphrase of a history, the critical elaboration of a fiction, is not only what constitutes that fiction in the first place; it is also the very condition of the subsequent critical acts performed in response to its reading. This is to say that criticism of a novel is always itself 'novel', a renewal of the fiction, a heretical revision of the text, such that the criticism itself approximates to the condition of telling a slightly different story. The most 'typical' novels, then, would be those which consciously rework earlier narratives, thereby incidentally making a criticism of those earlier writings. In this respect, a criticism like Eagleton's here bears some resemblance in impetus to a text like Jean Rhys's *Wide Sargasso Sea*, as a kind of feminist critique of Charlotte Brontë's *Jane Eyre*. In Ricoeur's terminology, this criticism 'appropriates' the world of the precursor work but produces a different 'world' or a different consciousness *vis-à-vis* the two narrated worlds. Eagleton, for instance, actually writes or articulates the rape which his precursor text, *Clarissa*, had euphemistically suggested; paradoxically, in some sense he has thus performed the *first* rape of Clarissa, the act for which he attacks earlier critics of the text. Yet this heretical narrative constructed by Eagleton ought to produce some degree of 'narrative knowledge', in Lyotard's phrase, and thereby authorise or authenticate itself in the shift of consciousness which it produces among readers both of *Clarissa* and of Eagleton's alternative version, *The Rape of Clarissa*. Clearly, of course, my own reading of Eagleton here is a further adulteration of *The Rape of Clarissa*, an adulteration of an adulteration. The important point, however, is that Eagleton has not 'stained' an otherwise 'pure' text; Richardson's *Clarissa* is already, in its very status as written artifact, an adulterated text. There is no *a priori* authority either in Richardson or in the text as pure, self-present object of consciousness; reading, critical reading, can only work 'ec-centrically', deviating from that text in order to disseminate authority through its extravagant letters.

The novel's proclivity for dealing with crime, a word related closely to criticism, stems perhaps from its sources in the criminal ballad. But such a mode of narrative, describing the death or execution of its own author, must be duplicitous, dialogical, a mode in which authority is already dis-seminated and dependent upon readers or interpreters to complete its fundamental aposiopesis, the death of the author. Such authority, of course, being 'criminal', is an authority precisely by dint of being 'legislated' against, and, 'delegitimised' in this way, the novelistic author is, as it were, removed from the *polis*, exiled from civic identity. As such, this authority is an anonymous source, one which, like some bourgeois notions of the female, has a mobile identity; but the other side of this coin of mobile identity is, as I have argued, multiple authority. The novel is itself inherently duplicitous and illegitimate; always digressing or heretically deviating from its own narratives, it becomes both historical and experimental. This study opened by examining some experiments in living; the eighteenth century, after seeing the 'world well lost' in the supervention of comedy over tragedy, had discovered that any such experiment, being a critical mediation of a societal or familial arrangement, is always firstly an experiment in writing. Authority is the fundamental question posed by these literary experiments, and they are formally a dissemination of authority. Demanding a critical reading, the novel generates readers who themselves con-struct alternative worlds, alternative narratives 'in front of' the text; if they are genuinely critical, these readers pursue the production of narrative knowledge and historical change or experiment. Such experimental criticism, of course, prod-uces hypothesised worlds or narratives which *differ* from the text which operates as the object or, better, stimulus for the criticism: it must therefore be 'betrayal'.

Betrayal of the text is as fundamental to the novel as it is to criticism, for the novel is constituted principally upon self-betrayal, a constant differing from itself. To return to some mythic originating monological source of authority in interpreting the novel, to return to a 'home' for which we feel nostalgia with a critic such as Hirsch, is, finally, to refuse an engagement with the text at all; it is certainly to marginalise, depoliticise and dehistoricise the act of reading or criticism. The 'historicist reconstructionist' in criticism has no real alternative to the position sketched out for Alceste by Molière: total withdrawal from social communication. A mode of criticism which complies, on the other hand, with the inevitable adulteration or contamination of the text has the advantage that, being fundamentally dialogical, spoken in the forked tongues of Swift's *Tale* or Derrida's *Glas*, it leads to the necessity of social, historical and political communication. A dialogical dissemination of authority, of patristic property and the ownership of meaning, is the result. Such a mode of criticism, further, works not to arrest the possibility of raising a dissenting voice in the socio-political consensus; rather, it should work to liberate such voices and to encourage their historical recognition as 'legislators' (readers/writers) in the context of a social collectivist mode of authority. Authority can thus be returned to those from whom it has been appropriated: not 'historicist reconstructionists' but active, historically constructive and critically conscious readers.

Notes

Introduction

Epigraph:

Tom Leonard, 'Good Style', from *Six Glasgow Poems*, repr. in Hamish Whyte (ed.), *Noise and Smoky Breath* (Third Eye Centre and Glasgow District Libraries Publications Board, Glasgow, 1983), p. 71; Geoffrey H. Hartman, *The Fate of Reading and Other Essays* (University of Chicago Press, Chicago, 1975), pp. 254–5; Edwin Morgan, from a letter to *Times Literary Supplement*, 28 January 1965, p. 67. Morgan's letter referred to Hugh MacDiarmid's poem, 'Perfect', which was quoted in its entirety as a 'small imagist masterpiece' in the *TLS* review of Kenneth Buthley's *Hugh MacDiarmid* (31 Dec. 1964). Glyn Jones wrote to *TLS* indicating that the 'poem' was a precise transcription (except for its first line) of a passage of prose in his own story, 'The Blue Bed'. MacDiarmid then wrote to *TLS*, trying to reconstruct a chain of events which led to his 'authorship', his 'writing' of the poem. It transpired that the relevant passage had been quoted by John Brophy in *The Listener*, in a review of Jones's story. MacDiarmid wrote: 'I either automatically memorized it and subsequently thought it my own or wrote it into one of my notebooks with the same effect' (*TLS*, 28 Jan. 1965, p. 67). Morgan's letter, then, posits the theoretical issue, especially given that, as he pointed out, the lines had been praised not only by Buthley but also by Walter Keir, in Duval and Smith (eds.), *Hugh MacDiarmid: A Festschrift* (1962) for its 'poetic' quality. The wider theoretical issue indicated by this, which my own study here examines, is of the relation between 'poetry' and other forms of discourse, specifically that of 'criticism': there is a sense in which 'Perfect' is already a critical writing.

1. See Walter Benjamin, 'The Work of Art in the Age of Mechanical Reproduction', repr. in Gerald Mast and Marshall Cohen (eds.), *Film Theory and Criticism*, 2nd edn (Oxford University Press, New York, 1979), and in Benjamin, *Illuminations*, ed. Hannah Arendt, trans. Harry Zohn (Fontana/Collins, London, 1973); Walter J. Ong, *Oral-*

ity and Literacy (Methuen, London, 1982), pp. 6 and *passim*; and cf. Julia Kristeva, σημειωτικη (Seuil, Paris, 1969), p. 181.

2. On the age of print and its relation to voice, see section 2 of this introduction. The 'Gutenberg Galaxy', as McLuhan called it, begins to cede place to the age of electronic communication in the mid-nineteenth century. Samuel Morse, a painter, constructed the first working model of the telegraph in 1835, and in 1839 transmitted the first telegraphic message, the 'Fiat Lux' of the electronic age, 'What hath God wrought!'. Meanwhile, in England Sir William Cooke and Sir Charles Wheatstone were developing the first British telegraph communications, around 1837; and Bell's telephone was operational in 1876. The Gutenberg age of print, then, perhaps stretches from roughly 1448 and the printing of the *Forty-Two Line Bible* to approximately 1835. In the last years of the nineteenth century Guglielmo Marconi was successfully transmitting radio messages over distances of twelve miles (in 1897). It may be useful to consider the age of print as 'the modern age', between medievalism and post-modernism. This would locate the works we call 'modernist' in the post-modern age, a seeming anachronism which can be explained by reference to Lyotard, who argues that post-modernism is actually the founding condition of modernism: 'A work can become modern only if it is first postmodern' (Jean-François Lyotard, 'Answering the Question: What Is Postmodernism?', trans. Régis Durand; in Lyotard, *The Postmodern Condition*, Manchester University Press, Manchester 1984, p. 79).

3. 'Bill' derives from *bulla*, and thus is informed with the notion of the ancient Sumerian script of around 3500 BC, the first 'writing'; a good example of such *bullae* can be seen in the Oriental Institute of the University of Chicago. For more information on this, see Ong, pp. 83–6.

4. This λεξισ corresponds roughly to the unit of the *lexie*, in the interpretative manoeuvres of Roland Barthes, *S/Z* (Seuil, Paris, 1970).

5. Ong, p. 131.

6. Alastair Fowler, *Kinds of Literature* (Clarendon Press, Oxford, 1982), p. 266. Fowler follows Hirsch here, arguing 'it must be said that E. D. Hirsch's powerful defense of the determinacy of literary meaning stands unanswered—indeed virtually unquestioned'. The present study aims to fill that 'gap'.

7. See Lyotard on the relation of knowledge to power; cf. also the work of Michel Foucault and Edward Said. Hans Blumenberg, *The Legitimacy of the Modern Age* (1966; trans. Robert M. Wallace; MIT Press, Cambridge, Mass., 1983), p. 139, defines modern historical humanity in terms of self-assertion and writes of Feuerbach's 'knowledge drive' as a basic instrument in such self-assertion, as a method which underlies the Nietzschean 'will to power' (pp. 440 ff.).

8. D. J. Gordon, 'Name and Fame: Shakespeare's *Coriolanus*', repr. in Stephen Orgel (ed.), *The Renaissance Imagination: Essays and Lectures by D. J. Gordon* (University of California Press, Berkeley and Los Angeles, 1975), p. 208.

9. Shakespeare, *Coriolanus* I. ix; cf. the similar case of a life being dependent on a name in Shakespeare, *Julius Caesar* III. iii, when Cinna the poet is confused with Cinna the conspirator.

10. Jürgen Habermas, *Legitimation Crisis* (1973; trans. Thomas McCarthy; Heinemann, London, 1976). Habermas's term 'legitimation' is used in the socio-political context of a critique of capitalism (the German title of the book is *Legitimationsprobleme im Spatkapitalismus*). Although I use the notion here, I also use a term of my own, 'legitimisation', when writing in the more specific context of the legitimisation of critical reading; there is, nonetheless, an overlap between these two terms.

11. Habermas, p. 46.

12. John Guillory, *Poetic Authority* (Columbia University Press, New York, 1983), p. 22, describes a similar state of affairs in relation to the 'genealogy of imagination' in Spenser and Milton: 'Milton chooses Spenser as his "original", eclipsing with his dark medium the Shakespearean sun. This displacement, the greatest usurpation in literary history, marks the new origin Milton finds for himself'. This origin, it transpires, is also as much an internal one, in Milton, as it is indebted to his construction of literary history or tradition.

13. *Coriolanus* III. iii.

14. Pierre Macherey, *Pour une théorie de la production litteraire* (François Maspéro, Paris, 1974), p. 22.

15. Paul de Man, *Allegories of Reading* (Yale University Press, New Haven, 1979), p. 17.

16. Fredric Jameson, *The Political Unconscious* (Methuen, London, 1981), p. 9.

17. Kenneth Burke, *Language as Symbolic Action* (University of California Press, Berkeley and Los Angeles, 1968), p. 37; cf. section 3 of the present introduction for a fuller consideration of this 'knowledge' and its relation to authority.

18. But see Paul Ricoeur, 'The Model of the Text: Meaningful Action Considered as a Text', in Ricoeur, *Hermeneutics and the Human Sciences*, trans. John B. Thompson (Cambridge University Press, Cambridge, 1981), on the text as a model for historical understanding.

19. Percy Bysshe Shelley, 'A Defence of Poetry' (1821), repr. in Edmund D. Jones (ed.), *English Critical Essays: Nineteenth Century* (1916; Oxford University Press, Oxford, 1971), p. 138.

20. Philip Hobsbaum, in conversation with me, November 1977.

21. For a fuller explication of this, see Christopher Butler, *After the Wake* (Oxford University Press, Oxford, 1980).

22. See J. L. Austin, *How to Do Things with Words*, William James Lectures (1955), ed. J. C. Urmson and Marina Sbisà (1962; 2nd edn, Oxford University Press, Oxford, 1982).

23. Ong, pp. 32, 91.

24. Johan Huizinga, *The Waning of the Middle Ages* (1924), trans. F. Hopman (Penguin, Harmonsdsworth, 1976), p. 9.

25. Terry Eagleton, *Literary Theory* (Basil Blackwell, Oxford, 1983), p. 16.

26. Harold Bloom, 'The Breaking of Form', in Bloom *et al.*, *Deconstruction and Criticism* (Routledge & Kegan Paul, 1979), p. 7.
27. Adin Steinsaltz, *The Essential Talmud*. trans. Chaya Galai (Bantam Books, New York, 1976), p. 273.
28. Geoffrey H. Hartman, *Saving the Text* (Johns Hopkins University Press, Baltimore, 1981), pp. xxi–xxii.
29. E. D. Hirsch, Jnr, 'Three Dimensions of Hermeneutics', *New Literary History* 3 (1972), 245–61; repr. in David Newton-de Molina (ed.), *On Literary Intention* (Edinburgh University Press, Edinburgh, 1976), p. 208.
30. Frank Cioffi, F. E. Sparshott and Quentin Skinner, all in Newton-de Molina, pp. 66, 113, 215, respectively. Original location of articles: Cioffi, 'Intention and Interpretation in Criticism', *Proceedings of the Aristotelian Society* lxiv (1963–4), 85–106; Sparshott, *The Concept of Criticism* (Oxford University Press, Oxford, 1967); Skinner, 'Motives, Intentions and the Interpretation of Texts', *New Literary History* 3 (1972), 393–408.
31. William Wordsworth, 'Preface to Lyrical Ballads' and 'Poems of the Imagination: XII', repr. in Wordsworth, *Poetical Works*, ed. Thomas Hutchinson, revised by Ernest de Selincourt (Oxford University Press, Oxford, 1904; repr. 1975), pp. 734, 149.
32. Ricoeur, 'The task of Hermeneutics', in Ricoeur, p. 52.
33. Ong, p. 106; cf. David R. Olson, 'From Utterance to Text: The Bias of Language in Speech and Writing', *Harvard Educational Review* 47 (1977), pp. 257–81, and Don Ihde, *Listening and Voice* (Ohio University Press, Athens, Ohio, 1976), *passim*.
34. Ricoeur, p. 52.
35. Geoffrey H. Hartman, *Fate of Reading*, p. 94.
36. Hirsch, in Newton-de Molina, p. 199.
37. Helen Gardner (ed.), *John Donne: Elegies and Songs and Sonnets* (Clarendon Press, Oxford, 1965), p. 187.
38. Hirsch, in Newton-de Molina, p. 207.
39. *Ibid.*, pp. 207–8.
40. Ong, *Ramus: Method and the Decay of Dialogue* (Harvard University Press, Cambridge, Mass., 1958), p. 121, and *Orality and Literacy*, p. 176.
41. Blumenberg, p. 269.
42. *Ibid.*, p. 404.
43. *Ibid.*, p. 137.
44. *Ibid.*, p. 565.
45. *Ibid.*, p. 569. 'Know-how', the implicit relation of knowledge to power, is made clear in this notion that 'anything can become of anything'. In a perceptive comment in his review of Peter Conrad, *The Art of the City*, Edward Mendelson picked up on an error in which Conrad's text confuses J. Edgar Hoover (FBI director) and Herbert Hoover (republican president of the USA, 1929–33): 'Four American presidents could not dislodge J. Edgar Hoover from the office of FBI director; one touch of Conrad's wand and Herbert

Hoover is there instead. It is a short step from the state of mind in which persons are indistinguishable to the state of mind in which they are dispensable' (*TLS*, 21 Sept. 1984, p.. 1050).

46. Lyotard, p. 27.
47. *Ibid.*, p. xxiii.
48. *Ibid.*, p. 13.
49. *Ibid.*, p. 31.
50. *Ibid.*, p. 36.
51. *Ibid.*, p. 36.
52. Edward W. Said, *The World, The Text, The Critic* (1983; repr. Faber & Faber, London, 1984), p. 29.
53. Habermas, pp. 107–8.
54. On another usage of this Gramscian distinction, see Edward W. Said, *Orientalism* (Routledge & Kegan Paul, London, 1978), pp. 6 ff.; clearly, there will be some degree of 'interference' between civil and political spheres, and the pragmatic aim of a work in the area of culture, such as Said's or my own here, is, fundamentally, to contribute to a disturbance or critical reconsideration in the political realm.
55. Jeffrey Mehlman, *Revolution and Repetition* (University of California Press, Berkeley and Los Angeles, 1977), p. 107; Bloom, in Bloom *et al.*, p. 6.
56. Mehlman, p. 107.
57. Eagleton, p. 165.
58. Jacques Lacan, *Écrits*, tome 1 (Seuil, Paris, 1966), pp. 157–8.
59. Ihde, p. 153.
60. Ong, *Orality and Literacy*, p. 34; cf. Ihde, p. 175, and Ricoeur, pp. 133–4.
61. Oliver Taplin, 'A Surplus of Signifier', in *Essays in Criticism* 26 (1976), 342.
62. *Ibid.*, p. 344.
63. *Ibid.*, p. 344.
64. Plato, *Ion*, trans. Percy Bysshe Shelley, in *Five Dialogues of Plato Bearing on Poetic Inspiration* (Dent, London, 1910) p. 1.
65. Plato, *Phaedrus*, trans. Benjamin Jowett; in *The Kama Sutra of Vatsyayana and the Phaedrus of Plato* (William Kimber, London, 1963), p. 75.
66. Theorisations of 'validity' in interpretation, a validity supposedly engendered or supported by reference to 'the text itself', are thus off the mark. A useful article which addresses itself to the problem in such terms is K. M. Newton, 'Interest, Authority and Ideology in Literary Interpretation', *British Journal of Aesthetics* 22 (1982), 103–14.
67. Ihde, p. 149.
68. Edwin Morgan, 'Message Clear', in *The Second Life: Selected Poems* (Edinburgh University Press, Edinburgh, 1968) pp. 24–5. This is only one of a whole series of what Morgan calls 'emergent' poems: see his *Poems of Thirty Years* (Carcanet New Press, Manchester, 1982).

69. See Jean Starobinski, *Les mots sous les mots* (Gallimard, Paris, 1971).
70. Interpretation of a printed text differs in this respect from interpretation of another speaking voice in a specific historical context, and the historical conditions affecting both modes vary, depending on the medium in which they are constructed. For a relevant example which shows up this problem, see Graham Greene's discussion, in *Getting to Know the General*, of the Panama Canal Treaty, signed by Omar Torrijos, but changed by the Senate of the USA *after* the signing.
71. Ricoeur, p. 141.
72. *Ibid.*, p. 142.
73. *Ibid.*, p. 174.
74. *Ibid.*, p. 177.
75. *Ibid.*, p. 178.
76. Ihde, pp. 145–6.
77. This is William James's phrase, quoted by Rorty in *Philosophy and the Mirror of Nature* (Basil Blackwell, Oxford, 1980), p. 10; and cf. Rorty, 'Introduction' to *Consequences of Pragmatism* (Harvester, Brighton, 1982), p. xxv, where James's more precise formulation is given.

Chapter 1: Experiments in Living

Epigraph: Charles Osborne, *W. H. Auden: The Life of a Poet* (Eyre Methuen, London, 1980), p. 328.
1. Jeffrey Stout, *The Flight from Authority* (University of Notre Dame Press, Indiana, 1981), pp. 2–3.
2. W. J. Bate, *The Burden of the Past and the English Poet* (Chatto & Windus, London, 1971), pp. 4–5. For a similar problem of authority in the Renaissance, see also John Guillory, *Poetic Authority* (Columbia University Press, New York, 1983).
3. See, for example, Peter Laslett, *The World We Have Lost*, 3rd edn. (Methuen, London, 1983); Laslett, *Family Life and Illicit Love in Earlier Generations* (Cambridge University Press, Cambridge, 1977); Michael Mitterauer and Reinhard Seider, *The European Family*, trans. Karla Oosterveen and Manfred Hörzinger (Basil Blackwell, Oxford, 1982); Lawrence Stone, *The Family, Sex and Marriage in England 1500–1800*, rev. edn. (Penguin, Harmondsworth, 1979).
4. Amerigo Vespucci, *The First Four Voyages*, trans. M.K. from 1st edn, Florence 1505–6 (Bernard Quaritch, 1855), p. 5.
5. Samuel Beckett, *The Unnamable*, in Beckett, *Molloy, Malone Dies, The Unnamable* (John Calder, London, 1959), p. 386.
6. See James Turner, *The Politics of Landscape* (Basil Blackwell, Oxford, 1979), pp. 5–6, 153; and cf. Stone, p. 29.
7. See Charles Monroe Coffin, *John Donne and the New Philosophy* (Columbia University Press, New York, 1937), for a more specific examination of the relations between poetry and the new sciences. See

also W. J. Ong, *Ramus: Method and the Decay of Dialogue* (Harvard University Press, Cambridge, Mass., 1958), p. 121, for an examination of 'place-logic' in the thought of Rudolph Agricola and for Ong's attack on it.

8. M. A. Screech, *The Rabelaisian Marriage* (Edward Arnold, London, 1958), p. 14.

9. Mikhail Bakhtin, *Rabelais and His World*, trans. Helene Iswolsky (MIT Press, Cambridge, Mass., 1968), 135: 'Only relative seriousness is possible in Rabelais' world'.

10. François Rabelais, *Gargantua*, in *Oeuvres complètes*, tome 1, ed. P. Jourda (Garnier Frères, Paris, 1962), p. 190.

11. *Ibid.*, p. 189.

12. Bakhtin, pp. 138–9.

13. Rabelais, p. 204.

14. *Ibid.*

15. Bakhtin, p. 280n.

16. Rabelais, p. 189.

17. *Ibid.*, p. 197.

18. Thomas More, *Utopia*, ed. George Sampson (G. Bell & Sons, London, 1914), p. 81.

19. *Ibid.*, p. 75.

20. Giambattista Vico, *The New Science*, trans. from 3rd edn, 1744, by T. G. Bergin and M. H. Fisch (Cornell University Press, New York, 1948), p. 109.

21. More, p. 94.

22. See Vespucci, first voyage.

23. More, p. 130.

24. Quoted in G. R. Hibbard, 'The Country House Poem of the Seventeenth Century', *Journal of the Warburg and Courtauld Institutes* xix (1956), 159–74.

25. See Rev. T. T. Carter (ed.), *Nicholas Ferrar, His Household and His Friends* (Longmans, Green & Co., London, 1892); J. E. Acland, *Little Gidding and Its Inmates in the Time of King Charles* i (SPCK, London, 1903); H. P. K. Skipton, *The Life and Times of Nicholas Ferrar* (A. R. Mowbray & Co., London, 1907); Henry Collett, *Little Gidding and its Founder* (SPCK, London, 1925), for some representative examples of this valorisation of Gidding. A useful comparison between these and C. Leslie Craig, *Nicholas Ferrar Junior* (Epworth Press, London, 1950), might be made, to clarify the modification of attitudes to the place by scholars in the wake of Bernard Blackstone's notice in the *Times Literary Supplement*, 1 August 1936, 'Discord at Little Gidding'.

26. Bernard Blackstone (ed.), *The Ferrar Papers* (Cambridge University Press, Cambridge, 1938), letters XIV, XVIII, XXIV.

27. *Ibid.*, letter XXIV.

28. *Ibid.*, letter XXVII.

29. *Ibid.*, letter XXX.

30. *Ibid.*, postscript to letter XXXVIII.

31. *Ibid.*, letter XXXVI.
32. *Ibid.*

Chapter 2: *The Female Landscape*

Epigraph: John Donne, Elegy 19 'To His Mistress Going to Bed'; Tony Harrison, 'Doodlebugs', in *Selected Poems* (Penguin, Harmondsworth, 1984), p. 20.
1. Christian Norberg-Schulz, *Existence, Space and Architecture* (Studio Vista, 1971), pp. 18–19.
2. Augustine, *Confessions* trans. R. S. Pine-Coffin (Penguin, Harmondsworth, 1961) p. 24; cf. *ibid.*, pp. 45, 152, 170 and *passim*.
3. *Ibid.*, pp. 89–90.
4. Gaston Bachelard, *La poétique de l'espace* (Presses universitaires de France, Paris, 1957; 5ème éd., 1967), p. 24.
5. *Ibid.*, pp. 32–3.
6. *Ibid.*, p. 27.
7. Marcel Proust, *Sodome et Gomorrhe* (Gallimard, Paris, 1954), pp. 593–4; cf. Georges Poulet, *Proustian Space* (1963), trans. Elliott Coleman (Johns Hopkins University Press, Baltimore, 1977), *passim*.
8. Charles d'Orléans, 'Se Dieu plaist, briefment la nuee', in Brian Woledge (ed.), *Penguin Book of French Verse I* (Penguin, Harmondsworth, 1961), pp. 274–5.
9. *Ibid.*, p. 287.
10. Edmund Spenser, *Faerie Queene*, Book II, Canto ix, stanza 32.
11. Norberg-Schulz, pp. 258, 280.
12. See G. R. Hibbard, 'The Country House Poem of the Seventeenth Century', *Journal of the Warburg and Courtauld Institutes* xix (1956), 159–74. William A. McClung, *The Country House in English Renaissance Poetry* (University of California Press, Berkeley and Los Angeles, 1977), offers a slightly modified 'tradition': he takes over the poems by Jonson, Carew and Marvell as in Hibbard, but gives Herrick's 'A Panegyrick to Sir Lewis Pemberton' and adds Joseph Hall, 'Satire V, 2: Noble edifices, with unworthy inhabitants', Charles Cotton on Chatsworth in *Wonders of the Peake*, and Pope's 'Epistle to Bathurst'.
13. Thomas Carew, 'To Saxham', in Rhodes Dunlap (ed.), *Poems of Thomas Carew* (Clarendon Press, Oxford, 1949), pp. 27–9.
14. Andrew Marvell, 'Upon Appleton House', in James Reeves and Martin Seymour-Smith (eds.), *Poems of Andrew Marvell* (Heinemann, London 1969), pp. 78–106.
15. Ben Jonson, 'To Penshurst', in George Parfitt (ed.), *Ben Jonson: Complete Poems* (Penguin, Harmondsworth, 1975), p. 97.
16. See McClung, pp. 27–8.
17. Leslie A. Fiedler, *The Stranger in Shakespeare* (1973; repr. Paladin, St Albans, 1974).
18. John Donne, 'Elegie 19', in Herbert J. C. Grierson (ed.), *Donne:*

Poetical Works (Oxford University Press, Oxford, 1929; repr. 1979), p. 107.

Chapter 3: Degenerate Bastards

Epigraph: Walter Abish, *How German Is It?* (1979; repr. Faber & Faber, London, 1983), p. 250.

1. Samuel Johnson, 'Preface to Shakespeare', repr. in Bertrand H. Bronson (ed.), *Samuel Johnson: Rasselas, Poems, and Selected Prose* (3rd edn, enlarged; Holt, Rinehart & Winston, New York, 1971), p. 266.
2. Northrop Frye, 'The Argument of Comedy', in *English Institute Essays 1948* (Columbia University Press, New York, 1949); repr. in Leonard F. Dean (ed.), *Shakespeare: Modern Essays in Criticism*, (rev. edn; Oxford University Press, New York, 1967), pp. 79–89.
3. See Raymond Williams, *Modern Tragedy* (1966; rev. edn, Verso Editions, London, 1979).
4. Anne Barton, '*As You Like It* and *Twelfth Night*: Shakespeare's Sense of an Ending', in Malcolm Bradbury and David Palmer (eds.), *Shakespearean Comedy (Stratford-upon-Avon Studies 14)* (Edward Arnold, London, 1972), p. 170.
5. William Shakespeare, *As You Like It* I. iii. 134; subsequent references appear in the text.
6. The relation between acting and reality, in which acting itself becomes constitutive of 'reality' is manifest in the Sartrean waiter who 'plays at' being a waiter, and thus becomes a 'waiter'. In contemporary writing, an exploration of the idea is to be found in Milan Kundera's 'The Hitchhiking Game', in Kundera, *Laughable Loves*, trans. Suzanne Rappaport (Penguin, Harmondsdworth, 1975).
7. See, for example, Paul Valéry, *Cahiers*, in 2 vols., ed. Judith Robinson (Pléiade, nrf Gallimard, Paris, 1973), vol. II, p. 932; 'Le passage de la prose au vers; de la parole au chant; de la marche à la danse'. Cf. *ibid.*, vol. I, pp. 294–5; vol. II, pp. 1060, 1077–8, 1085–6, 1102, for comments which corroborate this view.
8. Lawrence Stone, *The Family, Sex and Marriage in England 1500–1800* (1977; abridged and revised, Penguin, Harmondsworth, 1979), p. 146.
9. John Keats, letter of 21 December 1817 to George and Thomas Keats; repr. in Richard Harter Fogle (ed.), *John Keats, Selected Poetry and Letters (Rinehart Press, San Francisco, 1969), pp. 307–9*.
10. Jan Kott, *Shakespeare our Contemporary*, trans. Boleslaw Taborski (Methuen, London, 1965; rev. 1967), p. 193.
11. For Kott, however, this history, as manifest in 'the Grand Mechanism', is itself repetitive and circular.
12. Stone, pp. 104–5.
13. Edward Said, *Beginnings* (Basic Books, New York, 1975), p. 81.
14. Belsey suggested this in a paper delivered at a 'Conference on Feminist

Perspectives' organised by Oxford English Limited in Oxford on 13 November 1982.

15. See Hans-Georg Gadamer, '*Logos* and *Ergon* in Plato's *Lysis*', in Gadamer, *Dialogue and Dialectic*, trans. P. Christopher Smith (Yale University Press, New Haven, Conn., 1980).

16. Shakespeare, *King Lear* I. i. 54–60; subsequent references appear in the text.

17. John F. Danby, *Shakespeare's Doctrine of Nature* (Faber and Faber, London, 1948; repr. 1982). In an interview on BBC radio's 'Kaleidoscope', Donald Sinden remarked that this, in fact, was how he played the part of Lear in the Royal Shakespeare Company's production of the play.

18. Joyce Carol Oates, in *The Edge of Impossibility* (Victor Gollancz, London, 1976), sees *Troilus and Cressida* as a tragedy in which infidelity is crucial. I extend this to apply it to the Shakespearean stage as a whole; and subsequently, to critical activity (see Ch. 8 below).

19. The relevance of this to the 'death of the author' is examined in Chapter 4 below.

20. When I delivered this chapter in a slightly different form during a conference on 'Rereading Shakespeare' in Oxford, 5 March 1983, Lisa Jardine remarked that there was an element of male appropriation of the female hymen in the argument, and advised me that women do not think of their hymens in the ways that I suggest. It seems to me, however, that the mediation of the female hymen, in symbolic terms as I offer it here, perhaps plays an important part in male consciousness, or even in both male and female unconsciousnesses. Jardine suggested that this might then be seen as a specifically 'male' contribution to a feminist critique; and as such, I retain the argument and offer it here.

21. See Shakespeare, *Romeo and Juliet* II. ii. 64; subsequent references appear in the text.

22. Shakespeare, *Othello* I. iii. 278; subsequent references appear in the text.

23. For a fuller explication of this argument, see T. G. A. Nelson and Charles Haines, 'Othello's Unconsummated Marriage', *Essays in Criticism* 33 (1983), 1–18.

24. It can also, clearly, be aligned with the Freudian 'fort-da' game, or the Lacanian 'mirror-stage'.

25. Frye, in Dean, pp. 86–7.

26. Leslie A. Fiedler, *The Stranger in Shakespeare* (1973; repr. Paladin, St Albans, 1974), p. 44.

27. See Stephen Heath, *The Sexual Fix* (Macmillan, London, 1982), *passim*.

28. Johnson, p. 269.

Chapter 4: Blood and Suicide: The Death of the Author?

Epigraph: Roland Barthes, 'The Death of the Author', in Barthes, *Image—Music—Text*, trans. S. Heath (Fontana/Collins, Glasgow, 1977), p. 142; Jacques Derrida, *Glas*, in 2 vols. (Denoël/Gonthier, Paris, 1981), vol. I, p. 153, left-hand column.

1. Hirsch would argue that anything 'more' in the word 'light' would be mere 'significance', and not intrinsic 'meaning'; Derrida, on the other hand, might regard such 'supplementariness' as essential to the very construction of meaning for the word; see Chapters 7 and 8 below.

2. See, for example, Christopher Hill, *Milton and the English Revolution* (Faber & Faber, London, 1977), p. 64, for an impressively long list, including Chapman, Donne, Drayton, Fletcher, Jonson, Massinger, Middleton, Bacon, Burton and others.

3. Augustine, *City of God*, trans. Henry Bettenson (Penguin, Harmondsworth, 1972), pp. 519–20. For current versions of the same sophistry, see for example, Ludwig Wittgenstein, *Tractatus Logico-Philosophicus*, 6.4311, and Albert Camus, *Le mythe de Sisyphe* (nrf, Gallimard, Paris, 1942), pp. 29–30.

4. See Rosemary Freeman, 'George Herbert and the Emblem Books', *Review of English Studies* xvii (1941), 150–65, and *English Emblem Books* (Chatto & Windus, 1948), *passim*.

5. Frank Kermode, *The Sense of an Ending* (Oxford University Press, Oxford, 1967, 1977), p. 89.

6. Dante, *Inferno*, Canto 10, lines 130–32.

7. *Ibid.*, Canto 19, lines 19–21.

8. Abraham Cowley, 'On the Death of Mr Crashaw', in A. R. Waller (ed.), *English Writings of Abraham Cowley* (Cambridge University Press, Cambridge, 1905), p. 48.

9. *Ibid.*, 129.

10. John Donne, 'Aire and Angels', in Herbert J. C. Grierson (ed.), *Donne: Poetical Works* (Oxford University Press, Oxford, 1929; repr. 1979), p. 21.

11. Augustine, p. 577.

12. Richard Crashaw, 'The Weeper', in L. C. Martin (ed.), *Poems of Richard Crashaw*, 2nd edn (Oxford University Press, Oxford, 1957), p. 81.

13. See Mircea Eliade, *Le mythe de l'éternel retour*, 4th edn (nrf, Paris, 1949), *passim*; and cf. Hans Blumenberg, *The Legitimacy of the Modern Age* (1966), trans. Robert M. Wallace (MIT Press, Cambridge, Mass., 1983), *passim*.

14. Crashaw, 'Easter Day', in Martin, p. 100.

15. Thomas à Kempis, *Of the Imitation of Christ* (Grant Richards, London, 1903), pp. 38–9; Book I, Ch. 23.

16. See John Carey, *John Donne: Life, Mind and Art* (Faber & Faber,

London, 1981); S. E. Sprott, *The English Debate on Suicide from Donne to Hume* (Open Court, La Salle, Ill., 1961). See also Mark Taylor, *The Soul in Paraphrase: George Herbert's Poetics* (Mouton, The Hague, 1974), pp. 4–5, where Taylor endorses E. M. Simpson's view (expressed in her edition, with G. R. Potter, of *The Sermons of John Donne*, vol. 10, p. 348), that Augustine was a precursor model for Donne, rather than Christ himself.

17. Thomas Carew, 'A cruell Mistris', in Rhodes Dunlap (ed.), *Poems of Thomas Carew* (Clarendon Press, Oxford, 1949), p. 8.
18. *Ibid.*, 26.
19. A similar pun occurs in Cowley, 'Coldnesse', in Walter, pp. 113–5.
20. Crashaw, 'On the still surviving marks of our Saviour's Wounds', in Martin, pp. 86–7. On violence in *interpretation*, analogous to this, see, for example, Jeffrey Mehlman, *Revolution and Repetition* (University of California Press, Berkeley and Los Angeles, 1977), p. 107; and Harold Bloom, 'The Breaking of Form', in Bloom *et al.*, *Deconstruction and Criticism* (Routledge & Kegan Paul, London, 1976), p. 6.
21. Crashaw, 'The Teare', in Martin, p. 84.
22. *Ibid.*, 131–2.
23. Robert Ellrodt, *Les poètes métaphysiques anglais* (José Corti, Paris, 1960), vol. 2, pp. 63 ff.
24. Cowley, in Martin, p. 72.
25. See Edward Said, *Beginnings* (Basic Books, New York, 1975), on the relation between heresy and alternative beginnings.
26. Thomas Browne, *Religio Medici*, in C. A. Patrides (ed.), *Sir Thomas Browne: The Major Works* (Penguin, Harmondsworth, 1977), p. 69.
27. Rosalie L. Colie, '*Logos* in *The Temple*', *Journal of the Warburg and Courtauld Institutes* xxvi (1963), 329; and *Paradoxia Epidemica* (Princeton University Press, New Jersey, 1966).
28. Colie, p. 329.
29. See, for example, George Herbert, 'Forerunners', 'Jordan (I)', 'Jordan (II)', in C. A. Partrides (ed.), *English Poems of George Herbert* (Dent, London, 1974), pp. 181, 75, 116, respectively.
30. Herbert, 'Sinne (II)', in Patrides, p. 81.
31. Stanley E. Fish, *Self-Consuming Artifacts* (University of California Press, Berkeley and Los Angeles, 1972), p. 190.
32. A. D. Nuttall, *Overheard by God* (Methuen, London, 1980), p. 7; cf. *ibid.*, p. 8.
33. Herbert, 'The H. Scriptures (I)', in Patrides, p. 77.
34. For a fuller explication of Herbert's meditational practice and its generation of the 'presence of a friend', see Louis L. Martz, *The Poetry of Meditation* (Yale University Press, New Haven, Conn., 1954; rev. edn, 1978), esp. pp. 56–61, 249 ff.
35. Milan Kundera, *The Book of Laughter and Forgetting*, trans. Michael Henry Heim (Penguin, Harmondsworth, 1983), p. 91, elevates the principle of 'denial' like this to that of the foundation of all writing: denial becomes crucial to the activity of writing at all.

36. Herbert, 'The H. Scriptures (II)', in Patrides, p. 77.
37. Chana Bloch, 'Spelling the Word: Herbert's Reading of the Bible', in Claude J. Summers and Ted-Larry Pebworth (eds.), *'Too Rich to Clothe the Sunne': Essays on George Herbert* (University of Pittsburgh Press, Pittsburgh, 1980), p. 21.
38. See, for example, Herbert, 'Good Friday' and 'The Sinner', in Patrides, p. 59.
39. *Ibid.*, p. 125.
40. *Ibid.*, p. 170.
41. *Ibid.*, p. 161.

Chapter 5: The Theatre of Indeterminacy

Epigraph: George Santayana, 'Tragic Philosophy', *Scrutiny* iv (1936), 369.
 1. Such omnipresence of death after the Civil War might be conceptually affected by notions of 'restoration' as a surrogate mode of resurrection. See, for instance, J. H. Plumb,. *The Growth of Political Stability in England 1675–1725* (1967; repr. Penguin, Harmondsworth, 1969), pp. 30–31, on the notion of Charles as king and martyr; and cf. Nicholas Jose, *Ideas of the Restoration in English Literature 1660–1671* (Macmillan, London, 1984), *passim*.
 2. Maurice Blanchot, *L'espace littéraire* (nrf, Gallimard, Paris, 1955), p. 164.
 3. Thomas Hobbes, *Leviathan* (1651; repr. edn, abridged by John Plamenatz, Collins, Glasgow, 1971), p. 123.
 4. *Ibid.*, 122–3.
 5. John Locke, *Essay Concerning Human Understanding* (1689–90; repr. edn and abridged by A. D. Woozley, Collins, Glasgow, 1977), p. 93.
 6. Cf. Simone de Beauvoir, *Force of Circumstance*, trans. Richard Howard (Penguin, Harmondsworth, 1968), pp. 671–4.
 7. Pierre Corneille, *Oeuvres complètes* (Seuil, Paris, 1963), p. 844.
 8. *Ibid.*, p. 844.
 9. *Ibid.*, p. 824.
10. This is the word Lucien Goldmann applies to the theatre of Racine, in his *Racine*, trans. Alastair Hamilton (1972; repr. Writers and Readers, London, 1981), p. 18.
11. Corneille, *Polyeucte*, in *Oeuvres complètes*, p. 293, lines 1–14; cf. line 775: 'Tout votre songe est vrai, Polyeucte n'est plus'. Subsequent line references appear in the text.
12. Nicholas Boileau, *L'Art Poétique*, chant 3, lines 359–72; in Boileau, *Oeuvres complètes*, (Garnier-Flammarion, Paris, 1969), vol. 2, p. 107.
13. Friedrich Nietzsche, *The Birth of Tragedy and the Genealogy of Morals*, trans. F. Golffing (Doubleday, New York, 1956), pp. 23–4.
14. See Leo Bersani, *A Future for Astyanax* (Little, Brown & Co., Boston, 1976), where Bersani argues that a central concern of *Andromaque* consists in whether a future can be generated for Astyanax. In Racine,

the question is how to generate such a future; in Corneille, such futurity is denied.

15. Robert McBride, *Aspects of Seventeenth-Century French Drama and Thought* (Macmillan, London, 1979), p. 13; from this, one can begin to detect similarities in the postures of Corneille and Descartes, who also builds on doubt.

16. *Ibid.*, pp. 13, 21.

17. Corneille, p. 824; the hubristic self-presence which results from the theory here bears a strong resemblance to the position of the spectator according to the theory of I. A. Richards, in *Principles of Literary Criticism* (1924; repr. Routledge & Kegan Paul, London, 1976), where the importance of the therapeutic effect of tragedy on the mind leads Richards to valorise positively the socially hygienic paralysis of the spectator.

18. Corneille, *Horace*, in *Oeuvres complètes*, p. 261, lines 1080, 1141–4.

19. Claude-Gilbert Dubois, *Le Baroque: profondeurs de l'apparence* (Librairie Larousse, Paris, 1973), p. 184.

20. Jean Racine, *Andromaque*, in *Oeuvres complètes* (Seuil, Paris, 1962), p. 118, lines 1205–8.

21. Corneille, *Discours du poème dramatique*, in *Oeuvres complètes*, p. 824.

22. Roland Barthes, *Sur Racine* (Seuil, Paris, 1963), p. 104, brings them into very close proximity with each other: 'Eriphile n'*est* rien, Iphigénie *a* tout'; cf. the confusion between Oreste and Pyrrhus in *Andromaque*, lines 1565–8, and the position of Thésée in *Phèdre*, in Racine, line 1004. Confusions such as these dominate the Racinian stage.

23. Blaise Pascal, *Pensées*, in *Oeuvres complètes* (Seuil, Paris, 1963), p. 528; liasse XV, 'Transition', fragment 201.

24. Racine, *Iphigénie en Aulide*, in *Oeuvres complètes*, p. 227, lines 115–6. Subsequent line references will appear in the text.

25. The modern manifestation of this, dramatically, is Beckett's *Breath*.

26. See Lucien Goldmann, *Le Dieu Caché* (nrf, Gallimard, Paris, 1955).

27. See Racine, 'Préface' to *Iphigénie*, in *Oeuvres complètes*, p. 225.

28. For a fuller explication of the philosophy behind this, see John Dewey, *Experience and Nature* (1925; rev. edn, Dover Publications, New York, 1958).

29. Pascal, p. 506; liasse II, 'Vanité', fragment 47.

30. T. S. Eliot, 'Burnt Norton', in *Complete Poems and Plays of T. S. Eliot* (Faber & Faber, 1969), p. 172.

31. Barthes, p. 109.

32. See, for example, *Phèdre*, in Racine, *Oeuvres complètes*, lines 44–5, 144, 156–7, 172; subsequent line references appear in the text.

33. Cf. Eliot, 'Tradition and the Individual Talent', in *The Sacred Wood* (Methuen, London, 1920; repr. 1966), p. 58.

34. Pascal, p. 516; liasse VIII, 'Divertissement', fragment 136.

Chapter 6: The Impossibility of Authenticity

1. See Pat Rogers, *The Augustan Vision* (1974; repr. Methuen, London, 1978), p. 234, on Johnson's dictionary: 'the new work marked a huge advance. It took a great step forward in its use of etymology. ... A larger contribution, however, lay in his choice of illustrative quotations. They are drawn to a large extent from classic authors, and indeed the *Dictionary* did as much as any single book to establish a roll of vernacular classics'. See also James Boswell, *Life of Samuel Johnson* (1791; repr. in 2 vols., Dent, London, 1952), vol. 1, p. 109, on the element of nationalism inherent in the construction of vernacular dictionaries. Johnson compares his own task with that of the French Academy in such a way as to demonstrate the 'manifest' superiority of the English people, not just the English language, Cf. *ibid.*, vol. 1, p. 110, on Johnson's etymologies: 'It is remarkable, that he was so attentive in the choice of the passages in which words were authorised, that one may read page after page of his Dictionary with improvement and pleasure; and it should not pass unobserved, that he has quoted no author whose writings had a tendency to hurt sound religion and morality'. Rogers, p. 234, comments on the same point that 'His remarks on the social acceptability of particular words meant that entries were able to sort and grade language'. There is some concern, then, with nationalist purification, a use of etymology to 'authorise' and demonstrate legitimacy—analogous, clearly, to the construction of a certain kind of familial heritage.
2. Reuben A. Brower, *Alexander Pope: The Poetry of Allusion* (Clarendon Press, Oxford, 1959), p. 2.
3. *Ibid.*, p. 8.
4. John Dryden, 'Of Dramatic Poesy: An Essay', in James Kinsley and George Parfitt (eds.), *John Dryden: Selected Criticism* (Clarendon Press, Oxford, 1970), pp. 55–6.
5. Dryden, 'Preface to *All for Love*', in *ibid.*, p. 152.
6. Jean Racine, *Oeuvres complètes* (Seuil, Paris, 1962), p. 225.
7. Racine alludes to various sources here, including Aeschylus, Sophocles and Lucretius.
8. Nicholas Boileau, *L'Art poétique*, chant I, lines 43–4; repr. in Boileau, *Oeuvres complètes*, (Garnier-Flammarion, Paris, 1969), vol. 2, p. 88.
9. *Ibid.*, chant III, lines 38–46, p. 99.
10. See Chapters 7 and 8 below for a fuller exploration of this.
11. René Rapin, *Réflexions sur la poétique* (1675); repr. ed. E. T. Dubois (Droz, Génève, 1970), p. 9.
12. *Ibid.*, p. 103.
13. *Ibid.*, 105; and cf. Rapin's comment, *ibid.*, 107: 'tout y doit estre dans le trouble, et le calme n'y doit paroistre, que quand l'action finit, par la catastrophe', a comment which accords with my characterisation of Cornelian *repos* in Chapter 5 above.
14. John Milton, 'At A Vacation Exercise', in B. A. Wright (ed.), *Milton: Poems* (Dent, London, 1956), p. 18.

15. *Ibid.*, p. 30.
16. Milton, 'The Doctrine and Discipline of Divorce', in C. A. Patrides (ed.), *John Milton: Selected Prose* (Penguin, Harmondsworth, 1974), p. 120; for further evidence of Miltonic nationalism, see Christopher Hill, *Milton and the English Revolution* (Faber & Faber, London, 1977), pp. 159, 279–84.
17. See, for example, Andrew Gurr, *Writers in Exile* (Harvester, Brighton, 1981), Eric J. Sundquist, *Home as Found* (Johns Hopkins University Press, Baltimore, 1979), Terry Eagleton, *Exiles and Emigrés* (Schocken Books, New York, 1970); and, more particularly, Hélène Cixous, *L'exil de James Joyce* (Grasset, Paris, 1968).
18. Pierre Corneille, *Oeuvres complètes* (Seuil, Paris, 1963), p. 824.
19. Maurice Blanchot, *L'espace littéraire* (nrf. Gallimard, Paris, 1955), p. 322.
20. D. H. Lawrence, *Lady Chatterley's Lover* (1928; repr. Penguin, Harmondsworth, 1972), p. 5.
21. Sophocles, *Oedipus Rex*, in Sophocles, *The Theban Plays*, trans. E. F. Watling (Penguin, Harmondsworth, 1947), p. 28.
22. *Ibid.*, p. 33.
23. See David Trotter, *The Poetry of Abraham Cowley* (Macmillan, London, 1979), p. 8.
24. Milton's 'Divorce' tract may be a relevant text here; but see also Frances Baumal, *Le féminisme au temps de Molière* (La Renaissance du Livre, Paris, n.d.), and Ian Maclean, *Woman Triumphant* (Clarendon Press, Oxford, 1977).
25. Corneille, *Horace*, in *Oeuvres complètes*, p. 250, lines 25–8; subsequent line references appear in the text.
26. Thomas Otway, *Venice Preserv'd*, in Robert G. Lawrence (ed.), *Restoration Plays* (Dent, London, 1976), p. 246; subsequent scene references in text.
27. See Lewis Mumford, *The City in History* (1961; repr. Penguin, Harmondsworth, 1979), esp. Ch. 12.
28. R. J. Kaufmann, 'On the Poetics of Terminal Tragedy: Dryden's *All for Love*', in Bernard N. Schilling (ed.), *Dryden: A Collection of Critical Essays* (Prentice-Hall, Englewood Cliffs, New Jersey, 1963), p. 87.
29. George Steiner, *The Death of Tragedy* (Faber & Faber, London, 1961), p. 353.
30. See François Millepierres, *La vie quotidienne des médecins au temps de Molière* (Hachette, Paris, 1964), esp. Ch. 3.
31. *Ibid.*, p. 53.
32. Molière, *Le Malade Imaginaire*, in Molière, *Oeuvres complètes* (Seuil, Paris, 1962), p. 651; Act 3, Scene 3.
33. Molière, *Tartuffe*, in *Oeuvres complètes*, p. 265, line 451; subsequent line references appear in text.
34. See Ferdinand de Saussure, *Cours de linguistique générale* (1915; repr. Payot, Paris, 1931), *passim*.
35. This was accepted only after some time, in the manner of a Kuhnian

scientific 'revolution'. See Millepierres on the slow acceptance of Harvey's work by the French Faculties of Medicine. But by the time Descartes was writing, it seems to have become a scientific axiom: see, for example, *Discours de la méthode*, ed. E. Gilson (Vrin, Paris, 1970), 113 ff., and *The Passions of the Soul*, in *Philosophical Works of Descartes*, (trans. Elizabeth S. Haldane and G. R. T. Ross; Cambridge University Press, Cambridge, 1911; repr. 1969), vol. 1, p. 333, art. VII ff. See also Thomas S. Kuhn, *Structure of Scientific Revolutions* (1962; 2nd edn, enlarged, University of Chicago Press, Chicago, 1970). The acceptance of Harvey does not, strictly speaking, constitute a Kuhnian 'paradigm-change'; but the rate of acceptance of the ideas is comparable with the usual speed at which scientific ideas change, according to Kuhn.

36. William Congreve, *The Way of the World*, in Lawrence (ed.), *Restoration Plays*, pp. 187–8.

37. Aristotle, *Poetics*, in *Classical Literary Criticism*, trans. T. S. Dorsch (Penguin, Harmondsworth, 1965), p. 35.

38. See Erving Goffman, *The Presentation of Self in Everyday Life* (University of Edinburgh Social Sciences Research Centre, Edinburgh, 1956; Penguin, Harmondsworth, 1969). Here, then, is a rupture between epistemology and pleasure; for a fuller explication of the philosophical grounding of such a rupture, see Hans Blumenberg, *The Legitimacy of the Modern Age*, (1966), trans. Robert M. Wallace (MIT Press, Cambridge, Mass., 1983), pp. 232, 404 and *passim*.

39. Walter Benjamin, 'The Work of Art in the Age of Mechanical Reproduction', in Gerald Mast and Marshall Cohen, (eds.), *Film Theory and Criticism*, 2nd edn; Oxford University Press, Oxford, 1979, p. 851.

40. *Ibid.*, p. 852.

41. See, for example, Arthur Tilley, *From Montaigne to Molière* (John Murray, London, 1908), pp. 77 ff.

42. Richard Steele, 'Advice to Ladies on Exercise and Education', *Tatler*, no. 248; repr. in L. E. Steele (ed.), *Essays of Richard Steele* (Macmillan, London, 1937), p. 235; cf. *Ibid.*, p. 285, on 'Matrimonial Happiness': 'indeed I have hardly ever observed the married condition unhappy, but from want of judgment or temper in the man'. This demonstrates the real impetus behind Steele's 'feminism': women are once again being used solely as a means of identifying the 'gentlemanly' male, and the comments are directed primarily towards male readers. Interestingly, Steele also comments in this latter essay that 'The truth is, we generally make love in a style, and with sentiments very unfit for ordinary life: they are half theatrical, half romantic'—that is, wholly fictional. For a fuller exploration of feminism in this entire period, see Katharine M. Rogers, *Feminism in Eighteenth-Century England* (Harvester Press, Brighton, 1982).

43. John Wilmot, Earl of Rochester, 'The Imperfect Enjoyment', in John Adlard (ed.), *Rochester: The Debt to Pleasure* (Fyfield Books, Cheadle, 1974), p. 65.

44. Congreve, in Lawrence (ed.), *Restoration Plays*, p. 173.
45. William Wycherley, *The Country Wife*, in Lawrence (ed.), *Restoration Plays*, p. 136.
46. This was in 1675; in the following year, Etherege repeated the same strategy, with reference to the word 'fruit' which 'lies heavily upon the stomach'; see *The Man of Mode*, in Lawrence (ed.), *Restoration Plays*, p. 508.
47. Molière, *Le Misanthrope*, in *Oeuvres complètes*, p. 324; lines 69–72; subsequent line references appear in the text.
48. See, for example, Octavien de Saint-Gelais, *Le séjour d'honneur*, ed. Joseph Alston James (North Carolina Studies in Romance Languages and Literatures, Chapel Hill, 1977); Jehan Marot, *Le voyage de Gênes*, ed. Giovanna Trisolini (Droz, Geneva, 1974). A typical example of the practice of the *rhétoriqueurs* is Jean Molinet's epitaph, punning on his own name: 'Dy moy qui gist icy?/C'est luy seul qui mouloit doulx motz en molin net'.
49. Ecclesiastes 3:1.
50. John Vanbrugh, *The Provoked Wife*, in Lawrence (ed.), *Restoration Plays*, p. 385.
51. For a fuller consideration of this, explicitly in relation to Hitler's *Mein Kampf*, see Kenneth Burke, *The Philosophy of Literary Form*, 3rd edn (University of California Press, 1973), pp. 40–45, 191 ff.
52. Lewis Carroll, *Through the Looking-Glass* (Dent, London, 1979), p. 79.

Chapter 7: Enthusiastic Carnal Knowledge

Epigraph: Alain, 'Que suis-je?', *Études*, présentées par Samuel S. de Sacy (nrf, Gallimard, Paris, 1968), pp. 29, 31–2; Michel Foucault, *Folie et déraison* (Plon, Paris, 1961), p. 181.

1. Richard Rorty, 'Deconstruction and Circumvention', *Critical Inquiry* 11 (1984), 1–23; and in conversation, School of Criticism and Theory, 1983.
2. Blaise Pascal, *Pensées*, in *Oeuvres complètes* (Seuil, Paris, 1963), p. 526, fragment 199. On Descartes as Cornelian 'hero', see Hugh Kenner, *Samuel Beckett: A Critical Study* (John Calder, London, 1962), Jacques Barzun, *Classic, Romantic and Modern* (Secker & Warburg, London, 1962), pp. 87–8; and cf. my comparison of this position in contradistinction to Pascal, in Docherty, *Reading (Absent) Character* (Clarendon Press, Oxford, 1983).
3. Basil Willey, *The Eighteenth-Century Background* (Chatto & Windus, 1950), p. 96.
4. Alexander Pope, 'Essay on Man', in John Butt (ed.), *Poems of Alexander Pope* (Methuen, 1963; repr. 1975), p. 506.
5. John Locke, *Essay Concerning Human Understanding* (1689–90) ed. and abridged by A. D. Woozley (Collins, Glasgow, 1977), pp. 141–2.

6. Isaac Newton, *Opticks* (1704; 4th edn, 1730; G. Bell & Sons, 1931), p. 249.

7. Voltaire, *Lettres Philosophiques* (1733), ed. R. Naves (Garnier Frères, Paris, 1964), p. 70.

8. See John Donne, 'The Flea', in Herbert J. C. Grierson (ed.), *Donne: Poetical Works* (Oxford University Press, Oxford, 1929; repr. 1979), pp. 36–7; Pascal, p. 526, fragment 199; Jonathan Swift, *Gulliver's Travels*, in Louis A. Landa (ed.), *Gulliver's Travels and Other Writings* (Oxford University Press, Oxford, 1976); William Blake, 'Marriage of Heaven and Hell', in J. Bronowski (ed.), *William Blake* (Penguin, Harmondsworth, 1958; repr. 1976), p. 96.

9. Pope, pp. 512–3; cf. *Dunciad*, Book I, lines 177–8, when the Dunce, Philemon (Colley Cibber) reiterates the same thought; cf. Foucault, *Folie et déraison* (Plon, Paris, 1961), 24–5, 181 ff., on the relation of bestiality to madness.

10. Samuel Johnson, 'Review of Soame Jenyns's "A Free Inquiry into the Nature and Origin of Evil"', repr. in Bertrand H. Bronson (ed.), *Samuel Johnson: Rasselas, Poems, and Selected Prose*, 3rd edn (Holt, Rinehart & Winston, New York, 1971), pp. 219–20.

11. *Ibid.*, p. 225.

12. John Milton, 'Paradise Lost', in B. A. Wright (ed.), *Milton: Poems* (Dent, 1956, London), p. 218 (Book IV, line 110), and p. 164 (Book I, line 253).

13. See Gilbert Ryle, *The Concept of Mind* (1949; repr. Penguin, Harmondsworth, 1978), pp. 186 ff.; and cf. Michel Butor, *L'Emploi du temps* (minuit, Paris, 1957), for a novel based on this problem.

14. Swift, *A Tale of a Tub*, in Landa, p. 310.

15. *Ibid.*, p. 261; cf. Richard Rorty, *Philosophy and the Mirror of Nature* (Basil Blackwell, Oxford, 1983), p. 61, on a similar eventuality in Cartesian philosophy: 'The Cartesian change from mind-as-reason to mind-as-inner-arena was not the triumph of the prideful individual subject freed from scholastic shackles so much as the triumph of the quest for certainty over the quest for wisdom'.

16. Swift, p. 321.

17. *Ibid.*, pp. 322–3; cf. Swift, *A Discourse Concerning the Mechanical Operation of the Spirit*, ed. Guthkelch and Nichol Smith (Oxford University Press, Oxford, 1920), p. 281.

18. Swift, *Tale*, in Landa, p. 243.

19. Swift, *Mechanical Operation*, pp. 271–2.

Chapter 8: Betraying the Text

Epigraph: Richard Hooker, *Of the Laws of Ecclesiastical Polity* (Dent, London, 1907; repr. 1954), vol. 2, p. 58 (Book V); Salman Rushdie, *Shame* (Jonathan Cape, London, 1983), pp. 76–7.

1. See, for example, William Wordsworth, 'Preface to Lyrical Ballads',

in Thomas Hutchinson (ed.), (revised by Ernest de Selincourt),
Wordsworth: Poetical Works (Oxford University Press, Oxford, 1936;
repr. 1975), 734; Samuel Taylor Coleridge, *Biographia Literaria*, ed.
George Watson (Dent, London, 1906; rev. edn, 1965), p. 173; Percy
Bysshe Shelley, 'A Defence of Poetry', in Edmund D. Jones (ed.),
English Critical Essays: Nineteenth Century (Oxford University Press,
Oxford, 1916; repr. 1971), p. 103.

2. John Locke, *Essay Concerning Human Understanding*, ed. and
   abridged by A. D. Woozley (Collins, Glasgow, 1964), p. 89.
3. Isaac Newton, *Opticks* (4th ed., 1730; G. Bell & Sons, 1931), p. 14.
4. Paul de Man, *Allegories of Reading* (Yale University Press, New
   Haven, Conn., 1979), 10; and cf. de Man's comments on Burkeian
   'deflection', *ibid.*, p. 8.
5. Jean–François Lyotard, *Rudiments païens* (Union Générale d'Éditions,
   10/18, Paris, 1977), pp. 50–51.
6. Alexander Pope, *Dunciad*, Book I, lines 187–8; in John Butt (ed.),
   Poems of Alexander Pope (Methuen, London, 1963), p. 729.
7. *Ibid.*, p. 733.
8. Jonathan Swift, *A Tale of a Tub*, in Louis A. Landa (ed.), *Gulliver's
   Travels and Other Writings* (Oxford University Press, Oxford, 1976),
   p. 253.
9. *Ibid.*, p. 339.
10. *Ibid.*, p. 265.
11. E. D. Hirsch, Jnr, *Validity in Interpretation* (Yale University Press,
    New Haven, Conn., 1967), p. 242.
12. de Man, p. 17.
13. Lyotard, p. 30.
14. See Michel Foucault, *Folie et déraison* (Plon, Paris, 1961), *passim*.
15. Swift, *Gulliver's Travels*, in Landa, p. 5.
16. Martin Heidegger, *Poetry, Language, Thought*, trans. A. Hofstadter
    (Harper & Row, New York, 1971), pp. 197, 215, as cited in Frank
    Lentricchia, *After the New Criticism* (1980; repr. Methuen, London,
    1983), p. 258. But cf., for example, Heidegger, *Being and Time*, trans.
    J. Macquarrie and E. Robinson (Basil Blackwell, Oxford, 1967),
    p. 208: 'Man shows himself as the entity which talks'.
17. Harold Pinter, *Betrayal*, Scene 1; in Pinter, *Plays: Four* (Eyre
    Methuen, London, 1981), p. 166.
18. Jean Starobinski, *Les mots sous les mots* (Gallimard, Paris, 1971),
    p. 29; the final word quoted here, *revient*, indicates the existence of
    these names as some kind of *revenants* or ghosts. There is an obsession
    with metaphors of the 'ghostly' in modernist writings, from Saussure
    here to Eliot's attention to 'the medium' in 'Tradition and the Indi-
    vidual Talent', and I. A. Richards's discussion of the 'phantom' aes-
    thetic state. In the earlier battle of 'modernism', that between ancients
    and moderns, there is a similar preponderance of such images,
    especially in Addison's *Spectator* Essays.
19. Swift, *Tale*, in Landa, p. 340.
20. See, for example, Pierre Michel (ed.), *Villon: Poésies complètes* (Livre

de Poche, Paris, 1972), pp. 119–21, 183, 163, 125.
21. Michael Riffaterre, *Semiotics of Poetry* (1978; repr. Methuen, London, 1980), pp. 67–8. Although the matrix is not the meaning of the poem, it does unify the poem, gives the text itself as the unit of significance (*ibid.*, p. 6), and such unification paves the way for the discovery of 'one symbolic focus' (*ibid.*, p. 12), the 'single sign' which constitutes the poem. Any cogent attack on Riffaterre's position must focus on his seemingly arbitrary decision to stress the unity of a given text. See Jonathan Culler, *The Pursuit of Signs* (Routledge & Kegan Paul, London, 1981), p. 81, where he complains, correctly, that Riffaterre does not argue for such unity, but rather merely assumes it.
22. Geoffrey H. Hartman, *Saving the Text* (Johns Hopkins University Press, Baltimore, 1981), p. 94; he further 'explains' or brings to enlightenment the elements of this shady name, ibid., pp. 94–5.
23. *Ibid.*, p. 82.
24. de Man, p. 17.
25. Kenneth Burke, *The Philosophy of Literary Form*, 3rd edn rev. (University of California Press, Berkeley and Los Angeles, 1973), p. 56.
26. A. E. Dyson, *The Crazy Fabric* (Macmillan, London, 1965), p. 4.
27. See, for example, Cleanth Brooks, *The Well Wrought Urn* (1947; repr. Methuen, London, 1968), p. 12, where Brooks indulges in a whole series of such heretical paraphrases of Donne's 'The Canonization'.
28. *Ibid.*, p. 161.
29. *Ibid.*, p. 162.
30. Harold Bloom, *The Anxiety of Influence* (Oxford University Press, New York, 1973), p. 94.
31. See Frank Lentricchia, pp. 319–21; and cf. Imre Salusinszky, 'The neo-Romantic Imagination in North American Criticism and Poetry since 1945', unpublished D. Phil. thesis, Oxford University, 1982, p. 281, where Salusinszky quotes Northrop Frye from a personal interview as saying 'in some respects, I am his [Bloom's] anxiety of influence'.
32. David Bleich, *Subjective Criticism* (Johns Hopkins University Press, Baltimore, 1978), p. 147.

Chapter 9: Experiments in Writing

Epigraph: Samuel Richardson, *Clarissa*, in 4 vols. (Dent, London, 1979), vol. 2, p.273; William Blake, 'Introduction', to *Songs of Innocence*, in J. Bronowski (ed.), *William Blake* (Penguin, Harmondsworth, 1958; repr. 1976), p. 26.
Sub-epigraph: John Updike, *Rabbit, Run* (1960; repr. Penguin, Harmondsworth, 1984), pp. 73–4; Walter J. Ong, *Orality and Literacy* (Methuen, London, 1982), pp. 111–12.
1. Stephen Heath, *The Sexual Fix* (Macmillan, London, 1982), p. 86.
2. Friedrich Engels, *The Origin of the Family, Private Property and the*

State (with intro. and notes by Eleanor Burke Leacock; from trans. by Alec [*sic*] West, 1942; Lawrence & Wishart, London, 1972), p. 134.

3. T. S. Eliot, *The Sacred Wood* (Methuen, London, 1920; repr. 1966), p. 50.

4. See, for examples, Richardson, *Clarissa*, in 4 vols (Dent, London, 1979), vol. 2, pp.442, 444 ff.; vol. 3, pp. 30 ff. 65 ff.

5. *Ibid.*, vol. 3, p. 94; subsequent volume and page references appear in the text.

6. Herman Melville, *Moby Dick*, ed. Charles Child Walcutt (Bantam Books, New York, 1981), pp. 138–9. Some clear modernist analogues to this might include the architecture of Ludwig Mies van der Rohe, or Richard Rogers's Centre Georges Pompidou in Paris, which is designed to appear to be 'under construction' as a dynamic building. Lennard J. Davis, in *Factual Fictions* (Columbia University Press, New York, 1983), p. 66, writes of the 'intermittent' production of serialised pamphlets in the eighteenth century, rather like the serialised and regular production of fiction-instalments in newspapers. Such fiction, I shall argue in this chapter, is dynamic in the same way as the modernist and post-modern architecture predicted by Melville; it is also a remarkably close analogy to the way in which the filmic image, that modernist cinematic form, is produced. Such 'draughts' or notes toward a fiction radically involve a reader in the activity of critical interventionist reading as a structuring principle in their formation or articulation.

7. Geoffrey H. Hartman, *Criticism in the Wilderness* (Yale University Press, New Haven, Conn., 1980), p. 131; Virginia Woolf, *The Waves* (1931; repr. Panther Books, St Albans, 1977), p. 26.

8. Henry Fielding, *Shamela*, in Douglas Brooks-Davies (ed.), *Joseph Andrews and Shamela* (Oxford University Press, Oxford, 1980), p. 330.

9. Davis, p. 58.

10. George Lukács, *Theory of the Novel*, trans. Anna Bostock (Merlin Press, London, 1978), pp. 74–5.

11. Alan Dugald McKillop, *The Early Masters of Modern Fiction* (University Press of Kansas, Lawrence, 1956), p. 80.

12. Viktor Shklovsky, 'A Parodying Novel', repr. in John Traugott (ed.), *Laurence Sterne: A Collection of Critical Essays* (Prentice-Hall, Englewood Cliffs, NJ, 1967).

13. Fielding, *Joseph Andrews*, in Brooks-Davies (ed.), p. 79.

14. Daniel Defoe, *Moll Flanders*, ed. Juliet Mitchell (Penguin, Harmondsworth, 1978), p. 28.

15. Terry Eagleton, *The Rape of Clarissa* (Basil Blackwell, Oxford, 1982), p. 61.

Index